Mosque

An Architect's Exploration of Form, Faith and Meaning

MARWA AL-SABOUNI

For all the free people in the world

'O children of Adam, take your adornment at every masjid,[1] and eat and drink, but do not be excessive. Indeed, He does not like those who are excessive.'[2]

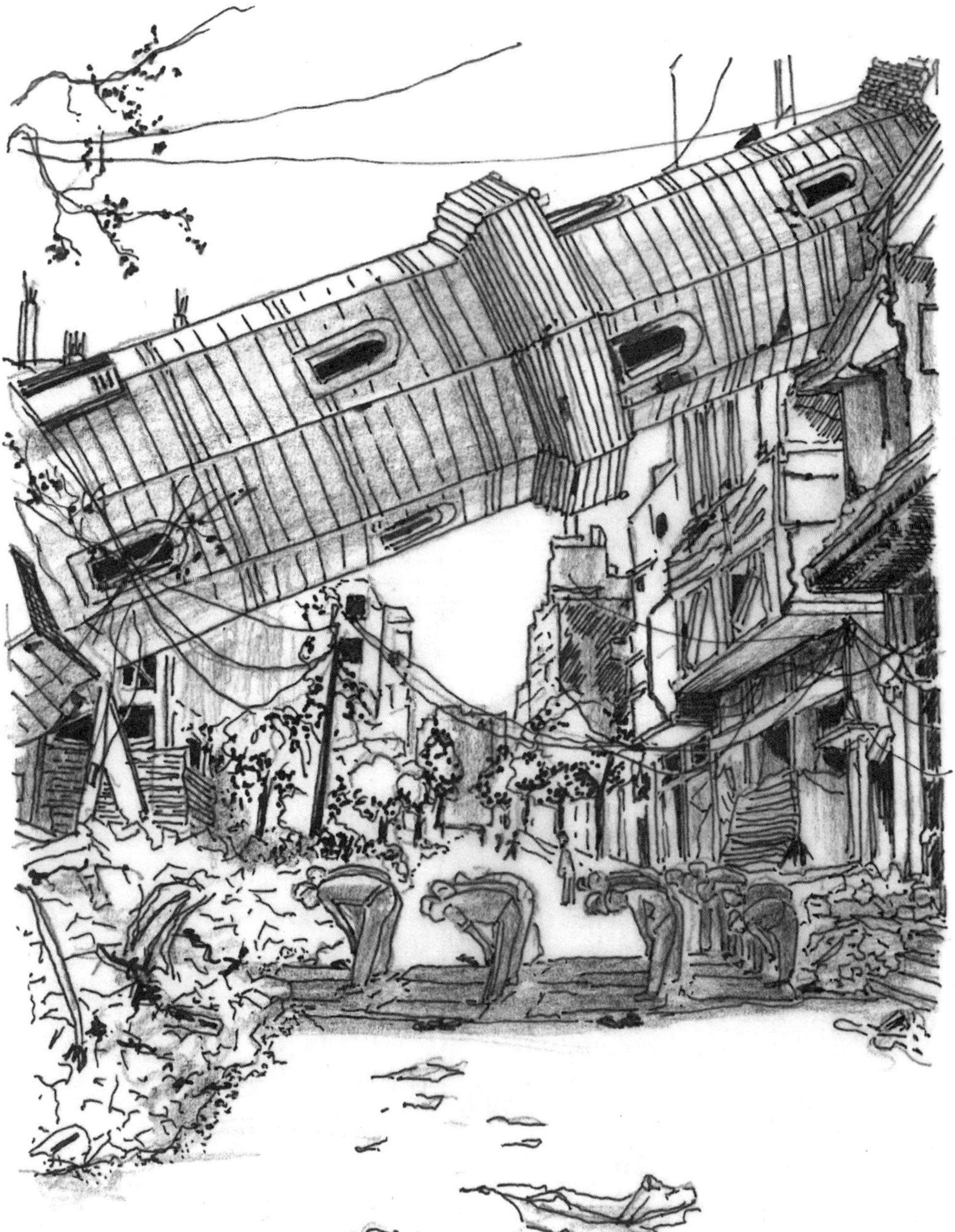

A group of men praying under a collapsed minaret in Gaza, shelled by Israeli forces

First published in the United Kingdom in 2026 by
Thames & Hudson Ltd, 6–24 Britannia Street, London WC1X 9JD

First published in the United States of America in 2026 by
Thames & Hudson Inc., 500 Fifth Avenue, New York, New York 10110

For illustration base sources, see picture credits on page 235

EU Authorized Representative: Interart S.A.R.L.
19 rue Charles Auray, 93500 Pantin, Paris, France
productsafety@thameshudson.co.uk
interart.fr

A CIP catalogue record for this book is available from the British Library

Library of Congress Control Number 2026938418

ISBN 978-0-500-02966-4
01

Printed and bound in Slovenia by DZS-Grafik d.o.o.

MIX
Paper | Supporting responsible forestry
FSC® C106600

Contents

Introduction

Like most devout Muslims, I pray five times a day. But, contrary to what one might assume, I do not go to a mosque, at least not frequently. This doesn't make my prayers any less important. It does, however, say something about the role of mosques in our times.

To be a Muslim is to testify, 'There is no god but God, and Muhammad is His messenger.' This is called the *shahada* (literally, 'testimony'; or 'declaration of faith'), and it is all that one needs to utter, with full conviction, to become a Muslim on the spot. The belief that takes off from that conviction is the core of Islam, and it is called *aqeedah* ('creed'). To maintain this belief, Islam has a meticulous legislative aspect, known as *sharia* (literally, 'correct path', the legal and moral system derived from the Quran and the Sunnah, or teachings and practices of the Prophet Muhammad). The purpose of these laws is essentially to safeguard two main things: faith and rights.

As much as it is simple and straightforward to become a believer, it can be complicated and overwhelming to follow the rules, because there are rules for everything at any given time. Non-Muslims often find that problematic: too controlling, too dogmatic. However, for Muslims, these rules – which we believe are God-sent, and not man-made – are very helpful. We think of them as the operating instructions of a machine sent by its maker.[1] Islam means submission: a deliberate giving in to a complete and unwavering faith in the Creator, who is compassionate, merciful and wise. Our commitment to the rules of that Creator comes out of trust, rather than a blind following of dogma.

Islam, like all religions, has a societal component. This begins with the way Islam enhances all aspects related to the individual, but always with an eye on the wider community in order to create a strong, collaborative society. Prayer is the first building block of that societal project. Praying takes place after ablution, and it is in itself an act of spiritual (as well as physical) cleansing – the Prophet Muhammad compared praying with bathing in a river five times a day – and it can take place anywhere, as long as the location is clean. I can pray in a hotel room or on the road, on board a plane or in my home, and I have done all of these. Of course, there are rules, and this book will shed light on some of them, but the question that arises here is: if anywhere on earth can be a place for prayer, what then is the need for mosques?

The mosque is primarily a place for group prayer, which is encouraged in Islam. While, first and foremost, the mosque is a house of God (there are meanings attached to this concept, which will also be explored in this book), it is also a symbol of faith, an architectural and societal landmark, and an attraction that functions like an open invitation for those who are visiting a place, or working nearby, or simply passing through, to take a break for the few minutes that are required for prayer. Ultimately, the mosque is the meeting place for the Muslim community, where, under the watchful eye of the Creator, both the *aqeedah* and *sharia* meet, and from whence various kinds of social activities have thrived in Muslim nations[2] since the first mosque was built by the Prophet Muhammad in Medina in 622 CE.

Since then, almost 3.6 million more mosques have been built around the world. They all vary in shape and in size, and also in their means and modes of architectural expression. However, there is a consensus among scholars, and even among casual readers of Islamic architectural legacy, on two main things. First, there is an undeniable unity even among the variety of mosques (and works of Islamic art and architecture in general, for that matter) that were built from the birth of Islam in the seventh century until the fall of the Ottoman Empire in 1922. Second, ever since that latter date, this unity has been shattered and the continuity interrupted, leaving behind a fragmented realty and a puzzling vacancy which has kept the creators of new mosques on a constant search for an agreeable alternative.

Interestingly, when it comes to the shape and form of the mosque, aside from some general guidelines, there are virtually no rules that specify any precise architectural style. This aspect of expression enjoys almost total artistic freedom. Thus, the question of the unified character of the mosque in the twelve centuries that preceded the Western colonial takeover of Muslim lands demands our attention. There is an underlying paradox when it comes to the two phases. On the one hand, a distinctive character and recognizable identity thrived freely during times that some would argue were marked by constrictions. On the other hand, in our 'free' modern era, attempts to establish a fresh new model that is in line with the times have proved to be conflicted and floundering.

There are a number of causes and contexts that will be explored in this book, in order to reach a true understanding of the extent of the conundrum around creating a new architectural model for mosques that might rival that abruptly discontinued legacy of Islamic architecture. It is important to understand that Islamic architecture was born in the womb of the mosque, which remains as its most distinguished indicator today, however lost it looks.

This lostness is most acutely felt in Western cities, whose skylines increasingly include the sight of a minaret. The debate around the architecture of the mosque and its building process is more intensely felt here than in the Muslim world, yet the conundrum of the two seems to be converging, even as our worlds drift apart. I experienced this first-hand when travelling to various European cities. Normally, I was hosted close to the centre of the city, where the 'action' took place. The mosque, on the other hand, was usually to be found at the 'edge', shrouded in mystery and possibly 'danger'. It brings to mind the comments made by the controversial French novelist Michel Houellebecq, in response to acts of violence in Paris, when he predicted a backlash: 'There will be attacks and shootings in mosques, in cafés frequented by Muslims.'[3] Such circumstances shift the need for understanding the mosque from timely to pressing.

Throughout its long history, the general style of the mosque never altered, no matter where it was located in the various regions where Muslim communities congregated, from China to Spain. While the mosque has always been a reflection of its own environment – in terms of local building materials, regional artistic preferences, and so on – that variety was always recognized in an overall unity, which was essentially an embodiment of a world view. Just as importantly, the mosque was never merely a place for prayer; rather, it was the axis of the Muslim city, around which all its human activity orbited. Comparing those realities with the state of today's mosque, one can immediately recognize the sense of reduction that has befallen not only the form of the mosque but also its very function.

I admit that, before taking on the task of writing this book, there was much that I was unaware of in regard to the form and function of the mosque. At various junctures, I had more questions than answers. The source of my ignorance was not due to lack of interest or poor research; it was, rather, because this process of reduction has left the mosque a shell of what it once was, and what it is supposed to be.

It is easy to jump to the conclusion that the legacy of colonialism is largely responsible for the sense of alienation that collectively afflicts modern-day Muslims, whether in formerly occupied Muslim countries or in the Western lands where Muslims have made their homes. However, it will lead us nowhere to put the blame entirely on colonial powers. Through telling the story of the mosque in this book, it is one of my intentions to demonstrate how what started as a colonial project to undermine the core of Muslim societies in fact ended up becoming a self-destructive act, which continues to this day.

Furthermore, across the globe we have become more and more united in our problems, even if their causes remain distinct. With globalism and the increase in communications, it is no longer possible for conflicts and the resulting population migrations, and all that these realities entail, to be brushed under any carpet; nor are they balls that can continue to be thrown in someone else's court. And since the different parts of the world are also united in having to deal with various degrees of governmental shortcomings, it falls on the shoulders of ordinary citizens who wish to live in a peaceful and harmonious society to seek understanding of the 'other' wherever it can be found.

When I started writing this book, I thought I was writing an account that could help in that task; namely, for the 'other' to understand the part of the world that I come from and the culture to which I belong. However, not too far down the line, I discovered I was on a personal journey to understand my own culture and religion before anything else.

Most books about the historical architecture of the mosque approach their subject either from a formative or stylistic perspective, or through a

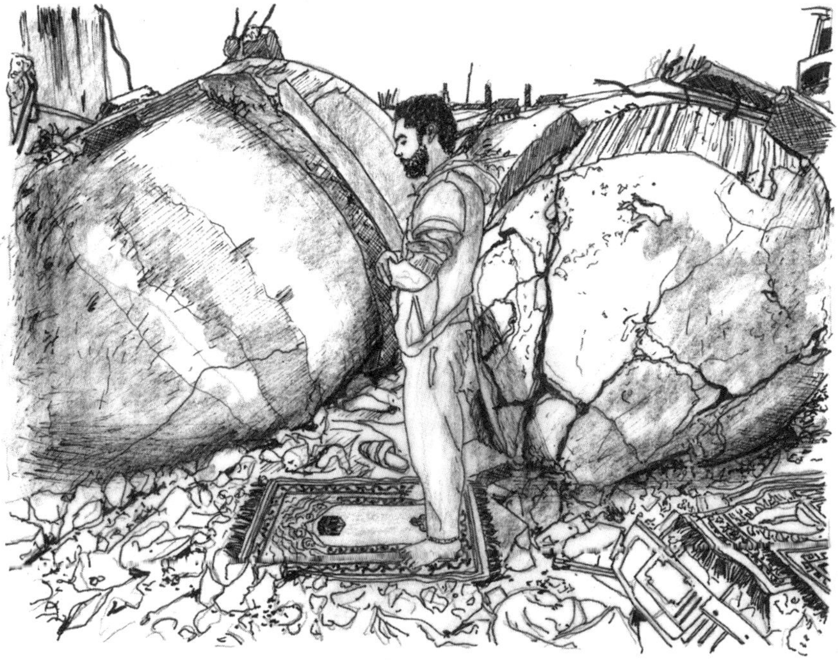

A man praying at the site of one of more than 1,100 mosques destroyed in Gaza by Israeli bombardment

chronological or evolutionary framework. Similarly, accounts that deal with the modern expression of the mosque often find themselves going down the same categorical or developmental paths in order to tell their story. But at the heart of all these approaches lies one main question, the answer to which seems to be elusive (whether to experts or the general public). It is a key question that keeps on slipping through the threads of narrative and history, coated with layers of misinterpretation and confusing terminologies: *what is the essence of the mosque*, both as a sacred place and as an architectural expression?

There are a number of challenges that lie ahead of delivering a fair answer to this two-fold question, most of which swim in the choppy waters between the West and the East. Whether you are a casual reader or an invested scholar, you will too often be confronted with orientalist myths and politicized stereotypes. You will also have to wade your way through the jargon of either a zealous romanticism or blind antagonism.

While many great works have been written about both ancient and modern mosques, and about Islamic architecture in general (with mosques and their art forms usually given as key examples), I nevertheless believe that I may have something to say when it comes to viewing the mosque in mediating terms: between past and present, East and West, form and meaning.

This is why I have chosen to examine the mosque from three angles constituting the three parts of the book. The first focuses on the fundamental reason for which the mosque exists; that is, the Muslim faith. The core of this part revolves around how Islam as a faith and a world view shapes the mosque as an object, and how the mosque in turn shapes Muslim life. In my view, this is the crucial point of departure, in order to truly appreciate the architecture of the mosque.

In the second part, having established a solid basis from which to look at the mosque as an orientation to the world, form becomes the focus. In order to tackle the various aspects of the mosque's form, we will look at the conclusions of those who have studied the mosque, and also put forward additional ideas in the light of acquired knowledge of faith and form.

Finally, the third part presents the mosque in a new light – the light of freedom, as a comprehensive and dominating force not only in the creation of the mosque but also in its life. I view this freedom against the ethos of both historic and modern Islamic structures, in an attempt to reach some conclusions around the future of the mosque.

By examining key concepts and key examples, and through debunking some of the myths around the architecture of the mosque (and Islamic arts and architecture in general), it is my hope that this book will be a step on the path towards bringing the mosque and its arts closer to the reader. By doing so, I hope I can help to bring two worlds which have drifted apart a little closer together.

It is a daunting task, so I send this book out into the world humbly, as I do my prayers.

Homs, Syria
Ramadan the 17th, 1446

Part I

Faith

Chapter 1

What is 'Mosqueness'?

'In the modern world the mosque, more than any other building type of Islam, signals and reflects the values both of client groups and of society, and thus becomes a manifestation of changes occurring in Muslim society.'

HASAN-UDDIN KHAN[1]

The mosque and its networks

At the corner, between the aromas of zaatar and the fragrance of hand-bottled perfumes, lies a small mosque. In my bag, I am carrying four tiny bottles containing a few last drops of scent made by a Damascene perfumer, famous for his talents in deciphering the components of fragrances. At the entrance to the covered souq, I was told that the perfumer's shop was tucked away 'a few steps past the "Fasi" mosque'. So I pass the walnut baskets, the dried apricots and the sugar-coated almonds. I look for 'signs' of the mosque under the roof of the covered Al-Buzuriyah market, and between the endless rows of compact shops spilling their wares into the main walking lane. I try not to be distracted by all the vibrant colours and wafting scents. And not to get run over by the packed trolleys that are whizzing by, chauffeured by young boys masterfully moving merchandise through the maze of the souq. A tray of warm chickpea salad passes over my shoulder – the delivery boy carries it overhead, as he manoeuvres his way seamlessly through the crowds. My eyes follow the tray, just as Alice in Wonderland followed the rabbit.

I must have missed the mosque, because I arrive at a rabbit hole at the end of the souq, a few steps below street level. A short dark corridor leads to what appears at first glance to be a small courtyard, but turns out to be the site of an old khan (trading post and hostel) that has lost its two wooden domes, of which only soaring stone arches and circular rims remain as traces. To my left, I finally spot the perfumer's shop, not because of a window display or a shop sign, but rather from the stacks of bottles and piles of boxes that frame the narrow wooden door of the 'Alghabra' shop. Alghabra is the last name of the family that have made perfumery their business in this historic quarter of Old Damascus. In fact, on my way several shops have had this family name on their signage, adding another layer of confusion to my expedition.

Inside, a long table occupies the space behind the door, covered with all sorts of bottles: big, small, plastic, glass, metal. The perfumer rises like a magician from underneath the table and asks me how he can help. The business of identifying the remnants of scents in my bottles, recomposing and refilling takes only a few minutes, during which time a boy referred to as 'Little One' is called upon to fetch some of the required ingredients from the piles outside. The ingredients are efficiently delivered, then, like an elf, Little One vanishes through one of the back doors. On my way out, I see him again, this time being harangued by a lady customer who delivers a sermon on the bad effects and negative image of a cigarette he has in his mouth. I can see she has completely lost him when she tells him he should be at school. Work for youngsters is part of the local culture; this is how family businesses have been built for centuries. Little One, however, is not part of a family business. Instead, he belongs to the Syrian generation of war, in which many fathers were lost, and many 'little ones' stopped being little all of a sudden. So, he shrugs off her remarks and pointedly asks for her 'real request'.

For a short moment before I re-enter the souq, the sky above me is framed by the two large stone rings of the khan. Then I'm faced with the bustle of the beehive again. This time, however, I have caught a glimpse of a small protruding minaret adorning the top corner of a structure at the intersection. This minaret was built as an integral part of the corner of the building – not perched on top of it – because otherwise it

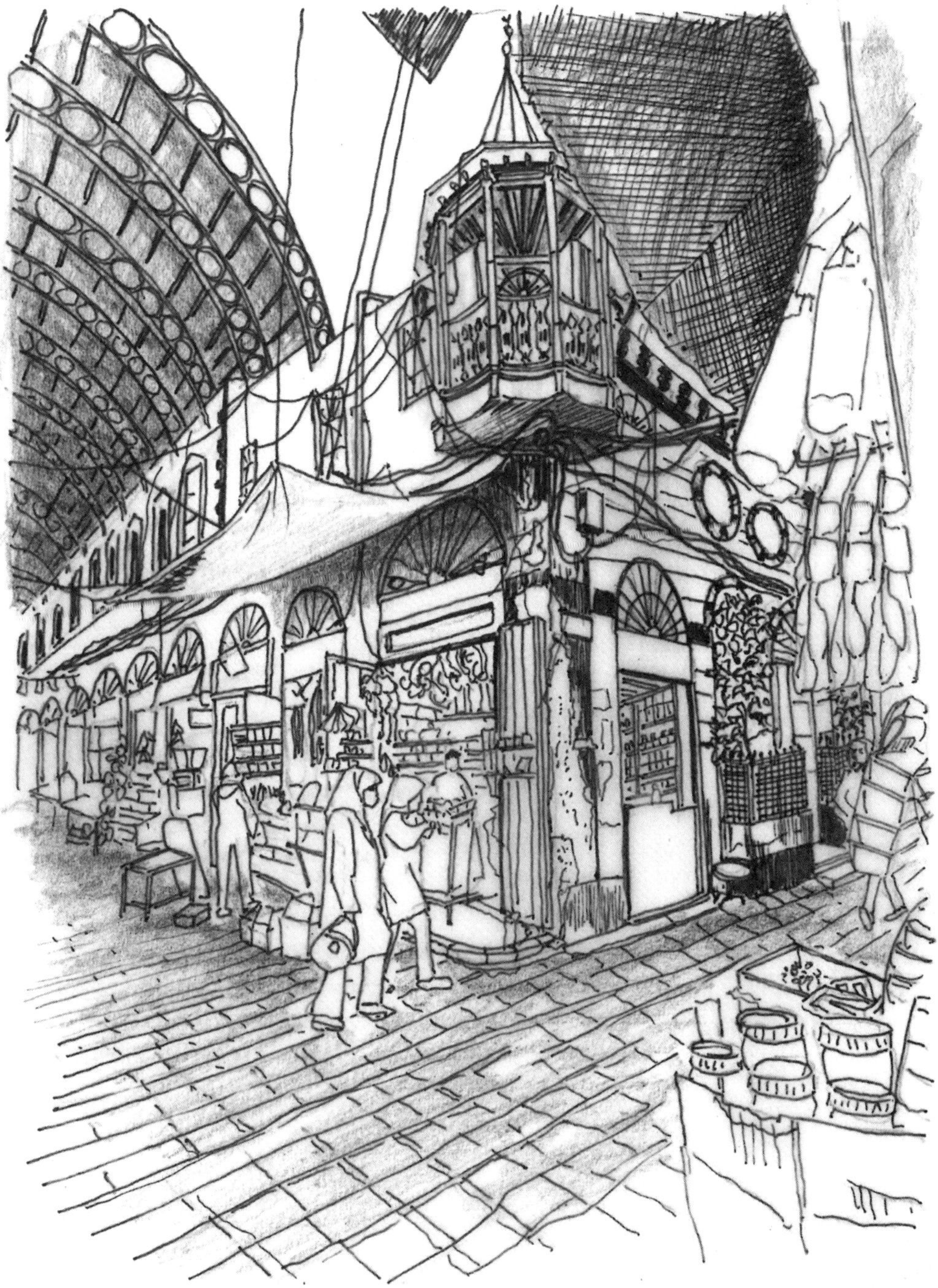

The minaret of Al-Farisiya Mosque,
at Al-Buzuriyah souq in Old Damascus, Syria

would be invisible to the souq's pedestrians. As a structure, it is primarily a small multi-angled balcony made entirely of wood, with a canopy hooded into a cone. Loudspeakers, with horns facing either direction of the two diverging alleys at the intersection, are fixed on the finely carved poles that spring from the concavely lobed railing. This miniature minaret performs its double function of delivering both visibility and audibility, with minimal disruption to – and in total harmony with – its surroundings.

Like the minaret, the door to Al-Farisiya Mosque is unassuming. Framed by nothing more than a climbing Araliaceae Juss. plant, the entrance of the mosque is simply part of the façade of the rows of buildings of the souq. The mosque used to be part of a madrasa (religious school), built by the Mamluk amir Faris al-Din al-Duadar in 1405; hence the name of the place, Al-Farisiya ('that of Faris'). However, al-Farisiyah is also the Arabic word for 'Persian', which has led to colloquial slippage, changing the 'Al-Farisi' into 'Al-Fasi' to avoid confusion. But the mosque has another colloquial name, which is the 'mosque between the two basins', in reference to two small basins that were reportedly built beside the mosque but no longer exist.[2]

Duos are definitively present in the mosque's architecture: besides the two basins, there are two anonymous tombs inside. Moreover, the mosque overlooks the street through two windows on each of its two façades. Additionally, the mosque's income is generated through two tiny adjacent *waqf* shops (shops set up, via the Muslim *waqf* charitable endowment system, to help fund the maintenance and upkeep of the mosque). According to a report prepared by Dr Layla al-Sabbagh, two German researchers worked on studying the history of the mosque, and interpreted the two basins in its colloquial name as in fact referring to two river basins.[3] The first is an offshoot of the River Barada: the River Banyas, which carries water from Al-Harir Khan in the old city to Al-Azm Palace. The second is thought to be one of the channels in the water network of Damascus's Straight Street, connecting the hammams (public baths) of the old city.[4]

As for the fifteenth-century madrasa, no trace is left. This type of religious school, which became prevalent during Ayyubid and Mamluk times, normally has a mosque attached. Importantly, these schools historically relied on a wide network of *waqf* properties, which sustained their high level of service and education. *Waqf* properties, land and funds given away by their donors in perpetuity (*waqf* literally means 'imprisonment' or 'prohibition', emphasizing its unchangeable status) enabled communities to establish not only madrasas, mosques and shops, but also baths, khans, hospitals, elements of public infrastructure such as bridges and canals, and many other types of structure for the benefit of the public good through means of piety. In this way, the *waqf* institution, as a civil entity that was completely independent of the state, was a major contributor to public welfare. Its networks, which developed freely around a physical property with a dedicated use, endured unchanged for generations.

The last days of every rule tend to be marked by all sorts of corruption, and the end of the Mamluk era was no exception: Mamluk manipulation of the records of *waqf* properties contributed to the demise of many madrasas. Then, the Ottomans revived *waqf* and strengthened the schools, only to fail them again by converting them to follow Western systems during the 1840s. In the later nineteenth and twentieth centuries, French and British colonial powers – as part of their so-called 'modernization' process – replaced the traditional *waqf* system with a governmental *waqf* ministry: this transfer of civil power to centralized state control (under an inefficient, and mostly corrupt, ministry) eroded the societal role of *waqf*, devastating social and economic networks by abruptly interrupting the development of Muslim civil society and inhibiting its civic role. The French, who occupied Syria from 1920 to 1946, dealt the last blow to the Al-Farisiya school (among others) by bombing it for good in 1940.[5]

The mosque, which survived, is referred to as a 'winter mosque' by historians, due to its lack of an open outside space. The building is made of stone, wood and mudbrick, but it has undergone three modern renovations to arrive at its current shape. The first was in 1989, in a collaboration between the Syrian *waqf* ministry, the committee that oversees protection of Old Damascus, the local merchants of Al-Buzuriyah market and the neighbours (and attendees) of the mosque. The two later renovations were undertaken solely by the local merchants.[6] The historical features of the mosque were left intact throughout. Visitors still enter through a one-metre-wide (40-inch) wooden door. To the left are the two anonymous tombs, clad modestly with a marble slab and a wooden frame. Squeezed beside them are the narrow steps that lead to the minaret. To the right is a drinking-water cooler and sinks for ablution. Ahead is the prayer hall with white lime paint and wooden panels covering the lower sections to prevent damp from showing through. The ceiling consists of open wooden beams, treated with tar. On the *qibla* wall (the wall that directs prayer towards Mecca) is carved a small *mihrab* (niche). Behind this lies one of the regular shops of the souq.

The Department of Antiquities of Damascus did not list Al-Farisiya Mosque as a heritage building, because it was classified as a newly built mosque with no archaeological relics of significance.[7] This raises questions around architectural significance as much as it does about the values of history. Regardless of any bureaucratic evaluation, however, the cobweb of historical events that seems to obscure a clear definition of this tiny mosque at the heart of Old Damascus – as do the shop signs and spice fragrances – should not prevent us from seeing how this building is a true example of living heritage. In fact, the ability of Al-Farisiya Mosque to exist as it does in our modern world should testify to the power of these buildings, which remain relevant to their communities, centuries from the date of their original creation.

The mosque's relevance stems not only from its being the spiritual axis around which the wheel of material work spins, but also from its role as the seed of the tree of social and commercial networks. Rooted as it is in place, it also forms part of spatial networks, such as the historical water-channel systems that have sustained its life. Damascus is no doubt a unique place, in the sense that no other capital in the world can compete with her for the throne of antiquity that she occupies.[8] Of course, in many places antiquity could also mean obsolescence, but not in the case of Damascus, and surely not in the case of Al-Farisiya. The question is: why?

Al-Farisiya is a living site, principally due to the networks of which it is a part and which have grown up around its existence. But the *nature* of these networks is equally important, because they reflect the moral structures of the community. While comprising the place of prayer of one of the wealthiest classes in Damascene society – the merchants of Al-Buzuriyah – Al-Farisiya has nonetheless remained low-key, despite multiple renovations. The mosque shows us how the life of a building does not necessarily rely on showy substance, and that identity does not have to be a boorish and superficial announcement of existence – which we can also deduce from those plain 'John Doe' tombs that have been carefully preserved and maintained inside the mosque. The merchants of Al-Buzuriyah have similarly felt no need to announce themselves or their level of devotion with any grand gesture; their status has never got in the way of their spiritual commitment.

But if the mosque, more than any other building in the Muslim world today, reflects the inner life of Muslim societies, what then do the 3D-printed mosques in the United Arab Emirates (UAE) and Saudi Arabia, for example, say about their societies? Or what about the monumental celebrations of hybrid historicism in politically motivated state mosques, whether in Indonesia or Morocco? Can the two extremes of humility and extravagance still be considered a true gauge of that inner life?

The problem of identity

The debate around the form of the mosque goes in parallel with that around the function of the mosque (on which Chapter 3 will expand). Since the mosque is no longer a building type that is strictly confined to Muslim-majority lands, the argument gains another layer of complexity. With the continuing waves of migrations, and the ripple effect of the ongoing colonial ambition of Western powers outside their homelands driving more and more people out of their countries, the need for places of worship but also for embodiments of native culture and bearers of identity has become an ever more pressing one. But it is not just on the landing grounds that the struggle for identity exists; it is equally present in the countries of take-off.

The root of the problem can be traced back to the collapse of the final representation of the Muslim *umma* (the worldwide community united by faith in Islam), after the fall of the Ottomans in 1924. Borders newly drawn by Allied forces during the First World War had already dissected the body of the Muslim world into English and French territories, which later mutated into a Frankensteinian jigsaw of 'independent' nations. These so-called 'modern states' were devised in a way that, needless to say, kept them subject to the colonial agenda. Being dysfunctional and corrupt, the new satellite states were governed against the people's will and aspirations. Meaningful civic roles were suppressed wherever possible (as in the example of *waqf*), and the seeds of internal conflict were sown. Islam – being not only a system of faith, but also a fully established system of governance – needed to be 'controlled'. To this day, a blockade of misleading information and literature can be found on the so-called 'clash of civilizations', whereas the truth is much simpler: namely, an unlawful and grasping desire to take over met with a sophisticated and self-sufficient system that was entirely independent.

Today, the corruption is as much 'insider' as it is 'outsider'. It is therefore too easy to oversimplify analysis by blaming problems merely on foreign players. Nonetheless, those foreign players are relentless in their interference (the list is long, but current examples include American and British intervention in Syria, Iraq, Libya, Sudan and Afghanistan, and French intervention in Mali, not to mention arms supply from the West in the recent death and destruction (which I regard as a continuation of the colonial project) in Gaza, so there is little space for self-reckoning or recovery.

Across Muslim lands, the newly imposed reality has resulted in an enormous disruption of self-image and identity, which still remain hopelessly conflicting and conflicted today. The mosque lies at the centre of the disruption, because it is the locus of Muslim life, where the duality of the spiritual and the material, the individual and the communal, the temporal and the eternal, should all be reconciled.

There are over 3.5 million mosques worldwide, and with every newly built one a step towards *a* direction is being taken. To make sense of the mosque is to make sense of oneself as a Muslim, and to make sense of a Muslim for the non-Muslim. The mosque is a building type that is like no other – even within the category of religious buildings – mainly due to the comprehensiveness and generative body of liturgical legislation of Islam, in comparison to the other monolithic religions. The mosque is thus central to the whole of Muslim society, as the locus for education, negotiation, law-making, meeting and bonding, as well as worship.

In today's volatile and divisive world, the mosque – with regard to both its activities and its symbolism – stands as a mysterious object for many. On the one hand, in its entirety, the mosque represents the constants of Islam as a religion and a way of life. On the other hand, there is pressure to keep its form and expression relevant and 'up to date', which puts the building in confrontation with its own meaning. Time seems to have stopped with the last, Ottoman-era representation of the *umma*. The fragmentation that followed, and the hollowness that ensued, left the builders of mosques (both as clients and architects) facing the conundrum of creating a model that would appeal to the public yet still convey the political, social and collective identity markers that this unique building type has been used to carry.

This is where mosques like Al-Farisiya stand out like lighthouses amid the turbulent seas of questions that engulf the meanings of today's mosque. To summarize the main matters of contention around the mosque today, we can consider two general issues. The first pertains to its 'form', which has found itself on a pendulum swing between outdated historical eclecticism and empty modernist shell. The second revolves around the 'message' of the mosque, as different groups have different expectations of the building. It is worth remembering that these two main challenges have one root cause; namely, the search for identity.

We must recall, above all, that these challenges are novel by-products of our present times; more specifically, they are the indirect results of that decisive moment in history after which Muslim lands no longer dwelled in that unified state of sovereignty and sobriety in which identity – whether national or individual – prospered concomitantly with everything around it. The Muslim world had, of course, faced countless times of turbulence and devastation before the fall of the Ottomans and the Western colonization that culminated in the mandates of the early twentieth century. However, the issue of identity had never before been so palpable, and its regaining of that former sense of unification had never seemed so unattainable. In the following chapters, more light will be shed on this change of hands in the various regions of the Muslim world, and what it meant for the development of the architecture of the mosque and its meanings. But, for now, it is vital to see that understanding the mosque as a building and as a concept is challenged by this modern dichotomy between what it historically represents and what it actually means today; namely, the disconnect between the Islamic religion as a spiritual force and structure, and the architectural articulation of the mosque as both a form and a process.

Al-Farisiya is a fine example of how the mosque – regardless of its size or scale – can grow like the root of a flourishing tree of networks. But there are conditions to that growth, which we will see throughout the course of this book, and they lie at the heart of the definition of what the mosque means. These conditions cannot be definitively prescribed, but one can glimpse something of their truth if one compares a mosque like Al-Farisiya with mosques that exhibit a high level of experimentation – the Federal Territory Mosque in Kuala Lumpur, for instance, dares to combine five different architectural styles (Ottoman, Egyptian, Moroccan, Malay and Persian) – or with mosques that challenge the centuries-old primacy of respectful and thoughtful craftsmanship by using, for example, prefabricated metal domes that can be purchased off the street in Indonesia.

Personally, I find such approaches problematic, not just because of the aesthetic choices that have been made, but because these kitsch architectural expressions place 'distance' between the mosque and its users. And by users, I do not mean simply those who actually pray in a mosque, but also those who pass, visit or live near it. The scale of the problem expands when the mosque is built outside the Muslim-majority parts of the world. There, the identity issue ceases to lurk beneath the surface, and becomes the axis around which civil conflict can potentially arise. An extreme example of an intersection of tensions is Park51, a planned project near the World Trade Center in New York, where the 9/11 attacks took place. Here, the disastrous public perception of Islam (due to criminals who identified as Muslims) and inflammatory propaganda regarding places of prayer being 'training grounds for terrorists' led to the cancellation of the project, which had been envisioned as a community centre – with a prayer space – for all New Yorkers.

Buildings, in general, implicitly carry different meanings and convey stories about their creators, contexts and compositions. Nevertheless, the mosque (as the main representation and generative engine of Islamic architecture) deserves special attention. For it is within an incredibly short space of time (by the mid-second century of *hijra* – the start of the Islamic calendar, marking the migration of the Prophet Muhammad from Mecca to Medina in 622) that the building was able to formulate and convey its own unique language of expression across enormous swathes of territory, populated with a great variety of races, ethnicities and tongues, and – more crucially – in the midst of surrounding civilizations that were at their prime. Henceforth, a fully developed character and an undeniable unity were maintained for almost twelve consecutive centuries, across those same diverse geographies. And from the mosque sprang similarly diverse but equally unified artistic manifestations to be, in their totality, read and understood as 'Islamic arts and architecture'.

To view this narrative in comparison with the current state of floundering and fragmentation that surrounds the modern architecture of the mosque must invite curiosity, if not regret. Architecturally, and beyond their immediate purpose of service, it is irrefutable that most of the mosques being built today are, at heart, attempts to tackle the question of identity. Pulled in every possible direction – whether by upholders of tradition or proponents of modernism, by conservative neighbourhood communities or ambitious heads of state – the mosque, as a shell of that quest, and racked by the dilemma of whether to open up or cocoon in, is left torn beyond recognition.

Like all buildings, mosques are 'read' by three main groups: the builders (whether official patrons or members of the general public), the users (whether frequent attendees or casual visitors), and the non-users (whether permanent neighbours or passers-by). Because identity is involved, the most radical requests usually come from the first and the last categories; namely, the builders who push for an agenda, and the non-users who act against it, or vice versa. Islam being so misunderstood today aggravates complexity and, in turn, this begets further misunderstandings in relation to a building within which form and function are never intended to remain confined, with no relationship to broader networks. Therefore, the most basic question becomes: what is a mosque?

Beyond the obvious – that is, being a place for prayer – the mosque is the beating heart of Muslim society. It constitutes the main locus for the diversity of all its expressions (whether religious, educational, cultural or social), and the fundamental forum of the multitudes of its peoples (of whatever age group, ethnicity, class or background). It is where networks are born, and where they are maintained. All these aspects revolve around belief in or respect for the central truth of Islam; that is, belief in the one God and sole Creator, and the message of his Prophet Muhammad.

Architecturally, the mosque is the first, finest and most central expression of the architecture of Islam. It is *the* object where style is formulated; then, from this hub, the various artistic and architectural trends that have taken form are reflected in the mainstream. In that sense, the mosque, as an object, can be viewed as the condensed formula of all the arts and architecture of Islam.

The terms 'Islamic architecture' (and 'arts') and 'mosque architecture' (and 'arts') are thus sometimes used interchangeably to refer to the artistic product of the faith. It is interesting that, despite the centrality of the mosque in Muslim life, there is a prevalent confusion surrounding the essential meanings of the mosque. In other words, there is a dichotomy between the mosque and what one might call 'mosqueness'; namely, the quality that should differentiate a mosque from any other type of building.

In creating new mosques, 'mosqueness' has generally become *the* sought-after quality – by both users and patrons. By this, I mean that the intent is for the building to be instantly recognized as a 'mosque'. This *image* of the mosque, as superficially perceived, is in fact at variance from its true reality. The history of Islamic architecture, spanning from the seventh century to the nineteenth century, reveals to us no such struggle to produce 'something' out of nothing; nor does it resort to blind repetitions and reiterations. For identity was not an issue, as it was lived and not borrowed. The mosque is a reflection of its times, and the current search for 'mosqueness' seems to be a search for a lost meaning and locus for public agreement. In my view, there should be no discrepancy between the mosque and 'mosqueness', which is only possible if one can truly understand the mosque as a building and as an object, as a form and a function, and, most importantly, as a place of meaning.

The first 'mosque' ever to have been built is actually different from the first mosque in Islam. While the Kaaba in Mecca is considered the first house of worship, built originally by Adam and then rebuilt by the Prophet Ibrahim and his son Ismail, this actually predates the formal establishment of Islam. It is the Quba Mosque in Medina, built by the Prophet Muhammad and his companions, that is regarded as the first mosque in Islam. However, Islam is an inclusive message, which looks at the history of humankind as one continuous pursuit to fulfil longing for the Creator and adherence to His teachings. 'Surely the first House [of worship] established for humanity is the one at Bakkah [Mecca] – a blessed sanctuary and a guide for [all] people,' states the Quran.[9]

Al-Alamin is the term that the Quran uses to refer to the entirety of humankind and creation. The 'blessed sanctuary and guide' is thus provided for *al-Alamin* everywhere and since the beginning of time, because the message of Islam recognizes all the monolithic teachings as pieces of one puzzle, the aim of which is the same: veneration of the one God and sole Creator. Likewise, all the prophets and all the messengers are equal in the eyes of God: 'We make no distinction between any of His messengers.'[10] The Prophet Muhammad himself summarized his role as the final messenger by saying, 'I have been sent to perfect good moral character.'[11]

There are those who think the next step, with regard to the collapse of identity, is to live in a post-identity era. However, such concepts are easily misunderstood and misused as an excuse to dissolve whatever remains of the Muslim character and reduce it to an over-simplified building block. For example, at the Abrahamic Family House, opened in Abu Dhabi in 2023, the idea of an overarching belief in the one God and the appreciation of good moral character has been misleadingly moulded into the conclusion that a mosque, a church and a synagogue can all be combined into one complex, made up of three separate cubes, representing each house of worship respectively.

This dissolution of differences seems problematic to me, because it ignores the fact that the distinct identity of each one of those three houses of worship means that they are essentially incomparable and encompass so much more than just a 'platonic form of building'. Despite the open invitation of Islam, the faith draws very defined boundaries around identity that start to formulate as soon as one enters into its realm. The Quran uses the words 'vow' and 'pledge' as indicators for what is understood as a contract with God ('Make good on your pledge to me, I make good on mine to you': Surah Al-Baqarah, verse 40). To enter Islam is to accept this agreement, which organizes the life of the Muslim around structures of dos and don'ts. If one can make the analogy, it is similar to accepting a new nationality, after which a person has to abide by the laws of that country.

On the other hand, while in essence the mosque as a place for prayer needs be no more than a space with an orientation towards the *qibla* (some go as far as reducing it to a wall, although I disagree with that notion, since the first mosque was in fact a building and not a wall), the mosque as a building – just like a church or synagogue – belongs to the field of art, provided this does not contradict the legislative rules of faith, and identity stems from this key factor. This incorporates a deeper type of orientation, one that is imbued in the faith, and thereafter influences a unique experience of interaction with the universe accordingly. This is how art is born with an expression of its own – one that distinguishes a church from a mosque, for instance, far beyond the obvious liturgical differences.

Although Muslims have lost their confidence, along with their identity, here it is enough to remember that, since its inception, Islam has been very clear about emphasizing its own identity, in lifestyle, behaviours and so on, and also in optics. The message is clear: to enter Islam is to enter a new life, a new agreement.

Prayer

In 622, on the very day that the Prophet Muhammad arrived at the outskirts of Medina, he personally laid the foundation stones of a primitive mosque. It was located on the southwestern edge of the city, near what was then the village of Quba, where the Prophet and his companions stayed before moving on to Medina itself. Over the next few days, they worked alongside locals to complete the construction. The Quba Mosque was reportedly a small square space, with a flat roof made of palm leaves and timber. With that first mosque, the building blocks of the new religion and the accompanying new society were laid.

In order to understand the mosques that followed, one must first understand the nature of the primary activity that the mosque houses: prayer. This was described by the Prophet as the 'main pillar of religion'.[12] These words express the centrality of prayer (*salat*, in Arabic) to the faith and life of the Muslim. It is not merely a ritual or an 'obligation' practised five times a day; it is a state of mind that accompanies the Muslim everywhere and at all times.

The Arabic word for 'mosque' is *masjid*, which literally means 'place of prostration', though prayer can be performed anywhere, as long as the location is clean.[13] The ritual of praying, which is an act of purification in itself, extends to all areas of the life of the Muslim. To place oneself 'in the hands of God' is how prayer is defined, and Muslims are encouraged to remain in this state of self-observance as long as possible, even after completing the ritual. One can pray alone and one can pray in a clean location when the time for prayer is due, but praying in a group and at the mosque is encouraged. The Friday prayer (*Jummah*) is the only mandatory form of congregational praying, and that applies solely to adult males. Otherwise, mosques are filled with congregations discretionarily driven by a desire to 'become closer to God'.

As long as I can remember I have prayed my five daily prayers, even though I was raised in what one might describe as merely a nominally Muslim household. This is to say that, despite our observance of some of the basic obligations, a true faith in Islam's spiritual meaning and a sincerely heartfelt practice were essentially absent. This state of affairs was not then – and is not now – the exception in the society to which I belong, although it is hard to be statistically precise when it comes to the practices of present-day Muslims. One of the disturbing manifestations of the identity crisis within the modern Muslim *umma* is that the prevalence of practice does not necessarily indicate a matching level of conviction. Prayer can be, for many, no more than a daily exercise. It does not 'lead away from bad deeds',[14] nor does it involve self-observance.

A serious issue that faces Muslims today – and, consequently, the general perception of Islam – is the muddling of tradition as a form of culture (which can be completely alien to religion) versus tradition as a genuine demand of faith. In my childhood household, we were led by the former, and praying was just another 'routine' of being confessionally Muslim. So, at a certain point in my teenage years, I started to question it all. In fact, it was through this questioning that I eventually found my faith, and ironically was able to break out from the shell to the core. But this is hardly a surprise: there are verses in the Quran that explicitly ask us to reflect on the 'evidence' in the universe and creation, in order to reach belief in God's existence and power. It is therefore vital not to simply accept Islam just because one was born into it, for it is not through imitation, but rather through investigation, that the way to faith is attained.

Reading about my own religion allowed me to view my praying in a completely new light. I was reminded that *salat*, which is derived from the Arabic word for 'connection', is the 'line' I should open with my Creator, where He will listen and I may speak. This encounter with the Divine cannot be more of a generous opportunity, as one scholar explained it: 'Imagine requesting an audience with a king. Naturally, your request may be denied and, even if it is actually granted, the terms for the meeting will not be set by you: when, where, how, and for how long you might wait at the threshold is completely beyond your control. Whereas with the Divine, who is the ultimate king and possessor of all creation, you are offered the *salat*, where all that is required is to show up, with a pure heart and body, so the meeting can go on as long as you wish, and it is you who gets to exit or re-enter again.'[15]

Indeed, Islamic prayer involves the whole being: it is mental, verbal and physical. Or, as architect and scholar Gülzar Haider has put it:

'Nothing expresses faith more succinctly yet symbolically, as *Salat*, the ritual prayer incumbent on every believer. It is a uniquely personal gesture where the body and all its constituents, mind and all its dimensions, and soul and all its harmonies participate.'[16]

The five canonical prayers form the basis of the ritual, to which one can add supererogatory (voluntary) prayers, as did the Prophet Muhammad. Each canonical prayer consists of a repeated sequence of standing, bowing, prostrating and genuflecting, accompanied by the murmured recitation of specific verses and prayers. This group of bodily gestures is repeated as a series of 'circuits'. It is worth mentioning that, at the beginning of every 'circuit', Muslims recite Al-Fatiha (literally, 'the opening' [of the book], i.e. the first *surah* – or chapter – of the Quran). In this short *surah*, an orientation towards the universe is set: the verse, 'It is You we worship and You we ask for help,' announces the central Islamic concept of the overlordship of God, who is 'merciful and compassionate, and the owner of the Day of Judgment', and to whom all praise and thanks are due, with a single plea 'to guide us to the rightful path'.[17]

It is a declaration which is key to understanding the state of mind behind the *salat*, and in consequence the state of mind that should lie behind the arts associated with the locus of the ritual. In his seminal book *Art of Islam*, Titus Burckhardt looks at the attitudes of prayer as representations of abasement before the Creator, guiding humans in their totality into a state of physical and spiritual equilibrium, which in turn imprints itself on the qualities of Islamic art:

> [I]t is in the upright position, which distinguishes man from all other animals, that the believer speaks to God, or that God speaks through him; bowing is an act of homage by the servant to what surpasses him, while prostration is the abandonment of oneself to the will of an all-powerful Lord .... it is this equilibrium, by virtue of which man is all and nothing before God, which confers on Islamic art its plenitude, sobriety, and serenity.[18]

The space of the mosque is thus shaped primarily through the action of prayer, as described by Burckhardt, and all that entails. Naturally, prayer and place are interlinked in any religious building. However, the fact that in Islam the whole earth is in itself a place for prayer negates the need for an absolutely prescriptive type of enclosure and places the emphasis solely on the act, time and place of prostration[19] – which begs the question of why mosques are actually needed. The apparent paradox between the open option of finding a place for performance of prayer and the restricted principles that guide the building of a mosque (whether involving religious aspects such as the orientation towards the *qibla*, or adherence to artistic and thematic elements as in any work of architecture) is instantly resolved once the distinction between the individual's practice and society's need is understood. It is similar to the difference between the open invitation of Islam and the guiding textbook of its contract.

Moreover, in building a mosque as his first act on approaching Medina, the Prophet Muhammad materialized a key principle in Islam, which is man's intended role in the world. The Quran describes humankind as a *khalifa* ('steward', 'vice-regent', 'inheritor', or 'successor') on earth. The *khalifa* is responsible for the *imar* ('building', 'maintaining', 'restoring', 'preserving' or 'refurbishing') of the earth. In his book *Deconstructing the American Mosque*, Dr Akel Kahera sheds light on the particular task of the *imar* of the mosques, as bestowed on believers in the Quran. He explains how the lexical term implies three main elements. The first is literal, through acts that aim 'to construct and preserve the physical quality of the edifice'. The second revolves around the notion that 'the prime objective of an edifice is to promote regular communal devotion since it is to be visited regularly and maintained'. And, finally, the third element is related to allowing Muslims 'to locate the textual meaning apropos to the primordial form of a mosque' – which is to say, the mosque is a form of 'spatial Sunnah', acting as an anchor to everything and everyone around it, speaking to an entire society, and perpetuating an order emanated through the example of the Prophet Muhammad that was set for all the *umma* that followed.[20]

The principles of space and love

While Quba Mosque on the outskirts of Medina constituted the first step in showing the nascent Muslim community the centrality of mosque-building in relation to the concept of *imar*, the mosque that the Prophet Muhammad built in the heart of Medina upon his arrival in the city (shortly after resting in Quba) became the prototype to which all subsequent Islamic religious building adhered. Despite being also a primordial edifice – i.e. constituting an archetype to follow and build upon, which (although basic, mirroring the state of Muslim society at the time, in which very little went a very long way) showed that a simple and genuine effort is all that is needed to bring on a force for good – the Medina Mosque (later known as the Prophet's Mosque) established the foundational formation of all the mosques to come.

Initially, the mosque at Medina was a simple rectangular enclosure measuring approximately 35 by 30 metres (115 × 100 ft). The roofs were made of beaten clay and palm leaves, supported by regularly spaced palm trunks. A door was cut into each of the walls, except for the northern wall, which became the first *qibla*, though at this time it was directed towards Jerusalem (rather than Mecca). The process of building the mosque inspired many tales of devotion, civil collaboration and comradeship, all of which qualities continued to thrive while the mosque itself flourished as the city's community centre, court of law and religious school. Following a Quranic revelation, sixteen or seventeen months after the *hijra*, the orientation of the *qibla* was changed to face Mecca, so a shaded portico (*zullah*) was added along the northern wall, where devotees gathered for worship. The resulting courtyard was often used as a civic space, and as an extra muros area for congregational worship on Fridays. Adjacent to the building, the residential quarters of the Prophet and his family were created. The mosque, in layout and general composition, mirrored traditions in the building of local residences. Across the various regions, inspired and guided by the Prophet's Mosque, mosque builders continued to look to the ordinary residence as the source of style and vocabulary of architecture in which the 'spatial Sunnah' would be manifested. These domestic origins are pivotal to the history of the mosque.

The call to prayer at Medina was made from a neighbouring roof; no minarets were built until the Umayyad era, by which time the mosque had already increased to four times its original size. Inside, there was nothing

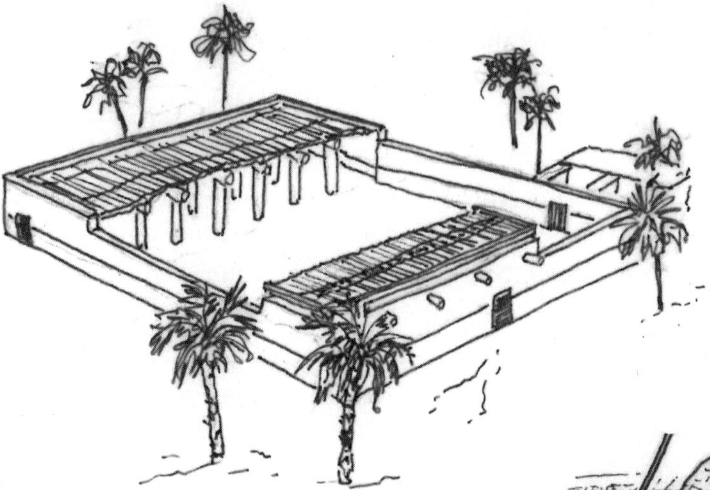

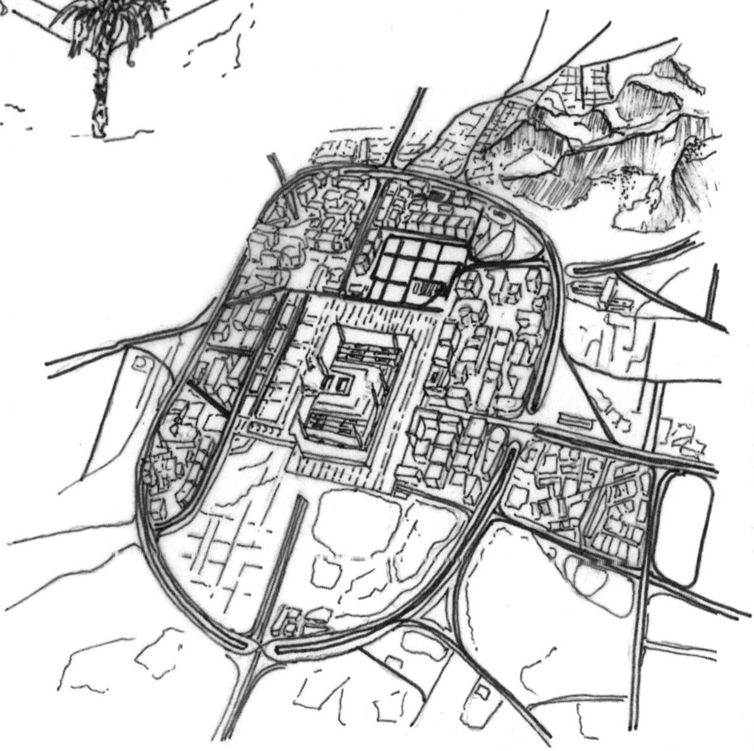

The Prophet's Mosque in Medina, Saudia Arabia: (above) a perspective showing how the mosque was during the Prophet Muhammad's time; (right) an aerial view of the mosque today; (below) a diagram showing the various expansions the seminal mosque has undergone.

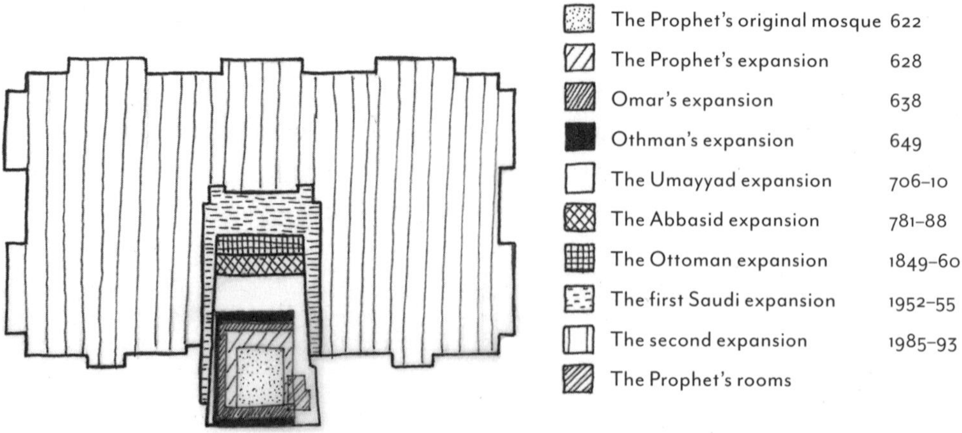

but bare ground. Even the *minbar* (pulpit) was not added until the crowds had increased in size so much that three makeshift wooden steps were put together for the Prophet to climb on and make his address.[21] Women prayed behind men in the same space, and all attendees were mindful that there should be no distractions from the purpose of prayer.

It is hard to imagine how the Prophet's Mosque in Medina, elementary as it was, formed the basis for the highly sophisticated mosque architecture that followed in less than two centuries. However, by examining the foundations of thought laid by this mosque, one can see past the liturgical elements and spatial formation. Since it is a fact that the Prophet's Mosque constituted a model that was adopted in various stylistic renditions of building across the Muslim world, the question is: how did this relatively simple and primitive structure evolve into undeniably masterful and brilliant architectural forms?

The complexity of the achievement is evident from the many different aspects to be considered. In addition to the orientation of humankind towards the universe, the space of the mosque has a directional axis; that is, towards the *qibla*. This plays a primary formulating role in the architecture of the mosque. By virtue of having all mosques – wherever in the world they are located – directed towards Mecca, a radial web of invisible axes is drawn. They all converge on that central point where the Kaaba is located, creating a collective sense of orientation that engulfs the whole of the earth. As historian James Dickie (also known as Yaqub Zaki) has explained: 'The notion of a directional axis operates on two levels: socially, as a focal point in relation to which the entire community, *umma*, is balanced, and liturgically, as the focus of prayer.'[22]

This relationship with the earth, space and population is extended through another factor, that is, the final physical posture of the prayer ritual. Prayer ends with a seated (specifically, kneeling) position on the ground, and it is also a seated position in which congregants listen to the address of the Friday prayer (*khutba*). In correlating this seated position with the ground of the mosque, Titus Burckhardt views this 'normal position of rest and contemplation' as the projection viewpoint of the whole interior space of the mosque: 'The interior of a mosque is made to be seen from this position, which amounts to saying that it relates to the earth and that its various components – pillars, columns and arcades – are distributed in such a way as to make each spot a center sufficient to itself.' As Burckhardt concludes: 'The consecrated element, if one may so describe it, is the ground itself.'[23]

The directional axis towards the *qibla* is thus a determining design principle according to which each spot – from the ground which is itself the 'consecrated element' – becomes a 'center sufficient to itself'. This is also how an absolute equality inside the mosque is achieved. This absence of hierarchy is *the* fundamental quality of space in the mosque, for it is there where every person stands equal before God to announce his or her total submission and renunciation of any temporal affairs, culminating in the act of communal prostration where all foreheads touch the ground together.

In the upright position, neighbours' shoulders must touch, and the rows must be tight, according to the commandments of the Prophet. This makes consideration of the rows another determining design principle, which is often disregarded in the modern architecture of the mosque. By choosing circular spaces or placing huge pillars inside the prayer hall, modern architects have overlooked one of the essential requirements and features of space in the mosque. Creating uninterrupted and extended rows should lie at the heart of the process of designing a mosque. Liturgically, the first row is prioritized. At first glance, this may seem like a paradox in comparison with the absence of hierarchy. However, in reality it encourages congregants to make attendance at prayer a priority.

Order also needs to be maintained with regard to another condition. For the task of designing a mosque, the tension between the axis of the *qibla* and the axis of the rows of congregants must be resolved into a state of balance. This is best explained by James Dickie in the following lines:

> For the architect of the mosque, two contradictory principles are involved. One of these stems from the insistence of Prophetical Tradition on the priority of the first row; that is, the first row of worshippers enjoys greater proximity to the source of blessing because it confronts the wall nearest to Mecca. There

> is then a *prima facie* case for extending the mosque laterally to accommodate as many as possible in the first row. But with a radial liturgy, the officiant in the middle would be invisible and inaudible at the extremities. As a result, two axes are in conflict; the primary liturgical axis of the *qibla* and the transversal axis, because of the superiority of the front row and the progressive inferiority of the rows behind. The success of a mosque architect may be measured by the degree to which he succeeds in reconciling these conflicting principles, taking into consideration the two axes and distributing mass and volume accordingly, to produce that impression of total equipoise which a successful mosque never fails to convey.[24]

Could this 'impression of total equipoise' in masses along two conflicting axes sum up 'mosqueness'? Or is it the same as the equilibrium which Burkhardt referred to as 'all and nothing before God', and which confers on Islamic art its generous qualities yet sober character? I believe that beyond the immediate answer, we must be wary not to fall for reducing the mosque to a mere design exercise, devoid of mystery and meaning.[25] Reductions have been produced around the mosque due to a process of hyper-defining. For example, is the mosque a civic gathering space, or is it a collective space of prostration? Is it a prayer hall, or is it a generic multi-purpose hall? Can it be simply a wall directed to the *qibla*, or does it have to be an enclosure? Does it have to offer a secluded spiritual retreat from the material world, or should it involve the civilian affairs of a community? In my view, the mosque combines many of these dualities as a representation of a religion that embodies dualism in its very structure – a dualism that is the essence of human life and the creation of the universe, for which Islam offers structures as a means of navigation and reconciliation. In my opinion, it is this mentality and those structures that are the true source of equipoise in mosque design.

One of the most important dualities, I believe, is that between rationality and sentimentality. What should be done, for example, when a mosque has outgrown its usage and needs to be expanded? We can start by taking a look at the Prophet's Mosque, which is today the second largest mosque in the world (after Al-Haram Mosque in Mecca). It is also the second holiest site in Islam, ranking between Al-Haram Mosque and Al-Aqsa Mosque in Jerusalem. Since its original establishment by the Prophet and the community of Medina, the Prophet's Mosque has undergone ten major renovations and expansions (for eight of these, see p. 38). The Ottomans were responsible for the sixth expansion, taking the size of the mosque to over 10,000 square metres (108,000 ft^2), supplemented with five minarets and five doors.[26] In turn, the Saudis conducted two more expansions (one in 1952 and the other in 1985), enlarging the mosque's footprint to an astonishing 98,000 square metres (over 1 million ft^2), with surrounding squares of 235,000 square metres (some 2.5 million ft^2). This was followed by the initiation of a third expansion in 2010, which is still ongoing. From the original three doors and no minarets to forty-one doors and ten minarets, the Prophet's Mosque has been transformed into a 'city' in its own right, adorned with twenty-seven automatically controlled sliding domes rimmed with over 67 kilograms (150 pounds) of pure gold and with 250 automated 'blossoming' canopies that look like an AI version of a palm grove.

In order to accomplish work on this gigantic scale, the Saudis demolished large swaths of the surrounding homes, mosques, schools and commercial areas. One might think that the highly sacred status of Medina could have spared it from the vandalism of the modernists, but what began with the destruction of the old city wall in the mid-1950s for automobile access and urban expansion has thus far ended with the ruthless erasure of the wide variety of urban premises and activities that had grown over the centuries around the Prophet's Mosque. These have been replaced with the sterility and exclusivity of gleaming commercial tower blocks, shopping malls and luxury hotels, along with a suffocating interior ring road, which together have strangled the life out of all the pre-existing human and natural networks.

In parallel with the modernist project for the city, there has been an official tendency to destroy all that is related to history, especially that which is beloved or venerated by the people. This destruction – reminiscent of the Iconoclastic Fury (*Beeldenstorm*) during the Protestant Reformation in Europe – can be explained by the adoption of the Saudi government of Wahhabism, which is 'vehemently opposed to anything

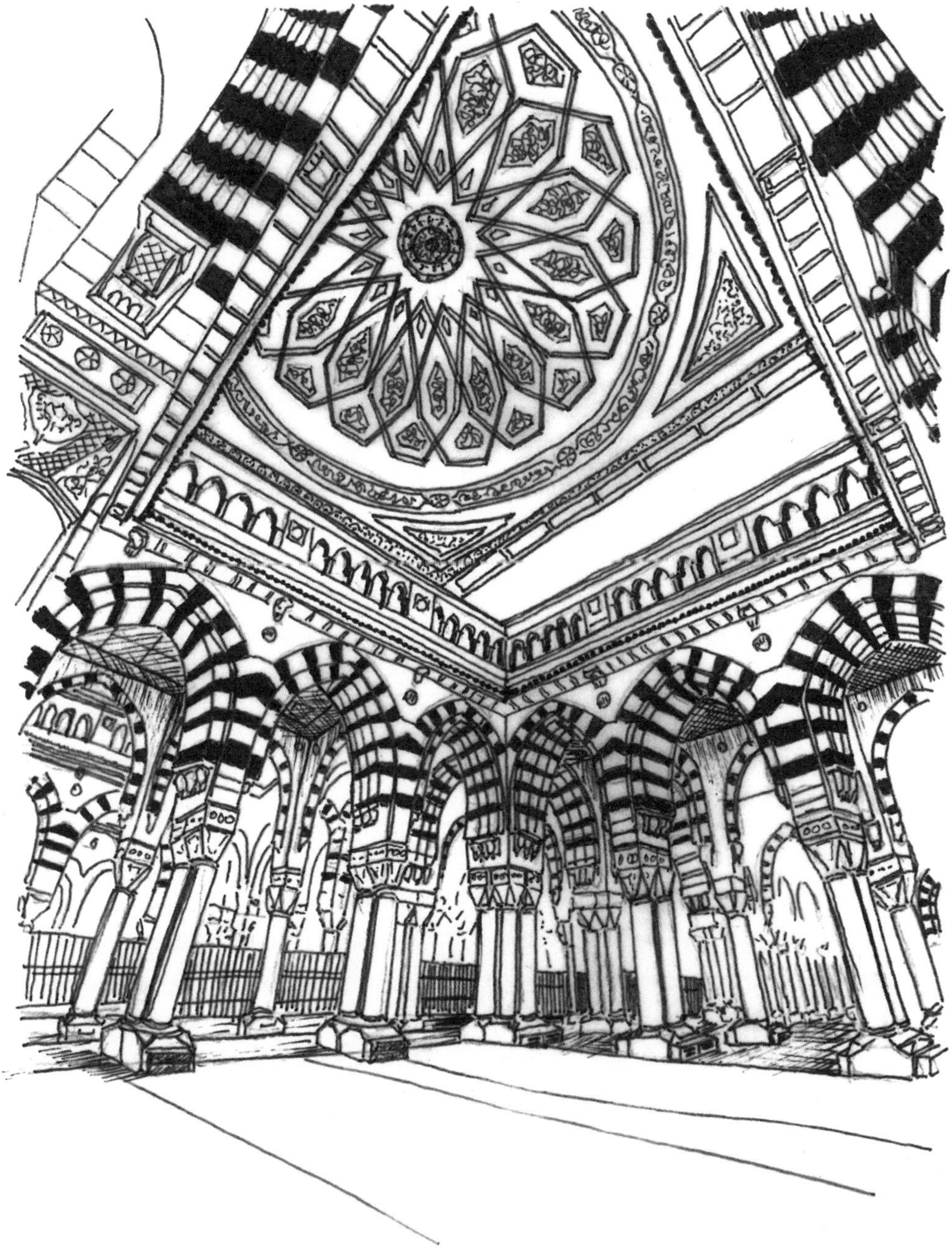

The Prophet's Mosque: an interior view

which might encourage Muslims towards idol worship'.[27] As a result of this thinking, 95 per cent of historic Medina (and Mecca) is estimated to have been destroyed in the past twenty years.[28] Even the burial place of the Prophet has become the target of a controversial plan to bring down the distinctive green dome on top, and possibly other traces of historic architecture.

Building a dome over a tomb is a relatively novel practice in Islamic architecture, introduced by the Seljuks and later heavily used by the Mamluks, eventually opening up space for the architecture of the shrine and mausoleum. There is a fine line between what can, in a religious sense, be accepted as a sign of respect and a visual marker, and what might fall into a dubious practice of sacralized veneration. But it is a line Muslims have mostly managed to walk at the Prophet's Mosque, since the installation of the original wooden dome over the Prophet's tomb, in 1279, by the Mamluk sultan Qalawun.

Since the time of the Umayyads, Muslim rulers have taken on the responsibility of safeguarding and maintaining holy religious sites. However, there is a special treatment when it comes to the Prophet's Mosque (and all that pertains to the Prophet, for that matter). This is because, for all practising Muslims (whether patrons of his mosque or wider members of the public), the Prophet Muhammad is a figure of sheer love. Beyond the respect and status he commands as a messenger of God and leader of *umma*, the figure of the Prophet enjoys the love of Muslims across nations as strongly as (if not more than) their belief in his teachings. Visitors to his mosque are not there simply for the reward of prayer; they are there for the reward of love. Indeed, eyes often start tearing up merely at the first glimpse of the green dome.

Personally, I haven't yet been to the Prophet's Mosque, not only because of the strict Saudi laws in regards to the *hajj* visa (which determines the age under which one is not allowed to make the pilgrimage to Mecca, in an attempt to regulate the overwhelming numbers to the holy sites), but also because, after the war in Syria began in 2011, Syrians were sanctioned by a politicized ban on *hajj*, which was only lifted after the toppling of the Assad regime in December 2024, marking a re-establishment of relations with Syria. Nonetheless, ever since I can remember almost nobody speaks of visiting the mosque; rather, those I have encountered who have been, talk of visiting the Prophet. It is not only place and ritual that are combined; it is also the individual and the divine. Yet the Prophet is not venerated like Jesus in Christianity (for his divine qualities). In Islam, all the prophets are messengers of God, equally human to any other man. Hence, the love of the Prophet is a personal love, immersed in gratitude.

I'm particularly touched by a poem written by the Syrian poet Anas al-Dughaim, describing his experience at the Salam Door (the door of peace) of the mosque in front of the Prophet's tomb:

> Alone at the Salam Door, I am solitary, and I am more than myself;
> for I am with you broadly and spaciously.
>
> I step forward with one foot and I retreat with the other;
> I, Oh Muhammad, coming and going.
>
> I walk and I don't. I arrive and I haven't. As if, while being alone
> before you here, I am pushing through crowds.
>
> Before you I stand broken, holding my posture,
> for I'm not propped up nor am I falling to the ground.
>
> I have found myself here because I lost it for a long while;
> away from you, everyone is lost.[29]

As much as these lines of poetry describe an individual emotional experience, they also seem to convey the consciousness of an entire population – a population that has a great sense of shame for abandoning many of the 'good ethics' the Prophet came to perfect, while still feeling the profound love and endless longing that were for so long present as a design ingredient.

Mohamed Kamal Ismail, the Egyptian architect hired in the 1950s by the Saudi king Fahd to supervise expansions of the Prophet's Mosque in Medina and Al-Haram Mosque in Mecca, seems to have been driven by the same sense of love. Ismail not only kept a discreet profile with regard to his assignment, but also reportedly refused to accept any fees for his work, viewing it as a service to God. Some would be pleased with the lack of payment, in view of the excessive ornamentation and the extravagance involved in the construction of the new architecture at the Prophet's Mosque, ranging from buying half a mountain of marble to adding adornments in gold and rare materials.

Personally, I wonder how much sense it makes to replace the organic life of the city with marble-clad squares, or living palm trees with gold-plated facsimiles. I also wonder about the sensibility behind the aesthetic choices advertised as 'pan-Islamic', as they appear on the website of one of the major artisans commissioned for the project:

> The style of the floral design for the Sliding Domes was developed [for SL GmbH, Stuttgart, Germany] especially for this project. Because the Prophet's Mosque is visited by millions of Muslims from throughout the Islamic world, it was felt that the ornament for these domes should be in a pan-Islamic, or universal, style that would appeal to all Muslims regardless of their country of origin.[30]

I find it bizarre to assume that such an ecumenical approach (completely reductionist of the spirit of Islamic architecture) would be considered unifyingly 'appealing' to all Muslims. Not only does this approach abolish style, but it also overlooks regional expressions and traditional tastes. This goes against the whole history of Islamic architecture, in which unity of faith went hand in hand with variety of expression. Once again we find ourselves, as Muslims, facing the dilemma of identity, overcompensating for the void with meaningless shortcuts, as well as imported technologies and standardized extravagance.

I cannot help remembering the first image of the Prophet's Mosque, and how the Prophet did not discriminate between the periphery and the centre of the city. On the contrary, by beginning from the modest periphery rather than heading straight to the coveted centre, he gave equal respect to both. His actions had an explicit objective: to establish that the mosque had no hierarchy in society. It is notable that this novel approach must have involved an adjustment on the part of the highly tribal societies of Medina and later Mecca, but they were evidently directed by their principled contract and devotional love, which took them in a matter of just a few decades from tribalism to civilization. By becoming the centre of human activity around the axis of spirituality, mosques brought people together around faith and virtue, but they were also reflected and radiated in the form of many networks, similarly to those at Al-Farisiya Mosque in Damascus.

It is true that there can be no possible comparison – in terms of scale or sanctity – between small neighbourhood mosques (which cannot even accommodate Friday prayer), such as Al-Farisiya, and mega-congregational holy sites like the Prophet's Mosque. However, the Prophet did plant with his mosque (before it expanded into its current incarnation) a seed of a prototype building, which grew into fully developed fruit across continents and centuries. Nevertheless, this did not happen unconditionally: within the structure of that first image of a mosque, there were frames of thought, which only got distorted and lost when we started using labels such as 'pan-Islamic'.

On the gravelled ground and under the shade of the pillars of palm trunks, the first Muslims prayed, and the first mosque was shaped. Orientation was determined, for both humans and space. Progress and civilization ensued. By remaining truthful to principles of justice and ethics, continually inspired by the universe and its Creator, and devoted to the teachings of His messenger, Muslims were able to create flourishing societies in all the places they went to. The evidence of this is the incredible wealth of arts and developments that speak in many tongues. But today progress and civilization are the very pretexts under which ostentation and extravagance go hand in hand with destruction, elimination and alienation. Perhaps all we need is to revisit the true conditions of so-called 'progress' and 'civilization'.

Chapter 2

What is the Nature of Islamic Civilization?

'While other religions conceive of the Absolute as an unattainable mystery or tend to divorce the path to that mystery from the conduct of life in this world, in Islam unity with the Absolute is attainable, and the path is revealed through knowledge, love, and correct conduct of life. In this world, in other words, Islam integrates the dual concepts of reality – the spiritual and material – and prescribes a ritual to help live the life of this world, yet be constantly reminded of the other.'

KAMIL KHAN MUMTAZ[1]

The meaning of civilization

'Are you civilized?' Few of us would answer 'no' to this question, for to be civilized is to be a human of a certain worth. Certainly, when it comes to evaluating other nations, this is the gauge that is often used by the Western measuring tape, and those who do not make the grade are stigmatized as 'barbaric' – a label that implicitly strips them of their humanity. 'Civilization' is generally defined in relation to advancement and development in areas of human society, culture, technology, and so on. However, does civilization revolve solely around such meanings? Are they not all intrinsically bound up in the very narrow measure of economic wealth?

In Qatar, the local population is among the highest paid in the world.[2] The relationship between wealth and civilization is obvious enough here to offer an answer to the question above. Like its sister nations in the Gulf region, Qatar stumbled upon enormous wealth overnight. In addition to its petroleum, and the pearls historically secured by its expert divers,[3] the country was able to exploit massive natural gas reserves discovered in 1971. I visited Qatar, and noticed that most of the faces – although rarely smiling – did not exhibit the appearance of cruelty that often accompanies the sudden fall of wealth into people's laps. In fact, native Qatari locals are even employed in a wide range of service positions, including behind counters and in drivers' seats, which is preferable to in other Gulf states, where the local presence – as opposed to imported low-paid labour – is confined to 'superior' positions.

Also evident throughout the fabric of the society is the 'modern English' touch, whether in the carpeting at the airport (as opposed to the region's usual hard floors for public buildings) or the highly regulated infrastructure of the roads. Overall, there is an exaggeration of scale – even down to the setting of the air-conditioning to degrees that force dawdling shorts-wearing Europeans to put on light jackets. The vast stretches of highway are virtually empty, except for large vehicles on the boiling tarmac, and the occasional appearance of sports bikes ridden by Asian men in full athletic gear.

My destination is a modernist mosque called the Education City (EC) Mosque, which is part of the larger building of the Qatar Faculty of Islamic Studies. In comprising both a religious university and a mosque, the building – which is also referred to as Al-Minaretein (Arabic for 'the two minarets') – replicates the concept of the madrasa. The architecture of the mosque, designed by Mangera Yvars Architects, could equally have been designed by the famously deconstructive Zaha Hadid Architects, or by AI for that matter.

Sinuously folding forms are coiled on five enormous inverted cones for pillars, which offer a clichéd representation of the Five Pillars of Islam. Each of these pillars features a verse from the Quran, written as part of a calligraphical scheme that predominates both inside and outside the building. Crossing the parking area, I am engulfed by a great sense of disorientation, which seems to me to be a general feature of the buildings in Doha. The pillars that raise the building, like the lifted hem of a dress, expose the glass façades that contain the entrance to the

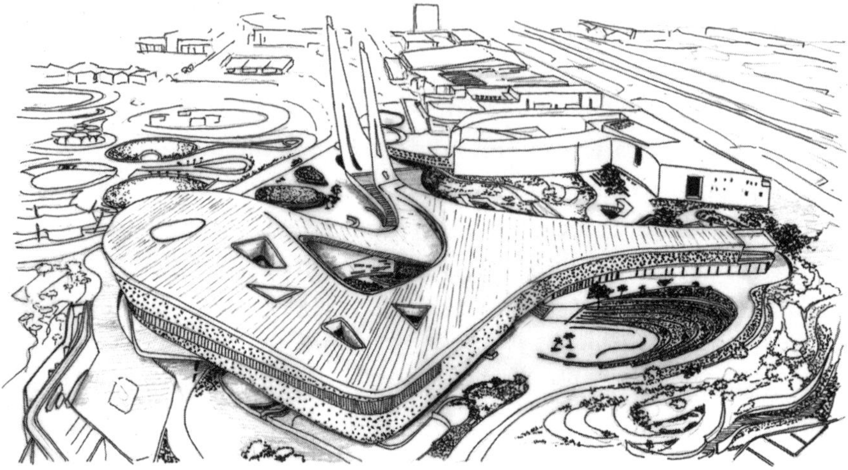

Education City (EC) Mosque in Doha, Qatar

library and the faculty, and also provide a refreshing space of cool shade, but I cannot yet see the entrance to the mosque. Everywhere I look, there is a worker with a mop or a broom – friendly and polite young men from India and Pakistan – but none seem able to offer any guidance. As I keep searching, I am in danger of falling into step-deep and foot-wide snaking streams, which I later learn are intended to represent the rivers of paradise. The general form of the building – wrapping around an inner garden, and dropping from the upper level into the ground, then ending back up with the soaring pair of abstracted minarets – looks like a giant 3D signature on the page of a manufactured landscape.

The official 'Visit Qatar' website, which advertises the building, draws attention to the vertical calligraphy on the body of the minarets. This was designed by Iraqi architect and calligrapher Taha al-Hiti, who is responsible for the works of calligraphy all over the mosque. According to the website, this vertical calligraphy 'sweeps upward, taking the viewer's eye heavenward in a contemplation of faith and meaning'. But, in reality, the minarets – which resemble the elongated tail of a plane – just look white and blank, distanced from the viewer under the glare of the sun. It is only when you climb up some stairs, leaving the minarets behind you, that you are faced with visible lines of calligraphy of substantial scale. These letters spelling out Quranic verses in metal, fixed on a mesh over the walls of the façade and surrounding the sunken garden, create an impressive space. Beautiful and striking as it is, however, it is the presence of poetry I feel, but not necessarily the divine.

I have arrived so far, but still have no clue as to where I can enter the mosque. To my right is a solitary little automatic door, lined with small sand bags, giving the impression that it is some sort of emergency exit. There are stairs in front of me, and stairs behind me. The amount of trouble in locating the entrance, for no discernible functional reason, seems baffling. I reluctantly approach the only other person here – a pregnant woman who is taking photographs of the calligraphy – and ask her if she knows where the mosque is. With a smile, she points at the solitary door.

Finally, I can enter the building. I am immediately greeted by the locker area where one places one's shoes, so I leave mine there. The floor is tiled, and a long corridor stretches ahead, leading to what turns out to be the administrative offices. At this point I'm bewildered as to where I should walk barefoot and where not, where is considered holy and where mundane, and I still have no idea where the prayer hall is. To be on the safe side, I decide to proceed barefoot. I go back to where I started, at which point I can now see a sign near the entrance warning that the place is monitored with cameras. I think to myself how weird it is to be threatened with cameras in the place where one should only feel the monitor of God. The curving rows of lined-up shoe racks only add to my impression of feeling like a rat in a maze.

So I go back to the corridor and decide to follow the light. I pass yet more closed offices, until I come to a spiral staircase lit by a skylight above. Down the stairs is an exhibition area where, barefoot, I read about the calligraphy works at the mosque. I climb up the stairs again, back to the shoe racks. This time, with more determination, I manage to get to a curved corridor that is punctured with another small automatic door. This, at last, opens into a carpeted prayer hall. The first thing I notice is that its ceiling feels too high, in comparison to the width of the space, and conjures up an auditorium rather than a prayer hall. A great effort has been made to make all the elements inside – including the *mihrab* and the *minbar* – look just as modern and reinvented as the building itself.

I look up and spot the mezzanine that accommodates the women's prayer hall, behind a CNC perforated screen. All I have to do now is find its entrance! On the second level, I arrive at last at the women's prayer hall. Like the downstairs hall, it is tucked away at the end point of a curve of the building, going against the natural flow of form and light. A woman immersed in her studies while rocking her child's baby carriage sits on the floor of the carpeted aisle, behind the screen, where low bookshelves and study furniture have been provided. We seem to be the only people in the building. So I leave her to her solitude and go on a final hectic search, this time to find my lonely shoes in the labyrinth of radial racks.

This award-winning religious building is supposed to be 'a commentary on the compatibility between Islam and modernity'.[4] The awkwardness and impenetrability of the planning, and the interrupted levels, shapes and scales of the spaces, open the success of this 'commentary' up to serious questioning. My impression is that the whole character of the place is the outcome of patching together clichés and introducing needless metaphors. In my view, no serious architecture

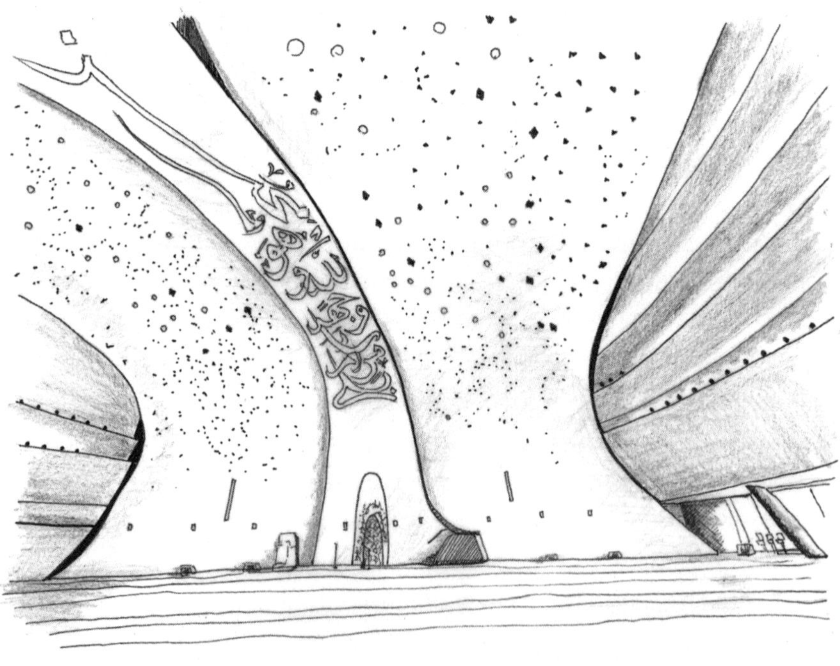

Education City (EC) Mosque: an interior view

can be achieved through literal symbolism (the five pillars, the Quranic garden, the rivers of paradise, and so on). More importantly, the essence of the mosque has been completely lost in this forced marriage between 'Islam and modernity', which could only be consummated by turning both worlds into pastiches. The third part of the book will come back to this specific issue – of how realistic it is to try to tie the knots between Islam and modernity – but here it is interesting to compare the historic form of the madrasa with buildings like this one.

The Education City (EC) Mosque in Doha is an example of the mosques categorized in *The Mosque and the Modern World* as 'mosques for public and commercial institutions'.[5] The authors of this book cleverly divided modern constructions of religious buildings according to the *intentions of their patrons*, arriving at six categories that make up the chapters of the book: 1) personal patronage (mosques built in honour of/for certain ruling figures), 2) state mosques (mosques built to represent the general official spirit and ideology of a state); 3) mosques commissioned by local government bodies (essentially, neighbourhood mosques, but built under governmental control); and 4) mosques for public and commercial institutions (these include mosques built for universities, such as the EC in Doha). The remaining two categories are for religious buildings constructed outside the borders of the Muslim world: 5) local community projects worldwide (mosques intended for the use of the Muslim community in Muslim-minority countries), and 6) Islamic centres in the West (buildings that mostly serve an Islamic diplomatic role). According to the authors, a mosque within the context of an educational institution – like the EC – represents 'a purposeful reinvention of (or return to) a tradition rather than a continuation of it'.[6] This deliberate divergence from the past has its roots in the colonial era,[7] to which many of these institutions have had to give a nod, whether for funding ties or to gain prestigious approvals.

Regardless of such considerations, the constant underlying argument that justifies stylistic choices revolves around the meaning of 'civilization'. Unlike the madrasa – which had no hidden agenda to project behind its existence – the mosque at the heart of present-day educational institutions is aimed at the subconscious of the 'enlightened' class. It sets the stage for the prescribed shape of the future – the values to which such buildings will adhere, and the (foreign) sponsoring entities who will appraise those values in embodied form, deciding whether or not they are 'progressive' and 'civilized'.

On the one hand, civilization is defined on the basis of advancements in the fields of knowledge and culture. But on the other hand, civilization cannot be separated from nation formation and relative status in comparison to other nations. If we investigate the ends to which the advancements of today are made, we will immediately discover the values they serve. Through examining the issue of scale, for instance, we will easily see that the value of the modern is quantitative. Whereas on the identity front – which distinguishes one nation from another – we are faced with a far more slippery slope.

Qatar combines two voices. One is aimed at the international front, as at the EC Mosque, announcing an embrace of the modern, the technological and the fluid. The other is aimed locally, as at the Imam Muhammad bin Abdul Wahhab Mosque (considered to be the Great Mosque of Qatar), which falls under the categorization of a state mosque. Named after the founder of Wahhabism, the mosque was inaugurated in 2011, but it shares none of the futuristic experimentation on view at the EC Mosque. With its barren walls and fortified look, and its sequences

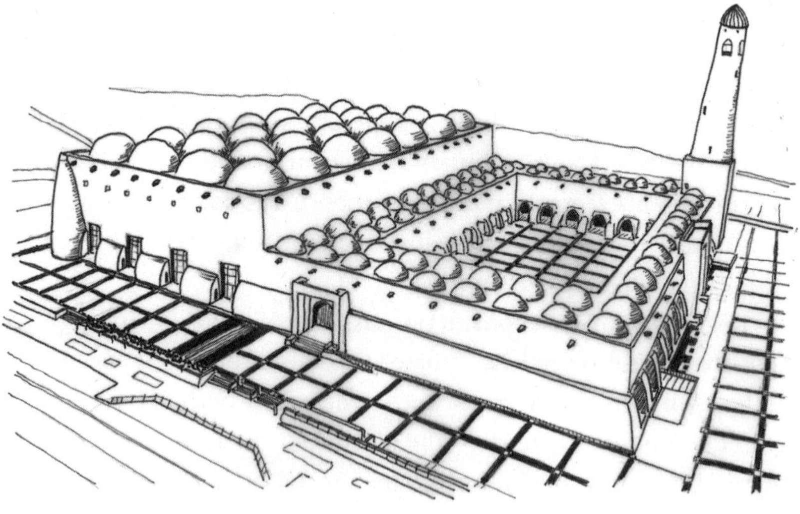

Imam Muhammad bin Abdul Wahhab Mosque in Doha, Qatar

of small domes and pointed arches, this mosque aligns with the Wahhabi principles of religious austerity and detachment. So does the appearance of the imam, the workers and many of the male attendees, whose shortened trousers and *jalabiya* robes indicate a literal interpretation of Islamic instructions to avoid ostentation. It is difficult to reconcile this restraint with the surroundings, where almost everything is marbled and luxurious – not just in the immediate environs of the mosque, but also in the hotels, shopping malls and other public spaces of Doha itself.

Mixed messages, which are prevalent all over the Gulf, are the sign of a rising ambition to be at the helm of the Muslim world – a seat that was established in Damascus under the Umayyads, the first Muslim dynasty who ruled the Muslim world.

Penetrating the wall of myths

At the bottom of a menu in a restaurant in Old Damascus, some famous lines by American author Mark Twain are quoted: 'To Damascus, years are only moments, decades are only flitting trifles of time. She measures time not by days, months and years, but by the empires she has seen rise and prosper and crumble to ruin. She is a type of immortality.'[8] Few, however, will look any further into what the 31-year-old Twain went on to write, after embarking with several dozen other Americans on a pleasure cruise across the Atlantic to the Mediterranean Sea in 1867. Arriving at the shores of the Levant, Twain and his companions hired a guide and continued on the backs of horses towards Damascus, crossing afterwards to the Sea of Galilee, and finally reaching Jerusalem.

As a result, Twain wrote *The Innocents Abroad* (also titled *The New Pilgrims' Progress*), which has been described as a travel masterpiece. In addition to the lines about the immortal Damascus, which are obliviously celebrated without any regard to their context, Twain expressed his disappointment – even disgust – with the city:

> I can understand how unspeakably beautiful it must be to eyes that are only used to the God-forsaken barrenness and desolation of Syria. I should think a Syrian would go wild with ecstasy when

> such a picture bursts upon him for the first time.... And when you think of the leagues of blighted, blasted, sandy, rocky, sunburnt, ugly, dreary, infamous country you have ridden over to get here, you think it is the most beautiful, beautiful picture that ever human eyes rested upon in all the broad universe!

Twain proceeded to point out that there was actually no need to venture any further 'into the paradise of Damascus', because:

> It is so crooked and cramped and dirty that one cannot realize that he is in the splendid city he saw from the hill-top. The gardens are hidden by high mud-walls, and the paradise is become a very sink of pollution and uncomeliness. Damascus has plenty of clear, pure water in it, though, and this is enough, of itself, to make an Arab think it is beautiful and blessed. Water is scarce in blistered Syria. We run railway by our large cities in America; in Syria they curve the roads so as to make them run by the meagre little puddles they call 'fountains', and which are not found oftener on a journey than every four hours. But the 'rivers' of Pharpar and Abana of Scripture (mere creeks) run through Damascus and so every house and every garden have their sparkling fountain and rivulets of water. With her forest of foliage and her abundance of water, Damascus must be a wonder of wonders to the Bedouin from the deserts. Damascus is simply an oasis – that is what it is.[9]

Regardless of the obscene prejudice that riddles Twain's 'masterpiece', his obsession with scale resembles that of a modernist, who is blinded from appreciating the *quality* of things by constantly seeking their *quantity*. However, such 'literature' has constituted the building blocks of the wall of myths that, to this day, separates the Muslim world from the Western world. It is a wall that has grown so high that no real understanding of what lies behind is possible any more.

Similarly contributing to the wall, Antoine Galland, the French orientalist and archaeologist who also served as a secretary to the French ambassador to Constantinople, became in 1709 the first European translator (and, in fact, compiler) of *Les Mille et une nuits: contes arabes*, known in English as *One Thousand and One Nights* (or *Arabian Nights*). From those pages, some of the greatest myths around the Arabs and the whole Muslim world were formed.

To my amazement, while researching this present book, I came across so many examples where the *Arabian Nights* were used as a foundation to discuss the architecture of the mosque! In his book *The British Mosque*, Shahed Saleem cites objections by members of the public to the proposed style of a local mosque, by conveying one man's concerns around seeing his area 'suddenly transformed into something out of the pages of the stories of the Arabian Nights!'[10]

Originally an assemblage of Indian and Persian anecdotes, the *Arabian Nights* is essentially not even Arabian. The only 'Arabian' part, which Galland failed to recognize, was the contribution of Hanna Diyab, a Syrian Maronite writer and storyteller from Aleppo, who worked as a travel companion and interpreter to the French 'tomb raider' Paul Lucas.[11] Until the information was unearthed by chance in both Diyab's and Galland's memoirs,[12] it remained unknown that Diyab had originated the best-known versions of the tales of 'Aladdin' and 'Ali Baba and the Forty Thieves', which were added to Galland's manuscript without credit.

The ensuing 'fascination with the East' is not news. However, when it comes to the architecture of the mosque, the mental image of a lavish palace, complete with bulbous domes, is apparently still too strong to undo. Likewise, Twain's myths of the 'glaring desert', the 'stunned Bedouin', and the 'crooked and cramped' Arab city have become such enduring memes that – for many – they turn out to be the dominant wellsprings of imagination and criteria of evaluation of all that is Islamic.

In *The Mosque and the Modern World*, Renata Holod and Hasan-Uddin Khan point out how the orientalists' publications in the nineteenth and early twentieth centuries constituted the foundations for the creation of what has become known as the 'image of the mosque'. This image is essentially different from the reality of the mosque, and it is fundamentally the source of much controversy around this building type. Citing works 'by Prisse d'Avennes, Goury and Jones, Creswell, Pope and others, and increasingly … the publications which have appeared since the 1970s', Holod and Khan note:

> These published works have been the mediators and led the way back to a far-removed past of architectural thinking and building traditions, from which the contemporary viewer has become cut off by the passage of time and by the transition from a pre-industrial to an industrialized society .... there are several versions of the new 'Islamic' image which have been created and disseminated worldwide: the Andalusian/Maghrebi version, the Ottoman and Mamluk version, and the Indo-Persian version. The link with the past is not a real one, but a willfully manufactured myth which has allowed for the realization of the new expression – an expression which has been named pan-Islamic, or even post-Islamic, architecture.[13]

The fact that the production of the ecumenical 'pan-Islamic' idiom – which is nothing more than a patchwork jumble – emanated from these 'willfully manufactured myths' leaves us with the question: why? Why were such myths crafted so willfully and systematically? I believe the answer can be revealed by looking into *how* such myths were formed and disseminated. In my view, it is only by penetrating the wall of myths that any actual grasp of the mosque, its architecture and its people is possible.

I have come up against that wall, firsthand, during my travels to Europe. Although I have never been to a desert, I cannot recall a single visit in which I was not confronted with its myth: I was lucky enough that the people were polite, and stopped at asking me if the weather wasn't too cold for my liking, and didn't go on to ask whether I realized that cars were not camels to hop onto! The depth to which the orientalists' mythical image of the East is engraved in the Western psyche is remarkable and astonishing. Even though modern technology offers information with a simple click, the dichotomy between the trope of the 'green, wet, developed and democratic' West and the 'bland, dry, chaotic and barbaric' East endures so powerfully – and, for some, so arrogantly. It is an image perpetuated by the media and politics, as much as it is by the domination of the Arab Gulf as the sole representation of the world of Islam, primarily through the flamboyance of its architecture.

In untangling the web of myths and fictions, we can start by looking at the issue of naming. First is the term 'Middle East', which was coined at the British India Office in the 1850s, and later popularized by the American naval officer Alfred Thayer Mahan, who used it in 1902 to designate the areas between the Mediterranean Sea and the Indian Ocean. If one thinks about it, it shouldn't take long for this Eurocentric oxymoronic term to reveal the idiocy of its implications. How can the East be 'middle'? Why is there no corresponding 'Middle West', or 'Far West', and so on?

Next comes the upgraded term, the 'MENA region' (meaning the Middle East and North Africa), which was intended to align the latter's cultural affinity with the so-called Middle East – even though North Africa sits directly below 'the West', i.e. Europe, on any traditional world map. In any case, where in the east are the borders of the 'Middle East' supposed to end? Do they stop at the Arabian Gulf? Or at the Caspian Sea? Is Turkey part of the 'Middle East', since Europe doesn't seem to want to embrace it? And how is it that Iran, which has a completely different cultural and ethnic heritage (being Persian, with Indo-European peoples and language), can be interchangeably considered 'Middle Eastern'?

Finally, the 'Global South' was intended to be a political correction of both terms, though of course no correction of the devastating colonial history has ever been forthcoming. Nonetheless, this new term remains equally problematic, simply lumping together anyone – regardless of culture, ethnicity or history – who is located below the upper shores of the Mediterranean, whether above the hemispherical line of the equator or beneath it. It goes without saying that historical cartographers oriented the world map to show the countries of the 'Global North' at the top – a hint as to their perceived superiority.

All of these terminologies may nonetheless constitute some form of progress in comparison to the previous denigratory Western categorizations. One ranked nations from 'First' to 'Third' World, with no guesses as to who was 'First'. Another differentiated between those who were 'developed' (because they were colonizers) and those who were 'underdeveloped' or 'developing' (because they were colonized).

Generally speaking, the term 'Middle East' – as used to refer to the lands that lie to the east of the Mediterranean and the Red Sea at one end, and to the west of the Caspian Sea at the other – seems to enjoy Western consensus. But in reality, the source of all this beating around the bush is the arbitrary colonial mapping that was agreed between the British and French diplomats Mark Sykes and François Georges-Picot in 1916, followed by the creation of Israel in 1948. Before those events, these regions enjoyed their native historical names, which referred to their actual geography rather than the clumsy doodling of bureaucrats. 'Pan-Islamic' is the outcome of those doodles, devoid of meaning and belonging to nowhere but vast stretches of desert. It is the expression of fantasies born in the minds of enchanted orientalists, in accordance with the unspoken goal of exploitation and annihilation.[14]

Bilad al-Sham (or 'the land of Sham') historically referred to the region of the Levant, which comprised the lands east of the Mediterranean and west of the Euphrates River, from the Taurus Mountains in the north to the Red Sea in the south.[15] Sham is another name for Damascus, so Bilad al-Sham follows Arab custom in naming the whole after the part, in order to bring to the fore the significance of the part; in this case, the importance of Damascus in relation to the whole of the lands of the Levant. Therefore, what is designated as 'of Damascus' or 'the Damascene', can be equally termed 'of Syria' or 'the Syrians'.

Indeed, Damascus – where the crystallization of Islamic arts and architecture first took place under the Umayyads – chronicles an alternative narrative to the culture of annihilation. Up until Western colonization, Syria, the Levant and Bilad al-Sham were all names of that same geography; and by using the native names of the different regions, the connections between geography and the habits and traditions of their peoples remain distinct, and the 'myth of the desert' loses its credibility. In the lands of Syria, diverse topographies and microclimates exist in close proximity. In response, different architectures were constructed, each with its own clear-cut character that remained unrefined and without potency until transformed by the unifying impetus of Islam. In this regard, Syria offered the ancient world its master masons, who under the wing of Islam brought their expertise to shaping

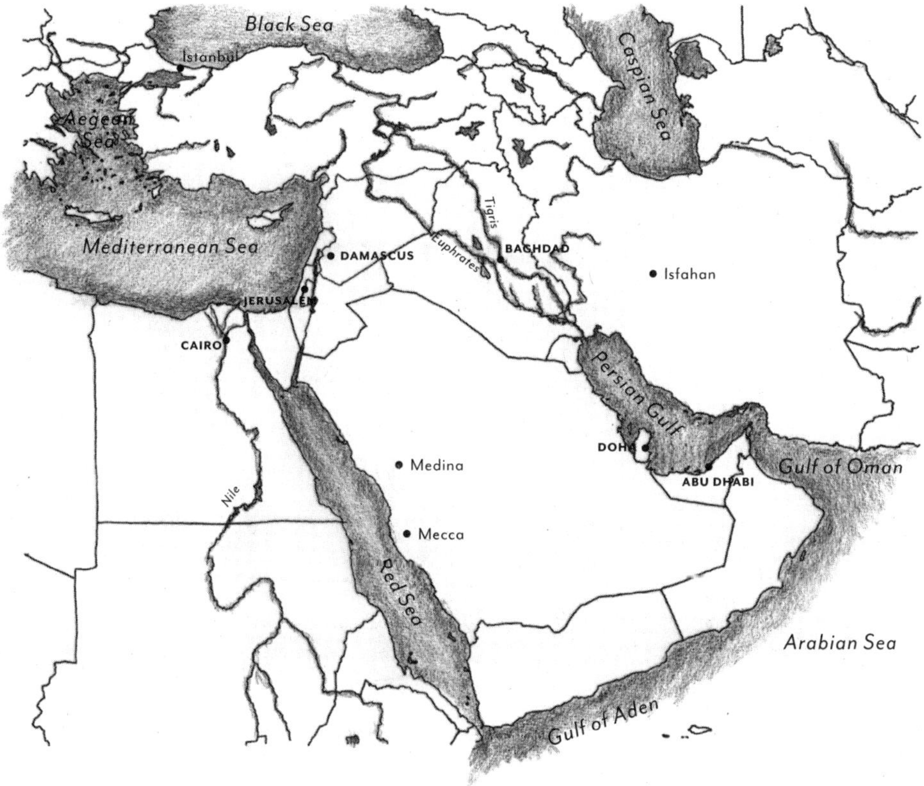

Map of the so-called 'Middle East'

the first mosques, and are also believed to have played a part in the construction and design of some of medieval Europe's most distinguished cathedrals.[16]

Here, we must note that, while the pernicious fictive wall has been built out of 'willfully manufactured myths', it teeters too on account of historical omissions. When it comes to high points of so-called 'civilization', a deliberate historical gap has been formed and retained. I remember being at a university library in Syria, doing some research for a history of architecture course I was about to give. In all of the Western books I had at my disposal, I couldn't find a single account of ancient Syrian architecture. The books covered some of the Mesopotamian contributions, and offer detailed histories of ancient Egypt, only to skip forward to other regions of the world, with no mention of the Levant's ancient peoples and kingdoms.[17] In order to learn about the countless Levantine contributions to alphabets, literature, agricultural breakthroughs and construction innovations, one has to conduct specialized research which, even then, provides only a fragmented viewpoint of the region.

In the end, falsified accounts have risen to the top, framing the Levant as desolate lands of warring tribes, rescued ultimately by foreign empires, whether Persian, Hellenistic or Byzantine. This of course couldn't be further from the truth, as those empires treated the Levant strictly as their colonies and never as part of their own (extended) territories. Reciprocally, the population of the Levant never adopted the alien ways and cultures of those empires, always remaining resistant to their influences and faithful to their indigenous culture.

The architecture of the mosque has, unsurprisingly, been read through an equally faulty lens, even by those who have the integrity to acknowledge that Islamic art and architecture ultimately took a route that was independent of outside influence. The missing link in this chain of events is the position held by Damascus, and the key role played by the urbanized artistry that was established and settled upon. This included a highly advanced understanding of geometry; specialist knowledge of complex techniques for masonry construction such as vaulting, arches and decorative stonework; innovative glass-blowing and glass-colouring; and longstanding prowess in other crafts besides. With its unique local character, which was highly cultivated and always embraced spirituality, Syrian architecture exhibited an ingenuity that was rewarded with worldwide continuity over the following centuries. This art was not Byzantine, nor was it Persian; it was *Syrian*.

Admittedly, it lacked the bold nature of other empires' arts, which empowers them with their definition and clarity, and makes them stand out as such. The nature of the Syrian is congenially embracive but not easily receptive to influence. This is very important to highlight, because it makes all the difference in our understanding of the ensuing formulation of an independent style, and the contrasting reactions the Syrian context displayed between the refusal of any coercion attempted by those foreign empires and the welcoming reception of Islam, which breathed resolute confidence into art forms that were previously lacking.

One example of the independence of the Syrian mind and character is also an example of historical omission. Apollodorus of Damascus was a Syrian architect, born in 60 CE. During the reign of the emperor Trajan, he built some of the most famous architectural features in Rome, including Trajan's Market and Forum, and Trajan's Column.[18] Many Western historians, however, omitted the 'of Damascus' from his name, and relied on the suffix '-dorus' to claim that the architect was Greek, although he was in fact born and brought up in Damascus (as his full moniker indicates). Despite being so visible and world-renowned to this day, the eastern legacy of Apollodorus,[19] which he carried with him onto Roman soil and into the Roman psyche, is rarely publicly acknowledged, or even discussed.

Influential incomers also played a key role in ancient Greek life, including Damascius (born in Damascus in 458 CE). He was the last director of the Platonic Academy in Athens, and is reportedly buried in Emesa (present-day Homs). Such historical omissions serve to place the East on the inferior receiving (i.e. passive, rather than active) end of history. As far as the West is concerned, the East would have remained barren and shapeless if it weren't for the civilizing forces of the Greeks and the Romans. But this myth only makes sense if the 'myth of the desert' is established. If it can be believed that the Levant was no more than empty swaths of sand and aimless tribes, then the myth of the 'white saviour' would not be such an outrageous lie after all.

In my view of history, there are essentially two types of civilization: one is military-driven and expansionist, with examples including the Romans, Persians and Hittites; the other is settled and trade-oriented, as found, for example, in the Levant and Mesopotamia. The first is an outlooker, impatient, seeing no point in self-reliance and believing in dominance, whereas the second is content with a smaller scale, especially when its position and resources provide abundance, which makes it coveted but not coveting. This latter type of civilization is generative (the term 'cradle of civilization' is still used to describe the Levant and Mesopotamia), but it is also strictly defensive: it makes no time for initiating wars, only for generating business. How, then, to reconcile this view with the perceived militaristic character of Islamic civilization as a whole? Military-driven and domination-seeking civilizations have a unified style to their products, just like a uniform, wherever they land. However, the variety that has been preserved in all the diverse Muslim lands, maintaining an unmistakably local stamp, proves that it was not the sword that built the civilization.

The regions of the Levant and Mesopotamia (the 'land of the Fertile Crescent') in fact enjoyed an uninterrupted sequence of civilizations of the second kind. Fertile land begets settlement and requires cultivation, which makes for a prime position on the crossroads of trade. While Bilad al-Sham (Syria, or the Levant) and Bilad al-Rafidain ('the land of the two rivers', i.e. Mesopotamia or present-day Iraq) were dissimilar in many ways, they were always intertwined in lands and peoples, and they exchanged knowledge and the baton of civilizations simultaneously. What they also both dealt with was fertility, which is historically linked to spirituality. It is in the nature of man to look to a higher power to seek protection of abundance, as well as the continuation of its provision. Praying for rain (the key to abundance, concealed in the heavens beyond man's reach) is at the core of ancient worship. It is around that fertility that the spiritual nature of the civilizations of the Fertile Crescent prospered. And it was over that fertility that raiding outside forces continued their assaults. Hence, as will later become important when it comes to the issue of mosque-building, the embedded tendencies to maintain settlement and to cultivate spirituality have always been the key formulating features of the productions of this region's peoples.

The Syrian character and the first Islamic style

On the walls of the Umayyad Mosque in Damascus exist some of the world's largest mosaics. To describe the Syrian population, historians and commentators repeatedly use the cliché of the 'Syrian mosaic', in order to describe the diversity of ethnicities, faiths and communities living in the compact cohesion of the Syrian context. Correspondingly, there are distinct geographies, landscapes and micro-climates that have contributed towards the *raison d'être* of such variety. In 705 CE, when the sixth Umayyad caliph Al-Walid ibn Abd al-Malik decided to build

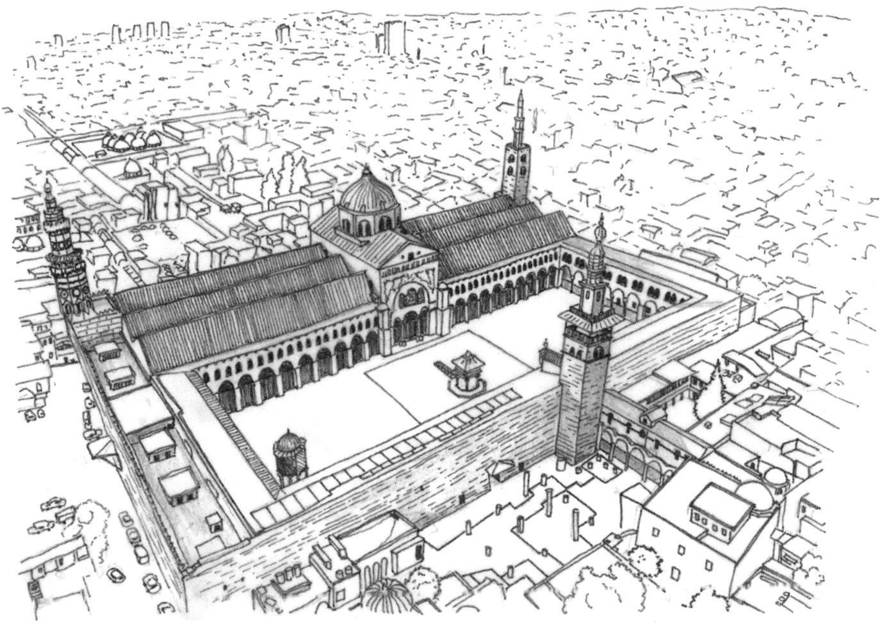

The Great Umayyad Mosque of Damascus

the Umayyad Mosque, which came to be known as the Great Umayyad Mosque of Damascus, or for short simply 'the Umayyad', he did not treat the location as a *tabula rasa*, nor conceive of the building as a kind of flag over territory, despite what some writers would like to argue.

Damascus had acquired Greco-Roman attributes under the Greeks (and later the Macedonian Greek Seleucids), followed by the Romans (and later the Byzantines, who emerged from the Eastern Roman Empire but also incorporated aspects of Greek culture). This era of rule lasted from the time that Damascus fell to Alexander the Great in 333 BCE until the arrival of Muslims in 634 CE. However, contrary to the assumptions of some Western scholars, the city did not remain passive, nor did it simply absorb the new Greco-Roman culture. On the contrary, as indicated above, Damascenes took an active role in the lives of both the Greeks and the Romans, and faithfully preserved their own Eastern character. Even if historical accounts based on key figures and narratives may be contested, urban plans cannot be. Despite the Greco-Roman grid that was imposed on its streets, and the Hellenization of its institutions, the oriental character of Damascus was retained, as was its language and way of life. As historian and architect Gérard Degeorge has stated: 'The Hellenization of Syria, pursuant on a determined policy of urbanization, was all in all a superficial phenomenon.'[20]

Thus, as in so much of life and in Islam itself, a city was formed with duality at its heart: one image that projected the undaunted spirit of its people, and the other that revealed their intrinsic skills in negotiation. Talal Akili, author of *The Great Mosque of Damascus: From Roman Temple to Monument of Islam*, describes it thus:

> Over that period, the image of Damascus, with its grid plan and urban form, looked like a city torn out of its setting, history and oriental urban legacy and annexed to the occidental Euro-Roman cities.... Thus, Damascus contained two urban images at the same time, one Greco-Roman and the other Aramaic-oriental. This defined it as a '*ville double*', as described by [French historian Jean] Sauvaget. Regardless of the form of transformation it went through, Damascus retained its former image after the end of the Greco-Roman period and continued its oriental urban evolution.[21]

This 'oriental urban evolution' is notable for the adaptability and flexibility of the local custom of inhabitation 'off the grid'. Akili explains how it was usual for the 'dwellers of Greater Syria', as much as the Damascenes, not to abide by the imposed Greco-Roman urban plans, but instead to revert to the norms that were in place before the time of Alexander the Great.[22]

In the same way that they guarded their oriental character, Syrians kept their places of worship. The fact that the location of the Umayyad is the same as that of the Temple of Hadad (the Aramaic deity of rain and thunder) testifies to the practice found across the lands of the Levant: spirituality is maintained, but progress is made as collective changes in values occur. In Islam, the story of belief does not begin with the Prophet Muhammad; it begins with Adam. It recognizes that there are times when faith gets eroded and practices get corrupted, which is when religion can ultimately turn into paganism, and when a new message is due to remind people of what they have forgotten. Excluding Judaism and

Christianity from the ultimate corruption, and taking the form of the last message, Islam is a declaration upon the future that it won't be due to amnesia, but rather to willful abandonment, that people may choose to disbelieve. There is thus no conflict in the idea that the Aramaic temple became a Roman temple dedicated to Jupiter, then in the fourth century CE turned into a Christian church, and in the early eighth century was transformed into a mosque. It was through negotiation and collective agreement that the Damascenes decided what would be worshipped in the key spiritual locus of their city.

Before growing in numbers, the new Muslims in Damascus shared the space with their fellow Christian citizens. Hence, the nucleus of the Umayyad grew out of the place taken by the Muslims at 'the eastern part of the inner courtyard of the Temple, in the remaining section of the southern colonnade, squeezed between the southern, triple doorway and the south eastern tower of the Temple'.[23] From this rectangular corner, the elongated rows of Muslim worshippers grew, enlarging northwards one row after the other, and correspondingly necessitating one new arcade after the other. This part of the mosque's evolution is often disregarded, but it is a misconception to think that a monumental religious building was suddenly dropped into the city, announcing victory over former creeds and peoples. The truth, however, is best encapsulated by Akili in the following lines:

> When Al-Walid succeeded his father Abdel-Malek as caliph in 705 A.D. seventy years had passed since the Arab Muslims conquered Damascus. The city had become the capital of a vast empire, from the Atlantic Ocean and the Pyrenees to the borders of China, larger than the Roman Empire at its height. The state had been well organized, the administration had been Arabized, coins had been minted, a navy had been established, the post had been regulated, offices had been created, construction had spread, and Damascus enjoyed its golden age... Damascus thus became one of the most important cities on earth.[24]

At the height of success, with access to such wealth and skills at his fingertips, no conqueror like Al-Walid would have waited seventy years to announce victory over Christian subjects with the implementation of a relatively understated mosque. It is true that, during those decades, the House of Umayya was under the pressure of the civil conflict that eventually resulted in the division between Sunni and Shi'a Muslims, which will be addressed later in the book, but nonetheless the rest of the history of Islamic architecture will confirm that it was not generally in the habit of Muslim rulers to build mosques driven by the burdens of any form of one-upmanship.

It is interesting to note how Al-Walid achieved compatibility between the new mosque and its context – a context that was, as mentioned above, notable for a relentless resistance to imposed new ideas. This comprehensive embrace can be explained only by the notion that it was through conviction, and not compulsion, that Syrians assented to the new idiom, and that they themselves were responsible for articulating it. This resulted in the splendid mosque that we know as the Umayyad, which exhibits extraordinary solutions to the wide variety of contextual challenges it faced. The construction demonstrates the genius of Syrian masons and craftsmen, as they dealt with the risks of seismic activity and the instability of porous ground over the basins of the underground tributaries of the River Barada. The mosque also had to connect harmoniously to the city's various networks of surrounding markets and its compact urban fabric, as well as to the different layers of extant buildings within the locality. To achieve the Umayyad as we know it was to succeed in weaving all these elements together, resulting in one brilliant work of sober architecture and flexible engineering that continues to serve its community to this day.

I first visited the Umayyad as a small child on a school trip. The stone-paved courtyard in which I found myself, after passing the big thick wooden door that opened up to the arcaded entrance, cried out to be run across. I sped towards the doves perched on the ground, which, as they flew away, lent me wings to circle the space of the courtyard, and then to embark on my journey inside.

Despite its enormous scale, a clear sense of orientation exists at the Umayyad. This is the outcome of the carefully considered engineering and mastery in geometry that was realized by Al-Walid's architects and masons. The architectural scheme, divided into five stages,[25] began with the clearance of all the previous constructions that were scattered throughout the site, while preserving the outer walls, the four corner towers, and the existing two gates on the western and northern walls. For the second stage, it was paramount to establish the orientational axes of the building in parallel to the southern wall, which became the *qibla* wall. This was achieved by first creating an eastern gate on the axis of the opposing western gate, and articulating it by flanking an elongated hall on either side of the eastern wall. The space for the sanctuary (the prayer hall) was determined by aligning its width with the eastern hall near the vestibule, and extending its length along the *qibla* wall.

In the third stage, Al-Walid's architects introduced an innovation to the architecture of the mosque, which would be used henceforward. This involved emphasizing the direction of the *qibla*, while simultaneously indicating the placement of the *mihrab* and the neighbouring *minbar*. To that end, a transept with a pitched roof was created: its central position and proportional scale were calculated geometrically, by doubling the width at the intersection points.

In the fourth stage, arcades flanking the transept to the east and west were installed, and the pitched roofs of the prayer hall were carried on three rows of two-storeyed stone pillars parallel to the *qibla* wall. The rows of pitched arcades were thought by Damascenes to zigzag like the wings of an eagle; they duly named the cupola over the gabled transept the 'Dome of the Eagle'. Finally, in the fifth stage, a colonnade (*riwaq*) was built to surround the courtyard (*sahn*), both functionally and visually tying the structure with the building's wall.

As a child, I didn't know that this architectural sensibility was behind the feeling of safety that accompanied my sense of liberty. The worst thing a child can experience in an open place is to feel lost, abandoned, swallowed into the belly of the space. However, at the courtyard of the Umayyad, even a small child can be guided by the centrality of the gabled transept that marks the entrance to the prayer hall and, at the same time, feel contained by the easily accessible flanking arcades. As we grow up, we keep this primordial apprehension of being lost, so we seek refuge in places where the logic of geometry governs.

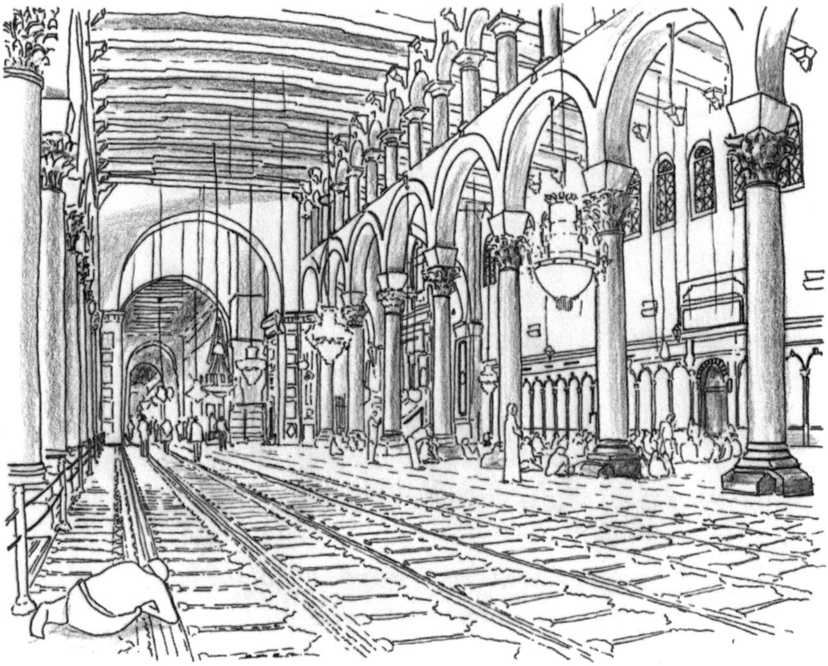

The Great Umayyad Mosque of Damascus: an interior view

However, geometry was not just a brilliant design aesthetic at the Umayyad, nor was its brilliance the reason the aesthetic became so widely adopted. The rationality springs from a totally different understanding, according to the Muslim mentality: geometry as a design phenomenon is not an abstraction of nature, nor is it a construct that departs completely from nature's forms. The key feature lies elsewhere. As Titus Burckhardt has put it, the art of Islam comprises not merely the 'experience of phenomena but awareness of the timeless'.[26] In other words, the world view of Islam places value on stability and continuity, aligning with the timelessness of God, the universe, and the message of the Quran. In the case of Islamic art, it is such qualities that the receptive viewer perceives. While the prototypes of the 'phenomena' may vary aesthetically according to local or individual preference, the ideals remain the same and constant. In Burckhardt's words: 'These prototypes are inexhaustible because they are true.'[27] At the Umayyad, the rhythms of its repetitions and the harmonious generosity of its spaces all contribute to the effect of a timeless sanctuary.

The site has, in fact, been a place of refuge throughout its long history. The head of John the Baptist (revered by Muslims as the Prophet Yahya) lies here, and is said to have been in situ since its arrival from the Church of Homs around the time of the mosque's construction. After its arrival, the granting of asylum became a right to those who took refuge in what was then still a church. In the same manner, the holy sanctuary of the previous pagan temple was a place where people and their possessions were inviolately protected.[28] In its turn, the Umayyad encapsulated this concept of refuge, where the presence of God, His protection and His plenitude were transmitted through the augmenting belief of the craftsmen who worked its very stones.

Since its inauguration in 715 CE, seven earthquakes and seven great fires (including the one lit by the Mongol leader Tamerlane in 1401) have left their devastating marks on the Umayyad.[29] Those multiple devastations have affected sections of the mosque to varying degrees. However, one of the constants of the Damascus skyline is the minaret built by Al-Walid, adjacent to the gate at the northern wall, and locally called Al-Aroos (the Bride's Minaret). This was the first minaret in Islam; it had no prior model. But the square minaret, with a height four times the width of its base, became an exemplar that was followed across the world, even by Christians. Talal Akili has noted: 'This model prevailed throughout Greater Syria until the early 20th century A.D. It speared to North Africa and Andalusia. It influenced the Gothic towers of European churches.'[30]

Due to its shape and the soundness of its construction, Al-Aroos never fell (despite sustaining some minor damage). In later phases, two more minarets were added to the Umayyad: the Jesus Minaret was built at the southeastern corner in the thirteenth century, while the Qaitbay Minaret was built at the southwestern corner in the early fifteenth century and named after the Mamluk sultan Al-Ashraf Qaitbay, who repaired the minaret in 1488 and gave it its current form. Both of the minarets fell, either partially or completely, at a certain point in their history, due to the various catastrophes that befell Damascus and its mosque. However, they were always repaired and rebuilt, as were other sections of the mosque, including the Dome of the Eagle. On every occasion, the mosque was saved by the Damascenes, who lived in its great shadow and cultivated life around it. Although it was the rulers who initiated the campaigns to restore the building to its glory, each construction ultimately relied on the donations and the volunteered efforts of the people to bring the Umayyad back to life – which is to say, back to their life.

Through the eyes of an architect, I look at the Umayyad today and I see the impeccable balance between the sense of movement given by the array of double arches and the stability of the building's rectangular proportions and square minaret. Likewise, the 'wings' of its gables are pinned down with the sublimity of its transept, crowned with its elegant lead-covered dome. In its turn, the dome can only be glimpsed occasionally from the outside, which speaks to its constructional and spatial necessity, rather than its being thrown on needlessly like a hat.

Relying on the wall of myths, many scholars fall into the trap of misjudging the Umayyad as a transitional expression, borrowing from Byzantine Christian art, while simply complying with the 'rules' of Islam and the model of the Prophet's Mosque. This couldn't be further from the truth, because such a narrative ignores two fundamental factors, which are essentially responsible for the birth of the first Islamic architectural style. The first is the Syrian character, which was the raw cloth from which the new Umayyad art was cut. And the second is Islam's world view, according to which this architecture was tailored. By evaluating the space, it is easily recognizable that it was under the Dome of the Eagle that a new architecture was born. As Titus Burckhardt asserts:

> This is not space folded back on itself, as in a Roman or Byzantine church; the vast oratory opens onto the courtyard, and the daylight floods in from the front, hardly impeded by the screen of arcades; this space has nothing in common with a Graeco-Roman peristyle architecture, whose entire reality is that of the walls, columns and architraves. The true aim of Islamic architecture is space as such, in its undifferentiated plenitude.[31]

The world view of Islam and the creation of integration

Scholars who looked at the mosaics on the walls of the Umayyad Mosque were divided between those who interpreted them as representations of paradise and a minority who saw them as a reflection of the orchards surrounding Damascus, which are called Al-Ghouta. As expected, the dominant orientalists' view favoured the first. Like Mark Twain, they saw Damascus as an oasis in a blighted landscape, with the Byzantine artists (who they claim made the arts of the Umayyad) satisfying the yearnings of the Bedouin Muslims (as they pictured them coming from the deserts of the Hejaz to the deserts of Syria) with an imagined paradise, tiled on the walls as an afterlife prize to contemplate on their way to worship.

Such fallacies completely overlook the inner qualities of the Islamic art that found its expression brewing for *eighty years* (including the decade-long construction of the mosque) in the temporary structures that hosted the early Muslim congregation, as we have seen. Those accounts put a false emphasis on a race towards glory and a life spent without pursuit of meaning, whereas in reality, from the life of the seed at the Prophet's Mosque to the fruit of the crystallized expression at the Umayyad Mosque, the message of *tawhid* (the consciousness of divine unity) can be seen reiterated across the different regions and the various cultures of the Muslim world, before it had its earth scorched in the aftermath of the Second World War at the hands of the colonizing powers. What I'm describing as the relation between the seed of the concept and the fruit of the style is phrased in the works of other scholars as the overarching principle of 'unity in variety' and 'variety in unity'. Prior to modernity, Islamic art and architecture were able to produce a sense of unity in character and style, which allowed one to recognize them as such. At the same time, those productions were diverse and expressive of their local cultures in the widely varying regions where Islam was practised.

Ismail Serageldin is among the experts who have provided terms to explain this distinct expression of regionalism within the unity of character, introducing what he calls 'societal specificities' and 'overlay'.[32]

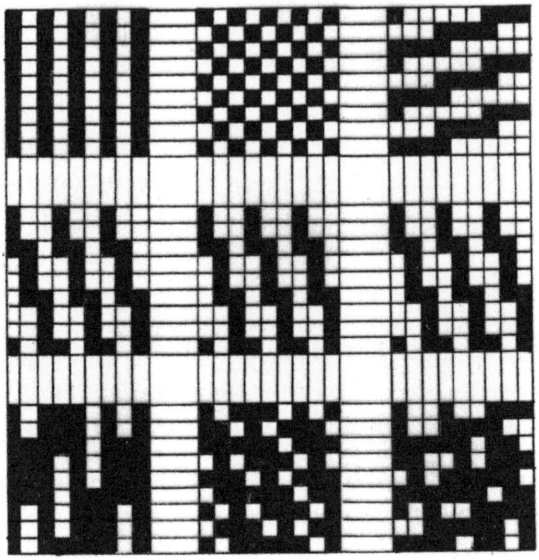

Societal specificities, overlay, and the Islamic cultural outcome; diagram after Ismail Serageldin

Societal specificities include the countless characterizations of local geography, climate and social practices defining of a particular environment, while the implementation of overlay refers to 'a process by which the cultural manifestations of Islamic principles in any Muslim society interact with, enrich and create new syntheses with existing cultures – Muslim and non-Muslim alike – with which they have extended contact'.[33] In short, Islam's world view.

To that end, Serageldin interlays two webs: one that is various and changeable from one context to another (societal specificities), and the other that is unified and constant like a foundation (the overlay). Crossing the two webs over each other, one will end up with a specific pattern; a pattern which will change with every new layer of context. However, this pattern will hold the steady underlying features of the constant foundation.

Islam's world view, which is the source of this unity, revolves around the encompassing axis of *tawhid*, but also the concrete structures that the religion provides through the legislative body of the Quran and the Hadith (the Prophet's sayings). In Serageldin's words:

> Muslim civilization ... exported no clearly defined architectural language from Arabia to the vast and varied regions that it ultimately encompassed. It spread a more subtle, yet ultimately much more powerful presence through a way of defining self and society in a non-physical sense by the 'codes of conduct' outlined in the Quran and the hadith.[34]

In my view, what requires more focus in Serageldin's premise is the determining role of the nature of settlement of certain people as the crucible of what he called 'societal specificities'. I will bring that to the fore in the following chapter, but for now it may suffice to be reminded that by being pre-eminently a religion of unity on all levels – ontological, social and political – Islam endowed all of its arts with a unity of purpose and form. This unity therefore exists *a priori*, in the form of detachment from the temporality of this world but, at the same time, in the form of appreciation of and devotion to its eternal Creator. As Titus Burckhardt explains:

> For a Muslim artist or – what comes to the same thing – a craftsman who has to decorate a surface, geometrical interlacement doubtless represents the most intellectually satisfying form, for it is an extremely direct expression of the idea of the Divine Unity underlying the inexhaustible variety of the world. True, Divine Unity as such is beyond all representation because its nature, which is total, lets nothing remain outside itself; it is 'without a second'. Nevertheless, it is through harmony that it is reflected in the world, harmony being nothing other than 'unity in multiplicity' ... the same as 'multiplicity in unity'.[35]

Does this mean that Al-Walid's architects and craftsmen at the Umayyad would necessarily have been presciently conscious of the effects their arts would produce? Absolutely not. Rather, it was through their immersion in the spirit and world view of Islam that the incipient style emerged. At the same time, of course, art never appears *ex nihilo*: while the success of the synthesis on view at the Umayyad might be unrivalled, one need only look at a cross-section to see how the strata of history were reused, whether parts of the pagan temple's pillars or the various layers of tiling that measure more than 80 centimetres (over 30 in.) deep.

However, the synthesis in Islamic architecture overall exceeds the simple act of combining or recycling various components in order to achieve a harmonious whole; it involves a *mental synthesis* that is able to regard all the components of the universe as elements of one single creation, the significance of which lies solely in being all-striving for that one ultimate goal of glorifying the one Creator. Man in this equation is a humble servant, not the centre of the universe (*homo universalis*); nor is he the 'measure of all things' (*panton metron anthropos*).[36] His job as a *khalifa* is to do no more than direct the earthly forces entrusted to him as an *amana* ('entrusted responsibility'), in order to fulfil the task of building civilization and elevating the state of the world through *imar*. In the Quran, it is made clear that this *amana* is more of a heavy burden than a flattering honour: 'We offered the *amana* to the heavens and the earth and the mountains, and they declined to bear it and feared it; but man undertook it. He was indeed unjust and ignorant.'[37]

Hence, Islamic art and architecture, as constructed by *khulafa* (plural of *khalifa*), are concerned with the earthly realm. They do not involve any attempt to materialize paradise, nor to approach the divine in any shape or form, other than through facilitating submission to the Creator and a constant striving for devotion. There was never any need for paradise to be depicted in images, because it was richly described in verses in the Quran. Moreover, especially in times when Muslims were so close to the original message, it would not have been part of Muslim thought that a worshipper might be preoccupied with the reward, instead of focused on the path. The idea of paradise being depicted on the walls of a mosque is entirely at odds with the Islamic faith that instigated the rest of the Umayyad, making the whole claim a non-starter. But it is through that ludicrous logic that we see the recurrence of bogus metaphors in today's mosques, like the 'rivers of paradise' I almost fell into in Doha. Furthermore, we see the idea of paradise being wheeled out once again as part of the old desert trope, to signify a Muslim yearning for an unattainable environment, and a departure from a lived scarcity to a dreamt reward. As before, we are in the realm of myth.

As to the view that the mosaics of 'paradise' were created by Byzantines (and its implicit casting of the Byzantines as sophisticated artisans, in comparison with the inferior, invading Muslims), this goes against the nature and the history of production of Islamic civilization, in which local expressions (and societal specificities) are always pronounced. In particular, it goes against the history of the Levant, whose populations have for millennia revolved around generative skill and local character. No: it is much more consistent to see the mosaics of the Umayyad as they must, in fact, be: a Muslim mirroring of the source of life and abundance in Damascus (that is, its Ghouta orchard), in something like a rain dance, but numinously bowing in a dual spirit of celebration and submission to the one God.[38]

The evolution of Islamic art, with its growing central focus on geometry and organic articulations such as the arabesque, meant the eventual abandonment of mosaic art in favour of interlacing and similar arts, which will be examined in the 'Form' part of this book. Nevertheless, the impact of the Umayyad on the architecture of the mosque continued, radiating from Damascus, and carried thereafter by Umayyad princes as well as Damascene artisans and masons all the way to Andalusia, and throughout the whole world.

By comparison, the 'image' that has been disseminated throughout the reshaped Muslim world from the twentieth century onwards has represented a wholesale failure of integration, in which the two layers of 'societal specificities' and 'overlay' have been misplaced. In *Deconstructing the American Mosque*, Akel Kahera explains how resurrecting the image of past Islamic styles is essentially 'concerned with satisfying an emotional condition that has historical efficacy for the immigrant Muslim community'.[39] However, the hankering after a familiar image from the past is rooted in the failure of the current productions to deliver meaning, as much as it is a yearning that can never truly be satisfied because that 'image' is generally – as shown – merely a shadow of what 'willfully manufactured myths' have constructed.

In 2016, back on the streets of Doha, an attempt was made to crack the code by the London-based firm John McAslan + Partners (JM+P). In designing the Jumaa Mosque (literally, 'Friday Mosque'), they devised a solid and honest off-white cube for the prayer hall, fronted by a small courtyard which in turn is entered through a rectangular box with a clearly defined entrance and straightforward axis. An unadorned free-standing minaret, nearly 30 metres (100 ft) tall, is placed near the entry, almost like a flagpole. Apart from the CNC-ed ornamental surfaces and the cast-bronze doors, the blocks of the mosque resemble giant pressed sheets of paper hanging in the air.

With the single exception of the decorative patterns, which have nothing to do with the principles of Islamic ornamentation (more light will be shed on this area in the 'Form' part of this book), JM+P have made good on their word when they said that they 'rejected pastiche'.[40] Moreover, unlike the modernist EC Mosque, which speaks to international aspirations, or the traditionalist Imam Muhammad bin Abdul Wahhab Mosque, which announces a state ideology, Jumaa Mosque seems to be satisfied with its small scale and quiet voice, with no hidden agendas apart from delivering a serene space for contemplation.

It is so quiet a voice, though, that it is almost inaudible. The design is too obvious, too direct, almost too bland. Its cubic form – which, on the inside, fails in spatiality by offering a cramped programme – gives away the unfamiliarity of its designers with the horizontally elongated rows of the typical mosque space. Moreover, in its minimalist approach, the mosque is almost reductionist. Even with their best intentions to learn about Islamic architecture, foreign architects have little chance of accessing its true essence – not due to any intrinsic shortcomings on their part, but rather due to the wall of myths, the idea that wealth leads progress, and the interruption in 'meaning' that has unfortunately been sustained.

Touring Doha's mosques, I couldn't help missing what Burckhardt (in reference to the Umayyad) described as 'undifferentiated plenitude'. Nods to 'civilization' are made merely in the shape of technological advances, beyond which no real address of the human condition is made. This makes me wonder: do advanced systems offer more to civilization than what filtered through the old stone colonnades? Should the soaring calligraphies on the abstracted minarets of the EC Mosque be more celebrated than the sundial of Ibn al-Shatir that once stood on Al-Aroos

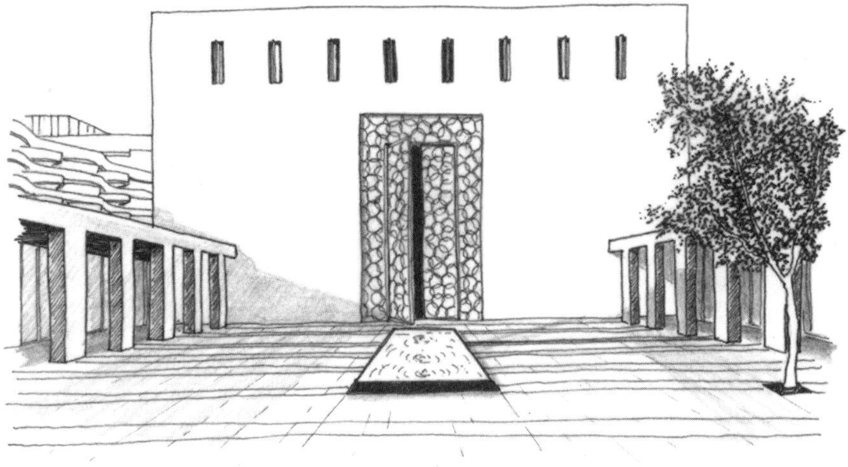

Jumaa Mosque in Doha, Qatar

minaret? And how have we lost a refuge where even the Muslim treasury could be kept and housed safely,[41] only to find ourselves under the watchful eye of monitoring cameras seeking to replace the angels over our shoulders?

This is not to entirely disregard the Qatari attempt to set a departure from the Gulf model, in which ostentation and self-glorification practically overshadow divinity. Along with its wealth, Qatar seems to be boosting its own confidence in order to grab the dropped flag of leadership that once flew over the lands of the Levant – a prize for which it competes with Turkey today. Nonetheless, even when speaking strictly about the building and cultivation of the mosque, one cannot overlook the conflicting gestures that are visible with regard to its architecture (also on view in Turkey). Are these the symptoms of misunderstanding the meaning of civilization, or of pandering to Western influence, or perhaps a mix of both? One cannot tell for certain. In any case, the question of who leads in the Muslim world today, and to what end, is highly relevant to personal ambitions as much as to the geopolitical strategizing of Western powers. It is not a stretch to say that the mosque and its architecture lie at the core of the matter.

Chapter 3

What is the Role of the Mosque?

'Without Islam, the Arab thrust of the seventh century – even supposing it to have been possible without the religious impulse – would have been no more than an episode in the history of the Middle East; decadent as they may have been, the great sedentary civilizations would have made short work of absorbing these hordes of Bedouin Arabs, and the nomadic invaders of the cultivated lands would have finished, as is generally the case, by accepting the customs and forms of expression of the sedentaries.'

TITUS BURCKHARDT[1]

The rulers of Islam

In 1963, an almost month-long war erupted between Algeria and Morocco. The war was called the Sand War, because it was the culmination of a long conflict between the two neighbouring countries over the demarcation of the mess of borders left between them by the colonizing/administrative French. The Western Sahara was torn between Algeria's upholding to the principle of *uti possidetis* (i.e. the maintenance of existing borders) and Morocco's irredentism (i.e. the reclamation of historic borders). The discovery of underlying mineral resources, along with lurking colonial interests, also fuelled the war. In effect, the foundations of a lasting and hostile rivalry between the Arab socialist government of Algeria and the long-established monarchy of Morocco were laid.

The Sand War was soon reflected in a mosque war. In 2013, the minaret of Al-Hassan II Mosque, Casablanca, became the tallest in the world, at an astonishing 210 metres (689 ft) high – only to be outshone in 2019

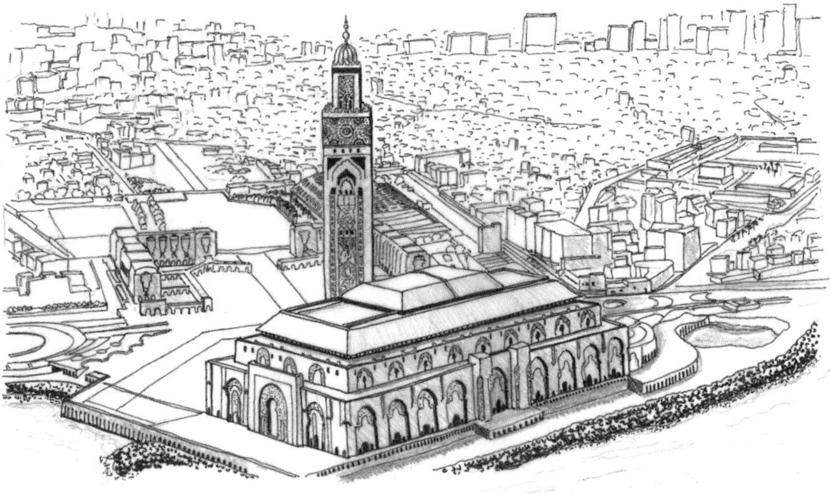

Al-Hassan II Mosque, on a promontory overlooking
the Atlantic Ocean in Casablanca, Morocco

by the minaret at the Great Mosque of Algiers, which soared to a height of 265 metres (869 ft). Like two alpha roosters vying for dominance, the mosques have vaunted their stature in an architectural competition over records and prestige, while also acting as a conduit for the politics their nations championed.

Morocco is in the race to become Africa's premier home to major international corporations, as it transitions out from its Francophone history and into the English-speaking global economy, offering up its beaches as resorts and transforming its heritage into tourist destinations. However, Al-Hassan II Mosque, which was completed in 1993, owes its creation to those Francophone attachments just as much as it does to the domination of fantasies. Known as 'the king's architect', the Frenchman Michel Pinseau was an obvious choice for the task of building the monarch's dreamt-of edifice on water. Rising over the Atlantic Ocean, the mosque was built by the French construction company Bouygues, partially on land and partially over the ocean. The mosque's design reverts to one of the three main pan-Islamic images (see p.58), as it celebrates the Andalusian/Maghrebi version of the global style.

Kickstarted with money arriving via public subscription, the inflated funding of the mega-project – which aspired to become second in rank to the joint holy sites of Mecca and Medina – ended up being secured through loans from Western countries. Later, restoration works required due to the erosional effect of the ocean further increased the cost. The level of embellishment is incredible: thousands of specialized artisans were recruited to work on decorating the edifice with the finest of their creations in wood carving, stucco, tiling and marble cladding. With a retractable roof, the prayer hall can be bathed in sunlight or illuminated with starlight in order to enhance its dreamy aura, albeit with an atmosphere disturbed by the puncturing laser beam directed from the top of the minaret towards Mecca! The complex includes a religious school, a library, and a museum commemorating the building process. The isolative location of the project, however, gives the impression that the mosque is 'running away' from Casablanca, almost as if it is embarking on a sea journey like a refugee. The building, with its myriad artistic decorations, seems to lack a uniting harmony. That all-encompassing sense of 'unity in variety', which ensues from the proper understanding of this perspective as regards the universe, appears to be missing.

To my eye, whether it is in the properties of the framing elements in the mosque or in the interrupted lines of the stuck-on *muqarnas* (honeycomb vaulting), an overlay of Art Deco bizarrely combined with Art Nouveau presides over the disjointed application of what is supposed to be 'traditional Islamic art'. The discordant layers of decoration placed over the structural elements show dividing lines, which cut through like the scars of a sharp knife. Although the discussion around form belongs to the second part of this book, what serves the discussion here is to examine how form has been voided of meaning by politics overriding faith.

In order to understand the context, one needs to note some core tenets of the Islamic faith. To begin with, the Christian principle which renders unto Caesar the things that are Caesar's and unto God the things that are God's does not exist in Islam. In Islam, there is no such dichotomy between the 'secular' and the 'sacred'. These terms have no meaning, because *all* things belong to God, and the role of the human being, as we have seen, is simply to carry out *amana* (entrusted responsibility).

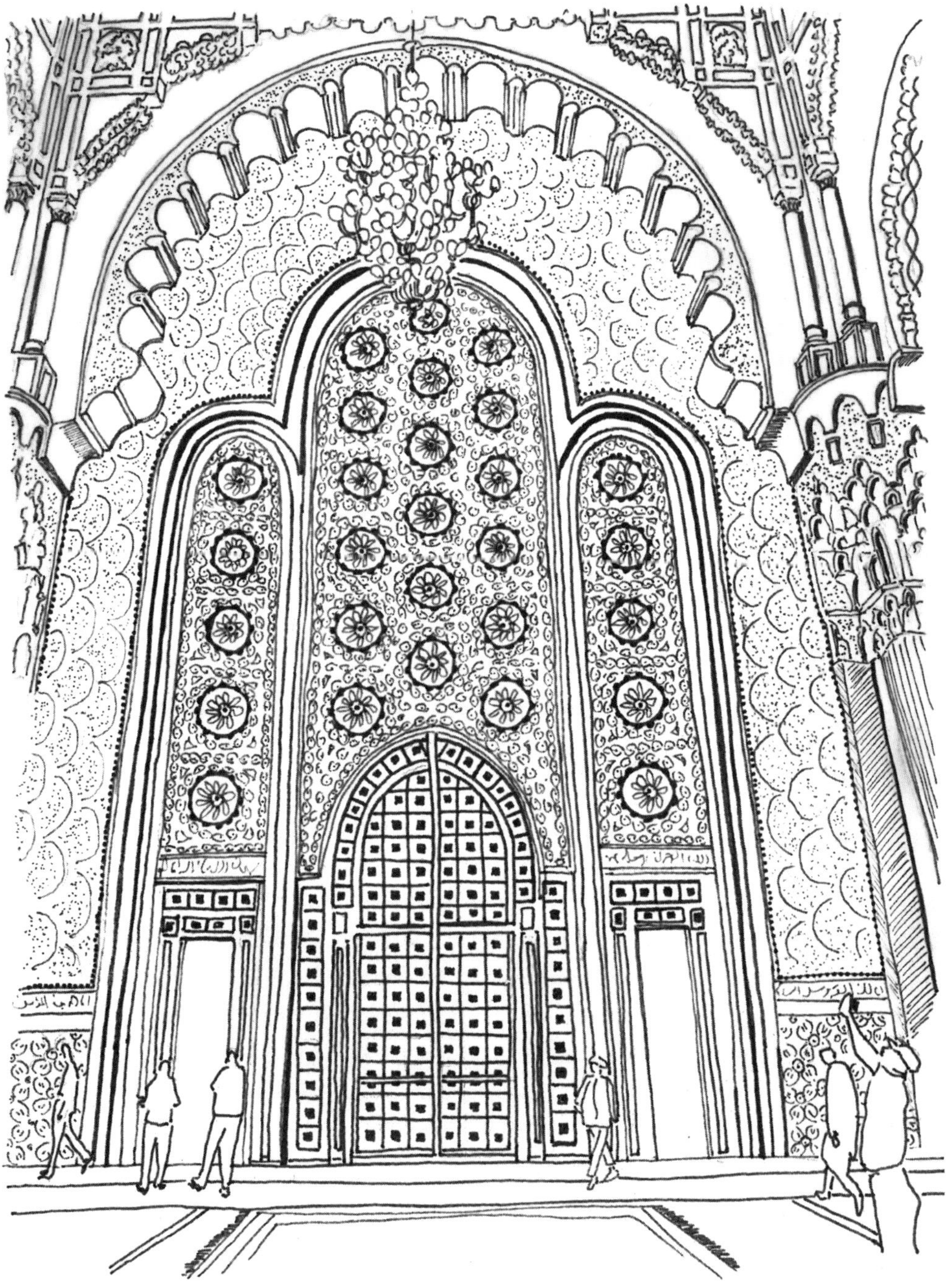

Al-Hassan II Mosque: an interior view

Hierarchy within the religious institution does not exist either, because there is no institution; religion is knowledge (*ilm*), which is derived from the Quran and the Hadith – accessible and open to all, with no mediatory persons required. Scholars (persons of knowledge, or *ulamaa*) are individuals who have dedicated their lives to studying these sources. However, like any scientist, they are highly regarded for their excellence, not simply for their role.

Through the Quran and Hadith, Islam is provided with a method for governance, a divine constitution which governs all aspects of life, in the form of guiding principles and formative recipes from which endless derivatives can be made. So, it is a mistake to think of the governing body as corresponding to a rigid unyielding message sent by God: it should, rather, be understood as a generative system that is capable of growing branches and leaves from the solid and alive trunk and roots. The second mistake many Western scholars make is to project their own understanding of law and religion – with its division of secular and sacred – onto the experience of Islam. This leads them to conclude that, in Islam, God is essentially Caesar. This is unfounded: firstly, because in Islam no human can be compared to God, who is the ultimate and omnipresent, the all-knowing and all-commanding; and, secondly, because the idea of overlay and societal specificities also applies to legislation in Islam, whereby a constant legalistic body is provided through major given principles, and the pathways for life's variables are then created according to specific contexts and cases. Since Islam is the religion of both the society and the individual, it has an ingrained political aspect to its message.

In this sense, the mosque is not merely a locus for spirituality, but also a house for political legitimacy. This is mainly what makes it controversial in non-Muslim countries (a point to which I will come in the third part of the book). Confining the discussion here to the Muslim nations, though, it is important to remember that, from the days of the Prophet, the leader of the nation was the same as the leader of prayer (that is, the caliph, or his representatives in the provinces). This is evident in the constitution of the mosque, as James Dickie has noted: 'Islam does not distinguish between spiritual and temporal power. The juxtaposition of the *mihrab* and *minbar* expresses their co-identity in the ambivalence of the *imam*, who uses both.'[2] In other words, with the *mihrab* (prayer niche) representing the key religious space behind which the rows of faithful align and the *minbar* (pulpit) representing the political position from which the faithful are addressed, the inseparability of religion and governance is clear to see.

Both are led by the core figure of the imam, whose title means leader, whether of the prayer or the nation.[3] In the latter sense, the head of state was historically the imam of Muslims, and he also led the *Jummah* (Friday) prayer. In our modern day, after the enforced change of governance following the fall of the Ottomans, imam is a title given to the leader of prayer, who is usually employed by the *waqf* ministry to address people at the *Jummah* prayer and to be present at the mosque.

The biggest change occurred in the aftermath of the colonial project in the Muslim nations, when appointed leaders and rulers often prioritized the interests of the former colonizing powers, thus fostering ideological divisions between client monarchs and socialist regimes. Islam was then deployed as a manipulative tool – a carrot and/or a stick – and used merely as a front to appease and control the masses. With Islam now in the hands of governmental administrators (as also happened in the *waqf* system), a substitute was put forward for the core identity that had been taken away from the people. This took the form of nationalism. As Arabism, it became one of the contrived 'isms' that the so-called independent Arab states threw at their societies, causing endless civil conflicts.

In 2008, Algeria initiated the start of a new legacy project: the Great Mosque of Algiers. When it came to the mosque's construction, its planners tried to distance themselves from the aspiration of reproducing a pastiche historical image, but they did this from a starting point of political ambition and competitiveness. They also made the mistake of seeking to merge the same old poles: localism and modernity. When it comes to Islamic overlay and societal specificities, foreign architects seem to struggle to pin this down: they either ignore the overlay and focus on localism (resulting in a pastiche of vernacularism) or they resort to symbolism and clichés that land them not far from the myth of the *Arabian Nights*! Modernity, in the form of technology, then becomes *the* saving rope to cling to.

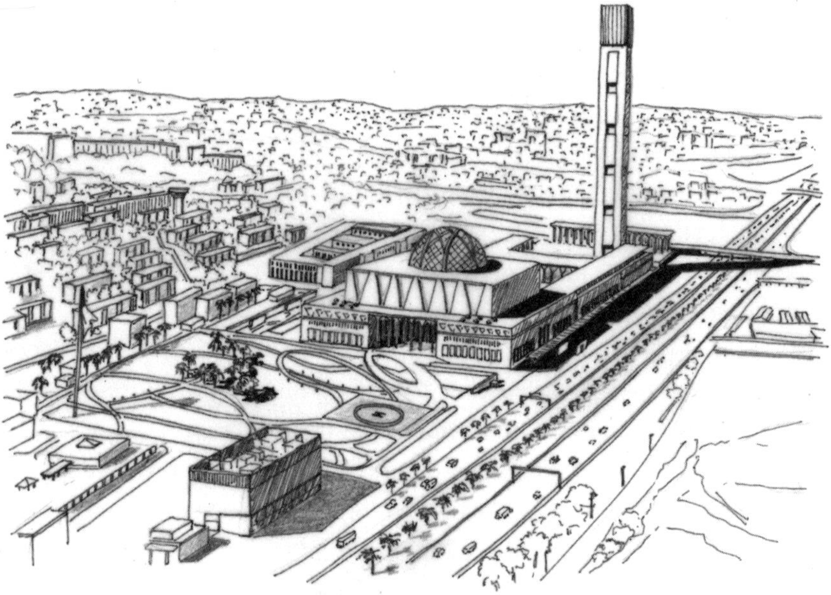

The Great Mosque of Algiers, Algeria

The Great Mosque of Algiers, known locally as Djamaa El-Djazair (Mosque of Algeria), is also nicknamed the 'Bouteflika Mosque', in reference to the former Algerian president Abdelaziz Bouteflika, who was forced to resign after twenty years of rule in 2019. The complex has been read as 'a kind of architectural concretization of the political project of opening up to moderate religiosity but also as a monument to himself'.[4] Competing in scale and height with its rival in Casablanca, at the time of its official opening in 2020 the Great Mosque became the world's third largest, after the holy sites in Mecca and Medina. Costing a staggering one billion dollars, the complex – which houses multiple facilities, including an imam school, a cultural centre, a library, a museum and a research centre – was designed by the German firm KSP Jürgen Engel Architekten, who won the bid through the architectural competition launched in 2008. Their approach is explained on the company website as an answer to designing a mosque in the twenty-first century: 'The Grand Mosque of Algiers pursues a lofty idea of connection: It combines Maghreb tradition with European Modernism.'[5]

Designed on a linear module of four sequenced squares, each measuring approximately 150 × 150 metres (490 × 490 ft), the complex has three main features that stand out. The first is the prayer hall, which – depending on how you look at it – occupies the first (or the fourth) square of the line of four. As we have seen, it is habitual for foreign architects to make the mistake of creating a square space, instead of the requisite elongated form. Fitting the rest of the programme becomes more challenging, and the whole sense of orientation and row creation gets lost. The resulting space is one created by extruding a recessed inner square into a higher block, which in turn is crowned with a massive dome that has no structural justification. From the outside the building resembles a Mesopotamian ziggurat, while inside the prayer hall space is left folded on itself, almost drained centripetally.

The second feature is the repeated loadbearing pillar, which, according to the architects, is meant to be 'an ingenious allusion to the local palm trees, [where] the overarching design motif is a floral column'. This 'forest' also serves multiple technical purposes, such as ventilation, drainage, and improved acoustics. Although Algeria is more famous for its olive groves, argan trees and Atlantic cedars than it is for its palms,

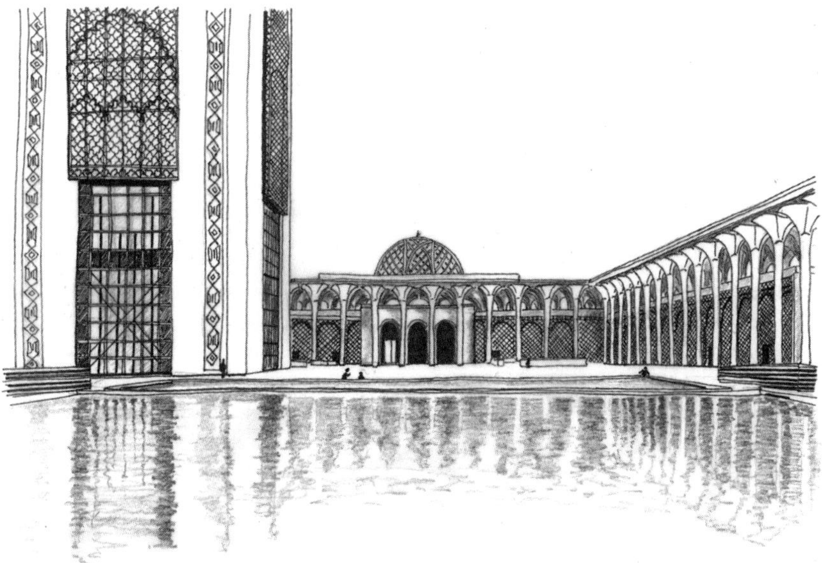

The Great Mosque of Algiers: a view from the courtyard, showing the base of the huge minaret block and the entrance to the prayer hall

the 'myth of the desert' persists. This is even used to explain the use of travertine, as an expression of 'the materiality of the desert'.[6] In addition, the Great Mosque of Córdoba is cited as a source of historical reference, but with no acknowledgment that, while a similar density of rows of pillars can be observed there, it has an entirely different sense of space, structural integrity and aesthetic sensibility. I won't dwell on the irony of such a comparison here, however, because our focus is on the political role of the mosque. The contract for its construction was signed in the presence of German chancellor Angela Merkel in 2008, during a time that was considered 'the golden age of oil revenues', before these were significantly reduced.[7] The hand outstretched towards the capitalist ambitions of Europe was also extended towards the socialist ones of China: the building works were entrusted to the China State Construction Engineering Corporation.

Finally, the third feature is the record-height minaret, which was built as a slender skyscraper (28 × 28 metres, 92 × 92 ft) and provided with panoramic elevators to take visitors to the various floors, which have different functions. The minaret hosts a museum of Islamic culture (fifteen floors), a research centre (ten floors), office areas and sky lobbies, in addition to a viewing platform at the glazed top. This hybrid minaret is visually divided, with the help of perforated screens, into five segments, based on one of the preferred clichés in modern mosque design: the Five Pillars of Islam. Marked by years of delays and cost overruns, as well as suspicions of corruption during the Bouteflika era, the complex was envisaged by its architects to function 'rather like the center of a town [to include] shops, restaurants, museums and a cinema'.[8] Regardless of how mundane and consumerist this vision is, the 'mosque' stands as a monumental suspension in the life of the city, separated from it by vast spaces of empty landscape, esplanades, and a great highway. This is the true desert.

Although the design does in many places deliver sleek and elegant details, it proves through its space and general conception that these factors are not enough to create a mosque. 'Mosqueness', as we have seen, cannot be achieved through historicism, nor is it found in 'inspired' modernism; it is a quality that can only be attained if the building is imbued with the spirit of Islam – a spirit which, even in Muslim lands, has been subdued into merely flickers here and there.

Generally speaking, as a building, the mosque evidently has an immediate religious role, but it also serves to fulfil educational, societal and political roles. The problem is that modern mosques like the Bouteflika morph these roles so that they fit comfortably with the presiding political ideologies and suit the needs of affiliates in the West, who believe that it is through the manipulation of the mosque as the abode of Islam that its role can fall under the control that is required for their own purposes. To that end, the religious role of the mosque needs to be restricted to individual practice: solitude, rather than solidarity. Likewise, its educational role needs to be cultural and historical, instead of innovative and contemporary; namely, confined to looking at the past from the perspective of its being a distant heritage, and no longer following the teachings and the knowledge of Islam to the level that they will allow for development and elevation, as was the case in the past. More crucially, the political role – the most dreaded of all – has to be suppressed and substituted with figure-serving ideologies, so the 'building' becomes a tourist attraction where the 'exquisite' dwells. In the third part of this book, I will shed more light on this source of dread, and show how fear is used as a tool of suppression in the interests of oppressive regimes, which will in turn lead to an analysis of the prescribed political role of the contemporary mosque, which is the replacement of the free-society mosque of the past.

In her book *The Transnational Mosque*, Kishwar Rizvi looks at four major powers responsible for shaping the contemporary mosque – both locally and internationally – in a fashion that serves their ideologies. Those four countries are: Iran, Turkey, Saudi Arabia and the UAE. Every one of those countries pushes forward its own ideology in the name of Islam, and for that they use what Rizvi has termed the 'ambassadorial mosque', which is the mosque built outside the territories of those countries. As Rizvi argues: 'Architecture, particularly that of mosques, manifests territorial as well as ideological connections by referencing historical periods and building styles and by enabling the rituals of inhabitation that augment the practice of religion.'[9] Those 'rituals of inhabitation' are precisely what those powers – with their ideologies and agendas – are seeking to transform, using the model of the mosque to shape both domestic policy and international diplomacy. From this perspective, the historical style of Al-Hassan II Mosque in Morocco, for example, becomes a clear shorthand for an ideology that seeks to invoke memories of the golden age of many pasts (Umayyad, Almohad, Andalusian), yet with a personal emphasis on power and glory.

Indeed, Rizvi deals in her book primarily with historical memory, with less focus on the modernist experimentation around the mosque. She insightfully recognizes the risks of transforming the mosque into a tool to gain political leverage both at home and abroad: 'the nationalist appropriation of Islam and the construction of transnational mosques emanating from the Middle East may be viewed as symptomatic of a twenty-first-century global imaginary that has turned to religious identity as a form of political agency'.[10]

Importantly, she reveals how the four countries often use contradictory 'images' of the mosque, when it comes to those that are built within the countries' own territories and those that are built outside, depending on their political audiences. What might be read as hypocrisy and betrayal of a prescribed local ideology at home by one audience is considered progress and openness by the other. For example, when it comes to religious principle, the Saudi rejection of memorial-building at home is somewhat tolerated when it serves an ambassadorial purpose, such as the Faisal Mosque in Islamabad built to commemorate the Saudi ruler Faisal bin Abdulaziz Al Saud and to accommodate the tomb of his Pakistani ally President Muhammad Zia-ul-Haq.[11] In cases of contradictory 'images', the architecture of the mosque is used as a cloak to forward certain ideas and impress certain minds, instead of being an honest manifestation of the collective spirit of the faith: 'The transnational mosque, as one of the most potent connections between the citizen and her state, lays bare the paradoxes and discrepancies in how countries in the Middle East frame their identities.'[12]

The Great Mosque of Algiers exemplifies the merging of paradoxes, in that the project seems to have become an arena for closing political deals, while disguised under the unassailable benignity of building a 'monument of Islam'. Perhaps a legitimate question at this point is: how are these buildings dissimilar from the Umayyad in Damascus, where scale, technology and innovative engineering were similarly deployed, but this time in support of realizing a true monument of Islam?

Commencing from their cut-off locations, the contemporary monumental mosques are not only a reflection of the isolative ideologies that produced them, but also an indicator of a misplaced adulation. The Umayyad's size and location were determined by what existed before it, with vigilant attention paid to what would continue to grow around it. The transition from the world of trade and materialism to the realm of the holy was maintained, in close association with both, as a constant reminder of the balance that should be struck between the two. Unlike the foreign architects who might have trouble experiencing what they do not necessarily have faith in, the builders of the Umayyad were making a house of God, not a throne on water or a skyscraper for culture. Articulating a space where unity, plenitude and harmony are manifested cannot be realized merely through the use of cutting-edge technology and the application of superficial symbolism. Most crucial is the role of the patron, who, in the case of the contemporary mosque, is the client, i.e. the person who is looking for an answer up the architect's sleeve, and not the agent, i.e. the person who has the responsibility and burden of *amana*, who would once have meditated on a place to manifest the spirit of *umma* and their longing for the divine.

The Quran tells the story of Haman, the chancellor of the Pharaoh: 'And Pharaoh said: O Haman, build me an edifice so I may reach the pathways; the pathways to the heavens and view the God of Moses of whom I believe he is lying.'[13] As an architect, these verses have always intrigued me: they made me think of my own profession as one that inconveniently demands rubbing shoulders with power. Not all architects can speak up to power as Apollodorus of Damascus did with Hadrian, who reportedly made him pay with his life for contradicting him and ridiculing his visions. Surely, no architect will lose his or her life to an emperor today, but it will certainly affect their livelihood if they oppose high-profile clients' visions, no matter how preposterous these may sound. On the other hand, building blindly for the Pharaoh should not be the way either. I remember the faces of an audience of architects to whom I defined our job description as being the 'king's mistress'; working to please the king (the client), to realize his visions, with a constant fear that we can be replaced at the slightest mishap.

Our role as architects is assuredly to fulfil visions. Indeed, especially when working on big projects, we must be under no illusion that the paying client will have no leverage whatsoever on our principles. The very commission of such projects lies in the realm of networking and building status among no less than the ruling class, in whose hands money and power converge in order to 'make dreams come true'. So, when it comes to the mosques of the past, where the implementation of power was in the service of God, it must have been so liberating for the architects to design a house for the Power that they knew how to honour. Nonetheless, even then the tone to the whole melody of the building was determined by that first key, which only the patron can hit by ordering what type of building it is going to be. For that reason, the different styles of Islamic art and architecture were named after the ruling dynasties that patronized them. These rulers played a decisive role, not only when it came to building, but also when it came to the cultivation of the special arts associated with the act of building.

In his seminal work *Art of Islam*, Titus Burckhardt illuminates a fascinating fact about the relationship between the origins of those ruling dynasties and their role in the conceptualization of Islamic art. His discussion highlights the nature of the geography of the lands of Muslims, which, as we have seen, were mistakenly characterized as undifferentiated desert, whereas they were in fact fertile regions bordered with different forms of arid steppe and actual deserts. This natural environment, which Burckhardt called the 'geography of Islam', facilitated the close proximity of sedentary communities and nomadic peoples (which had its pros and cons).[14] As Burckhardt revealed, it also meant that urban peoples have been ruled by nomads throughout the entirety of Muslim history: 'each dynasty coincides with the hegemony of a particular ethnic group.... [I]t can be stated without excessive generalization that there have been no founders of empire in the world of Islam who did not come either from the desert or the steppes, starting with the Arabs themselves who were in turn replaced by Turks, Mongols, and Berbers from the Sahara.'[15]

Ibn Khaldoun, the fourteenth-century Muslim scholar, attributed the fertility of the land and the resulting abundance to the lack of motivation and corruption to which urban settlers were susceptible. By contrast, in his view, nomads nurtured qualities of virtue, intrepidity and prowess, because their way of life confined them to the necessary and the essential. He explained 'civilization' in relation to settlement and urbanization, defining it as 'versatile in luxury and the refinement of craft'.[16] However, his major contribution is the insight he offers into the concept of *asabiyya*, which is the tendency to live tightly bound to one's kin and blood. This is the binding force in nomadic communities, and the force behind tribal thinking. Although Ibn Khaldoun saw *asabiyya* as the foundational principle behind any rule, regardless of the nature of its settlement, the history of civilization in the Levant and Mesopotamia tells a slightly different story.

In Mesopotamia, for example, the Sumerian people who created one of the earliest civilizations on earth, with highly developed irrigation systems and means of writing and registration, had relied on civic loyalty to the town, with its temples built to Sumerian gods, but this was replaced by the Akkadian hordes, who invaded from the steppe and instituted a military rule in which loyalty was turned only towards the ruler.[17] It is outside the scope of this book to follow all the threads of the peoples of the ancient kingdoms in the region (which will only cement this point), but what pertains to our discussion here is the possibility of shifting the centre of belonging from 'blood' (as it was for the Akkadians) back to 'place' (as it was for the Sumerians). With this shift would come the need to be governed by the higher power that only religion can offer, in place of the (temporary) dominant ruling figure.

In our modern societies, democracy represents the pinnacle of what that ancient sense of belonging to the town as governed by the gods once offered, and the spiral decline and corruption which this democracy is facing around the world is the result of our parting from that fundamental idea. Essentially, if the two possible loci of loyalty are 'blood' or 'place', then the two governing authorities to which affairs are reverted are 'Caesar' or 'God'. The most corrupt system is undoubtedly when Caesar becomes God. However, when voices of nationalism and populism pick up a religious narrative, one must also guard against God becoming Caesar. With processes of secularization, despite laws often being drawn from religious principles, God can be forgotten altogether.

Another vital binary point is the correlation between nomadism and urbanism, as the existence of the two modes of settlement is intrinsically intertwined. Burckhardt explains the contentious nature of this relationship in complementary terms: 'For the nomad, the sedentary is, as it were, his own prisoner, and for the sedentary, the nomad is a barbarian or even a savage. There is no doubt that these two ways of living are each favorable to different human qualities – different yet complementary; they represent something like the two halves of the totality that is mankind.'[18] The question is: how did nomadism under Islam succeed in flawlessly synthesizing those two halves into a complete whole?

If we consider how the various nomadic dynasties became the *avant-garde* sponsors of sedentary Islamic art, the conclusions actually defy the norms that used to govern our understanding of the two modes of living. Naturally, one of two scenarios occurs: either the conquering nomads get absorbed into urban life by accepting its norms, or else urban life gets vandalized and destroyed at the hands of the invaders who seek nothing beyond immediate reward. Burckhardt, however, eruditely phrased the answer to the question of synthesis, and he did it by turning to the mentality of Islam. It is, in my opinion, *the* most important question behind fully comprehending the copious brilliance of Islamic art, and consequently the essence of the mosque:

> The renewal of Islamic art by the contribution of the nomads is a phenomenon which cannot really be explained except in terms of a certain predisposition of Muslim mentality. The fact is that Islam bears within itself, on the spiritual level, the synthesis of two human attitudes, that of the sedentary and that of the nomad; the first chooses stability, which restricts him in space but allows him to count on the recurrent terms of time – he sows and reaps, dismantles and constructs – and the second chooses

> free movement in space, which places him, in a way, outside time and history, for nomadic life is not subject to transformation, remaining always at the point where it began. In the spiritual economy of Islam, the attitude of the sedentary establishes itself at a higher level as spiritual stability, while the attitude of the nomad establishes itself as non-attachment to ephemeral things.[19]

As Burckhardt states: 'If the sedentary knows the value of things, the nomad, for his part, is acutely conscious of their fragility....'[20] With such insight into the nature of the Muslim mentality, and the spiritual economy of Islam, the integrative character of Islamic art gains another dimension. More importantly, the unfathomable ability of Islamic civilization to hold its breath for twelve long centuries, inexhaustibly regenerating its product, finally makes sense. It managed, through Islam, to create that state of equilibrium between the ideals of nomadism and urbanism, which Burckhardt laments losing in the European model, reliant as it was on the Roman inheritance of 'universal *civitas*', possessing, he asserts, 'exclusively civic proclivities which are hostile to nature'.[21]

It is the same with European modernism, which the architects of the Great Mosque of Algiers tried to marry, through their orientalist overview, with the remnants of the Muslim ideal. Rulers such as Bouteflika have insufficient detachment to inculcate current creations with the breadth and sense of spirit that made the Islamic arts under past dynasties so marvellously surpassing. Even if the thousands of artisans who worked under Michel Pinseau at Al-Hassan II Mosque had been allowed to remember how to exteriorize their most intimate experiencing of the timeless, the reins of dogmatic glorification would have pulled them astray.

Under the dynasties, the mosque was a house of God, in which to worship and to learn, to exchange and to express, to see and be seen. The ruler was a leader of *umma*, a leader who, from the mosque, encouraged all that would nurture humankind with a loyalty that was placed in the service and love of the one Creator. Today, it is in the service of pseudo-rulers and masked colonizers that many of those meanings are lost, and in their place connotations of terror and destruction are aligned. Instead of being an *omphalos* (centre or hub), from which divinity radiates into all aspects of society, the mosque has turned into a temple where the sacred is either absent or kept in its box.

The nature of the sacred

> And [remember] when We made the House a place of resort for mankind and a place of safety, enjoining people to take the place where Ibraham stood as a place of prayer, as We commanded Ibraham and Ismail to purify My House for those who walk around it, and those who abide, and those who bow, and those who prostrate themselves.[22]

> And [remember] when Ibrahim was raising the foundations of the House with Ismail, [saying] 'Our Lord, accept [this] from us. Indeed, You are the all-hearer and the all-knower.'[23]

In these verses, the story of the construction of the Kaaba as a house of God is told. It is a pure place of refuge, built in a spirit of humility and submission, that seeks nothing beyond the acceptance of the Creator. It also embodies the continuation of the prophetical torch, passed from one messenger to the next, manifesting in physical form the unity of their messages. While the Kaaba is symbolic, it is – as a building made manifest – not in itself a symbol (unlike, say, the proliferated image of the Christian cross). In fact, nothing testifies more to the sincerity of Islam's commitment to the unity of faith than the fact that it is virtually without symbols. In all its rituals, ceremonies and practices, Islam offers no symbolism of form. Instead, it provides values and principles that leave space open for overarching manifestation. The holy is a governing realm, but it is not separate from life itself.

Some schools – particularly certain Sufi metaphysical currents and Orientalist writers – have proposed symbolic or esoteric interpretations of mosque architecture. In these interpretive traditions, the cube (or polygonal form) is understood symbolically to represent the earth, while the dome is seen as evoking the heavens. These interpretations draw on pre-modern cosmological ideas, which differ from the approach taken by architects who emphasize engineering principles and aesthetics over symbolic readings. In that sense, the two most misinterpreted edifices in Islamic architecture are those that belong to two of the most sacred sites in Islam: Mecca and Jerusalem.

According to the Hadith, the three most sacred mosques in Islam are: Al-Haram Mosque (the Sacred Mosque, or the Great Mosque) in Mecca,[24] the Prophet's Mosque in Medina, and Al-Aqsa Mosque (literally, the 'Farthest Mosque') in Jerusalem. Those at Mecca and Jerusalem are demarcated by rectangular territories, which host a holy centre, but the whole territory is referred to as *masjid*, i.e. a mosque.

In Mecca, the Kaaba – which is the roughly cubic structure built by the Prophets Ibrahim and Ismail, after Adam – lies at the heart of Al-Haram Mosque, and it is around the Kaaba that the circumambulation (*tawaf*) of the annual pilgrimage rituals takes place. The rituals of *ḥajj* (pilgrimage) involve a series of practices, reanimating actions taken by the Prophet Ibrahim's family. For instance, the *sa'y*, which is the complementary ritual to the *tawaf*, is a reenactment of the search for water performed by Hajar (wife of Ibrahim), as she went back and forth seven times between the two hills of Safa and Marwah. Hence, the space around the Kaaba *is* the mosque, where sacred events occurred and a collective memory was encapsulated.

Mistakenly, the emphasis of those who look at Islam from the outside is placed on the object itself. It is true that the Quraish, the ruling tribe of Mecca pre-Islam, practised paganism around and inside the Kaaba, desecrating it by building statues of their pagan gods and worshipping around them. But this, as touched upon in previous chapters (see pp. 31 and 66), is an example of how the message of faith in one God got lost in previous eras, and only a distorted residue of practice remained as an indicator. The renewal of the message of Ibrahim, by the Prophet Muhammad, restored the Kaaba and the sacred precincts around it to their original state of purity. Every Muslim prayer finishes with a plea that is for 'God to send prayers upon Muhammad and his family, as You sent prayers upon Ibrahim and his family, and to bless Muhammad and his family, as You blessed Ibrahim and his family'.

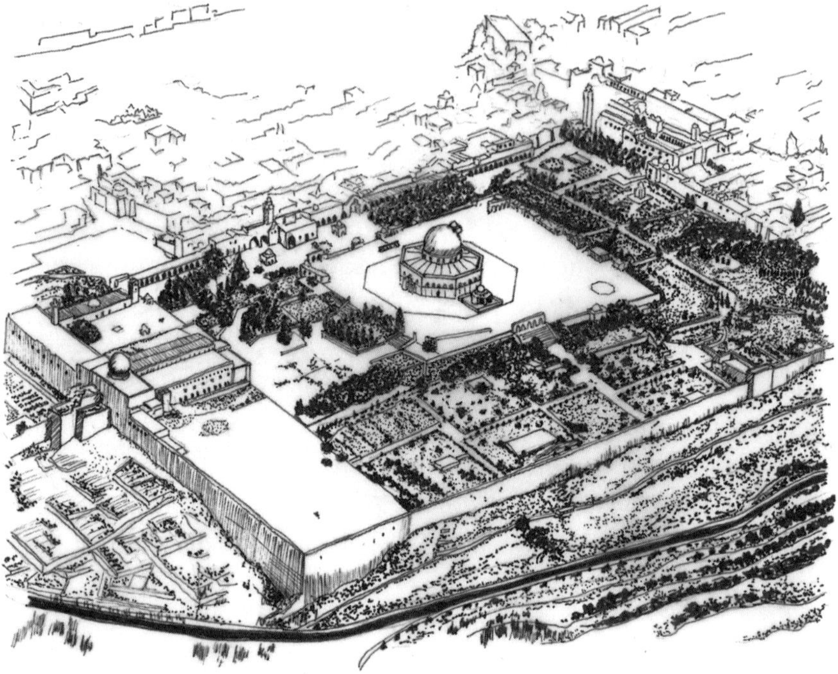

Al-Aqsa Mosque in Jerusalem

Between Ibrahim, the 'father' of the prophets, and Muhammad, the last of them, the arc of the Muslim faith is born and reborn.

Al-Aqsa Mosque in Jerusalem is the corresponding pole in sacredness to that of Mecca, since Jerusalem was the first *qibla* that Muslims prayed to, before shifting direction to Mecca shortly thereafter. As mentioned, this mosque is also demarcated by the rectangular territory it occupies, and not merely by the buildings that are constructed on the site. The Prophet Muhammad's night journey (*israa*) and ascension to heaven (*mi'raj*) is marked by a rock (during the ascension, the divine commandment for Muslims, which highlights the importance of prayer, was given to the Prophet – the only religious obligation that was not sent out to the Prophet, but, rather, he was summoned to receive in person). Upon this spot, the fifth Umayyad caliph Abd al-Malik ibn Marwan (father of Al-Walid) built the Dome of the Rock. This, in turn, is considered the inaugural edifice in Islamic architecture, being the most ancient surviving structure of Islam preserved in its complete architectural integrity.

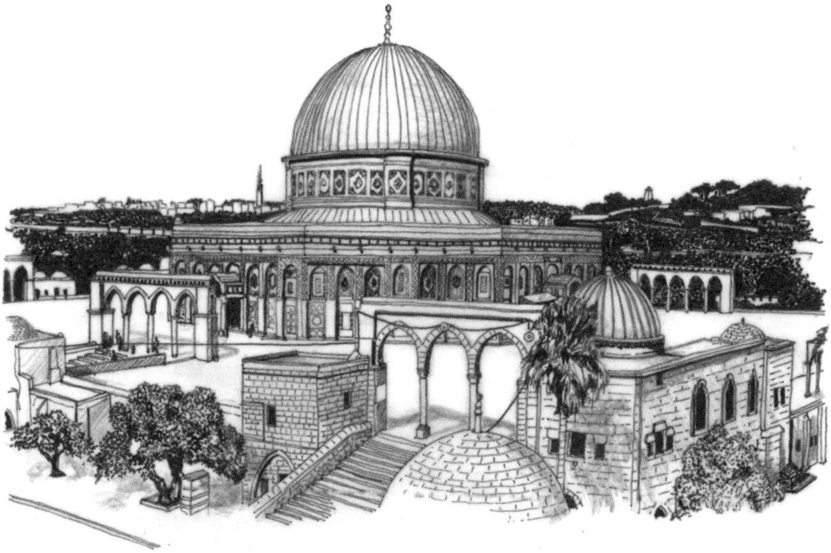

The Dome of the Rock at Al-Aqsa Mosque in Jerusalem

The Dome of the Rock (built between 685 and 691/2) is, next to the Kaaba, one of the most misquoted objects in Islamic architecture. Increasingly, we see it being used as a reference point and source of inspiration for modern mosque designs. However, the building – which is often incorrectly referred to as a mosque – is only a mosque insofar as the whole site on which it stands is a mosque. The site of Al-Aqsa, which is the walled area of approximately 144,000 square metres (1,550,000 ft^2) inside the old city of Jerusalem, is *as a whole* the mosque. Similar to Al-Haram in Mecca, the whole site is a sacred precinct. As a holy territory, it encompasses the history of the faith, having been the first *qibla*. And just as the Kaaba demarks a holy centre, so too does the Dome of the Rock. This is not in any way an equalizer between the two edifices; for the holiness of the Kaaba comes from the identity of its builders, whereas the Dome of the Rock hovers over the holiness of what lies under and around it.

Since the era of the Prophet Ibrahim, the Kaaba has been partially destroyed and rebuilt several times. However, every time, its builders would more or less preserve its form and dimensions within the general limits of its original conception. Many today confuse the Kaaba with an object of worship, but this contradicts the central tenet of belief in the one God. As the Quran noted, the Kaaba is 'surely the first House [of worship]', but this does not mean that it is a house to be worshipped. The best way to look at it is as a cadastral building, i.e. a building that indicates property boundaries, thus passing on knowledge of the whereabouts of a sacred place from one prophetical era to the next. In this light, any citation of the Kaaba's 'sacred geometry' loses all credibility.

This point also stresses the sacredness of the *ground* of both the sites in Mecca and Jerusalem, which endows their buildings with their significance. The Dome of the Rock gains its holiness from the prophetical touch (just like the stones of the Kaaba). Scholars have struggled to find a probable cause behind Abd al-Malik's decision to build his captivating octagonal edifice. The imagination of the orientalists led them to tell tales, as in the *Arabian Nights*, that the Umayyad rulers wanted to build the people of Bilad al-Sham a 'new Kaaba', contriving a story about revenge over a supposed banned pilgrimage.[25] Likewise, there is an orientalist hypothesis that Abd al-Malik was trying to divert the *hajj* to Jerusalem, in order to outsmart a rival whom he claimed was exploiting Mecca for political purposes.[26] All such preposterous allegations were categorically refuted by Muslim historians through conclusive historical evidence. However, the apparent lack of logical justification behind the creation of such a building suggests the clouded judgment of those with good intentions.

In appreciating the nature of the sacred in Islam, it becomes quite natural to understand how a builder like Abd al-Malik could have sought to protect the holy rock with a dignifying structure, especially when this is viewed within the context of the rest of the built structures on the Al-Aqsa Mosque site. At the time, the mosque itself – built by Omar, the second Muslim caliph and one of the Prophet's companions – was a rudimentary rectangular wooden prayer hall, located at the south wall of the Al-Aqsa Mosque site, on an axis with the rock. Before building the Dome of the Rock, Abd al-Malik replaced that structure with a stone construction, creating what is today called the Qibli Mosque (literally, 'the mosque in the direction of the *qibla*'). He also built the Dome of the Chain, an almost duplicate mini-structure of the Dome of the Rock, which, although it is hexagonal, looks like a prototype for the latter.

Over the following years, more than two hundred buildings – ranging from various mosques and domed structures to platforms and corner towers – were constructed on the Al-Aqsa Mosque site, transforming its multi-levelled topology into a religious complex, the totality of which is called Al-Aqsa Mosque: 'Whoever enters to pray at Al-Aqsa, whether under one of its trees, or under one of its domes, or at one of its many pulpits, or inside the Dome of the Rock, or at the Qibli Mosque; it is all the same.'[27]

In 1969, in a bid to bring on the apocalypse, Denis Michael Rohan travelled from Australia to Jerusalem, in order to torch Al-Aqsa Mosque, having dreamed of fulfilling an evangelical vision associated with the destruction of the mosque and the building of the Third Temple.[28] He thought the Qibli Mosque was Al-Aqsa, so headed there, carrying a thermos flask of kerosene, and set the inside of the place ablaze in three locations. Causing significant damage to the mosque, and totally destroying it in some parts, the fire also consumed the Minbar of Saladin – an unrivalled masterpiece of woodwork, carved and interlocked without the use of any joinery fastenings. In 1168, some twenty years before Al-Aqsa was liberated from the grasp of the Crusaders, the Syrian ruler Nur al-Din had commissioned the best carpenters of Damascus and Aleppo to create this *minbar*, with the aim of placing it in Al-Aqsa. The Crusaders at that time had been haphazardly using the mosques at the site for various purposes, whether as stores, stables or chapels. Chipping pieces off the Rock to be sold as trophies from the Holy Lands went in parallel to using it as an altar.

Those who are in favour of viewing the region as an empty vessel persist in attributing the architecture of the Dome of the Rock to previous Byzantine models, relying on examples of the octagonal martyrium idiom. Without turning this discussion into a game of rope-pulling, as it is surely true that civilizations are built in continuity, and that the overlaps and common grounds are necessarily essential to the thriving of humankind, we can nonetheless see that claims which strictly focus on crediting the architecture of the Umayyads to a previous imperial legacy do so by paving over the source of its character. It is important to highlight what was achieved architecturally and artistically between this point in history and the preceding period relating to the local eastern legacy of the Levant, in relation to these early monuments of Islam, because of the compatibility of the mindsets, in contrast with the mindsets of those who did not necessarily share similar orientations towards the universe. It is equally important to stress that, without Islam, the Levantine contributions would have remained comparatively muted in nature, thus rendering them particularly susceptible to outsider influence. It is by taking these factors into consideration that we will be able to view the architectural experience of the mosque with more depth.

It is the interaction of humankind with nature and typology (population patterns), and the chosen mode of settlement, that determines the shape of governance. Some nations, as in the Levant, develop a defensive nature that is prone to settlement and the establishment of mercantile relations, whereas other nations develop more belligerent attitudes, with an inclination towards expansion and exploitation. While the latter build mansions and palaces of power, the former build temples and places of worship. The spiritual view of the universe, which is as pivotal as the environment in determining those broad national characteristics, largely depends on two main concepts: the perceived nature of God, and the prevailing eschatology (i.e. beliefs and ideas about the ultimate fate of humanity and the world).

In Islam, life is not an end in itself: it is a means towards an end. This is called *al-hayat al-dunya*, which means the lower (inferior) life; whereas the afterlife is called *Al-Akhirah*, or the last and everlasting. On the other hand, it is only by honouring the means that we honour the end – albeit this must be done without mindlessly growing too attached and dependent on life. This means that a state of equilibrium must be achieved. As explained by Titus Burckhardt (see p. 94), it is through the embodiment of two natures – that of detached nomadism and that of settled urbanism – that the balance can be struck.

This equipoised spirit is what directed the energies of the Syrian builders and artists working under the Umayyads to produce work of such eloquence and confidence. The Dome of the Rock epitomizes this confidence. Pure in the quality of space, the building inside is uncluttered in comparison with its early Christian counterparts. The lack of liturgical programme (there are, for example, no altar or choir stalls to be incorporated), combined with the singular focus of worship (Islam has no saints to be venerated, for example), lies behind the structure's efficient yet soaring sense of freedom and lightness.

Although meant to protect the Rock, the building does not revolve around it, despite physically circling it. The design of the building, as a complex whole, has been formulated on its own terms, while seamlessly integrating the presence of the Rock. The two ambulatories created around the Rock, through the distribution of pillars and columns, underline a novel production of the unity of space, which would only advance in future buildings of Islam. With four doors distributed cardinally, the points of withdrawal and entrance are balanced with the total flow of movement.

The arrangement of the pillars and columns at the intersection points of the eight-pointed star-shaped polygonal floor plan results from the geometric module of the inner circle and the inscribed crossing squares of the polygon. Such an orientation in space is the result of two ideas. The first comes from the principle of *tawhid*, in which the centre of adulation is the all-encompassing Creator, and no specific object or liturgy is the locus. Through this, the focus of the architecture becomes the experience of the whole.

The second idea is the local mindset. To best explain this, it might be helpful to share an anecdote. Along with a group of architects and researchers, my husband and I were on a visit to a monasterial village in Italy, built defensively on the steep rocky slopes of a hill. Our destination was only accessible by mule or on foot. One of us, a Dutch researcher who was a specialist in mobility and accessibility, and was himself a paraplegic wheelchair-user, was now immersing himself in the antithesis of his area of expertise. Members of the group helped him get around, manoeuvering the endless steps that were the only means of connectivity at the site. However, the main challenge was the great staircase connecting the chapel, where we met to work, with the small diner down

CHAPTER 3

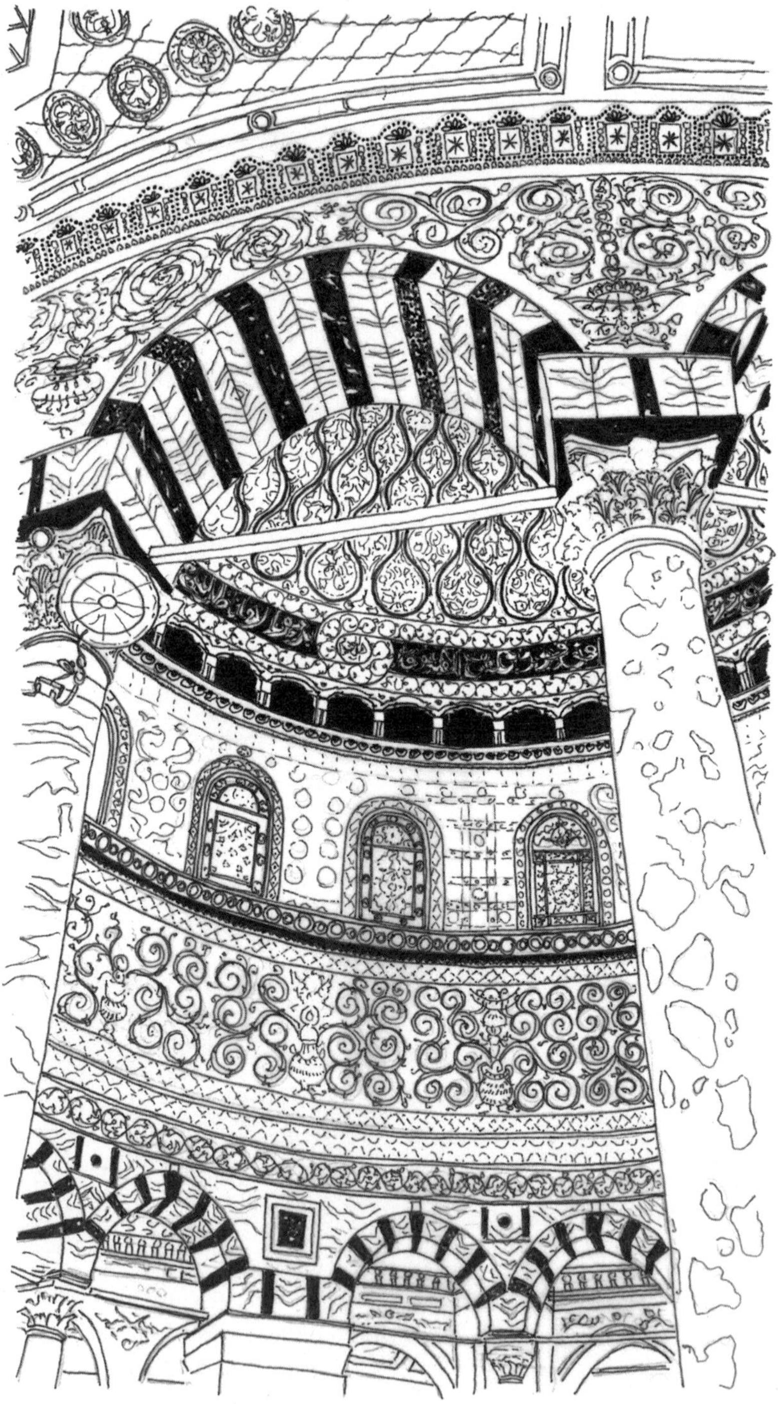

The Dome of the Rock: an interior view

the hill, where we rested. At the top of the stairs, the group tried placing rudimentary wooden planks ahead of every move the researcher might make. When that didn't work, they attempted to take him down backwards against gravity, but the steepness, along with the rocks, proved to be too challenging. At that stage, everyone could sense the frustration, which is when my husband asked for permission to interfere 'in his way' – whereupon he scooped the man up and headed off downhill, asking to be followed with the empty wheelchair. A Turkish member of the group shouted, 'Eastern thinking!' It is this flexibility in working *with* elements, and not *against* them, which characterizes Eastern thinking, and which can be found at the Dome of the Rock, infusing it with what Burckhardt called its '"Platonic" purity'.[29]

From the outside today, attention is dominated by the golden dome and the vivid blue of the tiled top section of the Dome of the Rock. Both of these, in fact, belong to later renovations. The Ottomans installed the tiles in the sixteenth century, in place of the deteriorating and damaged mosaics that originally covered the upper part of the building. As for the dome (which is actually a double-dome; the outer structure, originally covered in lead, is separated from the inner structure by a space of 1.5 metres [5 ft]), this has undergone various renovations, the last of which was carried out by the Jordanian government in the 1990s.

As much as the Dome of the Rock is not a mosque, it is not a shrine or a memorial either; it is a protective and cadastral building, on a holy site that constitutes the second of the two mosques of Islam where space is demarcated territorially. In his book *From Mecca to Las Vegas*, Ali Abd al-Raouf provocatively chooses to juxtapose the ultimate sacredness (the holiest city in Islam) and the ultimate desecration ('Sin City'). The point he tries to convey in the book is related to the desecration inflicted through the consumerist idiom of the luxury hotels and the Clock Tower built by the Saudis over Al-Haram Mosque. Kishwar Rizvi similarly highlights Saudi policy, by drawing attention to the reinstatement of the demolition campaign that was launched by the kingdom after its foundation: 'Starting in 1932 the new Kingdom of Saudi Arabia, which was established with the help of the British Army, unleashed a systematic agenda of destroying holy sites, a policy that has continued to the present day.'[30]

It is a cause for alarm that, through mosque building (and unbuilding), policies are shaped and governance is formed today. But the form of the mosque remains the field of Muslim expression through which we face the world, and face God.

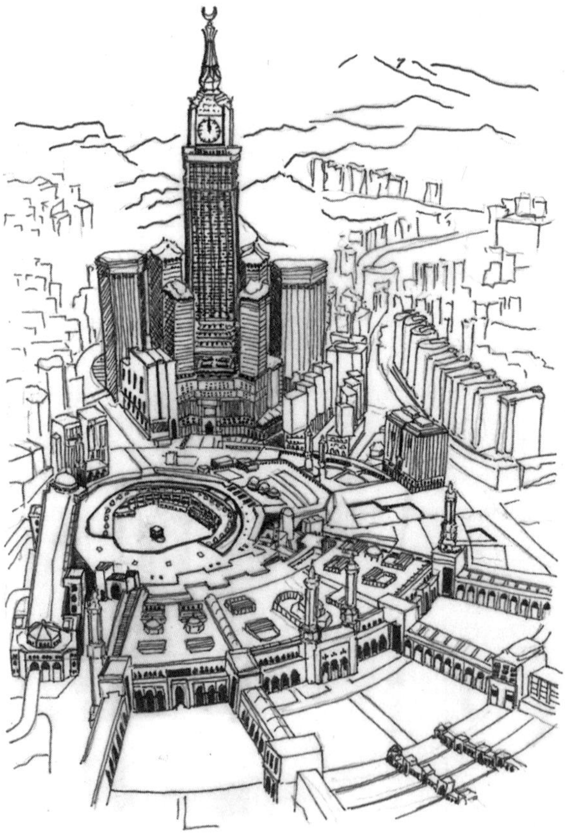

Al-Haram Mosque in Mecca, Saudi Arabia; the Kaaba is dwarfed by the Clock Tower

Part II

Form

Chapter 4

The Architecture of the Mosque

'It can happen, it will happen very often, that in becoming Islamicized a country adopts one of the many shades of colour that the huge triangular prism of Islam can offer when breaking up the white light of divine truth diffused by Islamic faith.'

TIERNO BOKAR, THE SAGE OF BANDIAGARA[1]

The modes of integration

China is as far as Islam went east. Although the rulers of China didn't convert to Islam, the new religion reached the region through two main routes: the Silk Road and the Perfume and Spices Route. The maritime Muslim merchants of the latter first arrived in the mid-seventh century via the port cities of Guangzhou and Quanzhou, and later Yangzhou and Hangzhou. There, Islam spread through daily dealings. By contrast, the land route was controlled by the geopolitics of expansionist powers. For example, the Chinese imperial force that headed westwards in the eighth century encountered Muslim forces, who stopped them at the frontiers of Transoxiana. By the thirteenth century, the Mongol conquest of China was aided by the 'great numbers of Muslims recruited from earlier Iranian and Central Asian campaigns',[2] complemented by the conversion to Islam of frontline Turkic tribes (such as Uyghurs and Karakhanids), which helped drive a wave of Muslim immigration – offering military and administrative support to the Mongols – into Xinjiang Province and the Chinese midlands. These Muslim communities settled, influencing Chinese society and remaining in place even after the Mongols were defeated in 1368.

According to Professor Luo Xiaowei, the result was two types of mosque architecture in China: 'one, brought from the Near East, occurs in the north-western region, including the Xinjiang province, and the other type is based on traditional Chinese architecture adapted to Islamic belief and ritual requirements'.[3] In her analysis, Luo explains how mosques of the latter type – those that developed alongside trade – 'ingeniously integrated Near Eastern Islamic influences with local architectural traditions, eventually producing a distinctive style for such buildings'.[4] This unique 'Sino-Islamic' idiom incorporated such elements as Chinese-style courtyards, tiled roofs and pagoda-like minarets.

Throughout its pre-modern history, the architecture of the mosque has followed the same evolutionary pattern, regardless of location. In southeastern China, just as in Medina or Damascus, the style went through two main phases before reaching its final phase of full crystallization. The first is the phase of emergence, where the mosque is built rudimentarily with a focus on merely providing a place for prayer to serve the nascent community of worshippers, while also taking into consideration the congregation's potential future need for more space. The next phase is the integration period, where connections with the local culture and modes of expression are sought, while relying on the solid foundations of the faith and its teachings. This is what was referred to in the previous part (see p.73) as the merging of 'overlay' and 'societal specificities', with Islam's world view as the conduit. Finally, in the third phase, maturity in style is reached, and with it the pinnacle of artistic and architectural expression is apotheosized.

With regard to the formulation of the Chinese style of the mosque, the three phases can be traced through the architectural manifestations within each phase.[5] Of the first two, the emergence phase brought mosques that were either a direct transfer from further west (in other words, a cultural continuation from neighbouring regions), as occurred in northwestern China, or else rudimentary structures built mostly in wood, as occurred in southeastern China. This period lasted for about 300 years (between the seventh and tenth centuries) before a Chinese architecture for mosques started to develop in the southeast, through the influence of local cultures. This next phase lasted for another three centuries, during which time 'efforts were made to integrate functional requirements, cultural expressions and building techniques from the western regions with characteristic local architecture, producing results which would be respected by Muslim and non-Muslim alike'.[6]

Huaisheng Si, which translates as the 'Mosque in Memory of the Holy Prophet', is considered to be the oldest surviving mosque in China. Located in the southeastern city of Guangzhou, which has been referred to as 'the cradle of Chinese Islam', due to its being the primary point of contact with the earliest Arab and Persian seafaring merchants, the mosque is thought to have been built in around 627 CE. Although it was rebuilt in 1350, and again in 1695 due to fire, and then its prayer hall was rebuilt in reinforced concrete in 1935, Huaisheng is regarded as one of the four great mosques along the South China Sea,[7] exemplifying cross-fertilization between China and Islam.

While the traditional orientation of the street façade to the south was maintained, the axis of the mosque was turned to be oriented east–west, with the narrow gateway preceding the prayer hall to be accessed from the east in order to face the *qibla* (with Mecca to the west). After access through the gateway, a succession of corridor spaces leads to

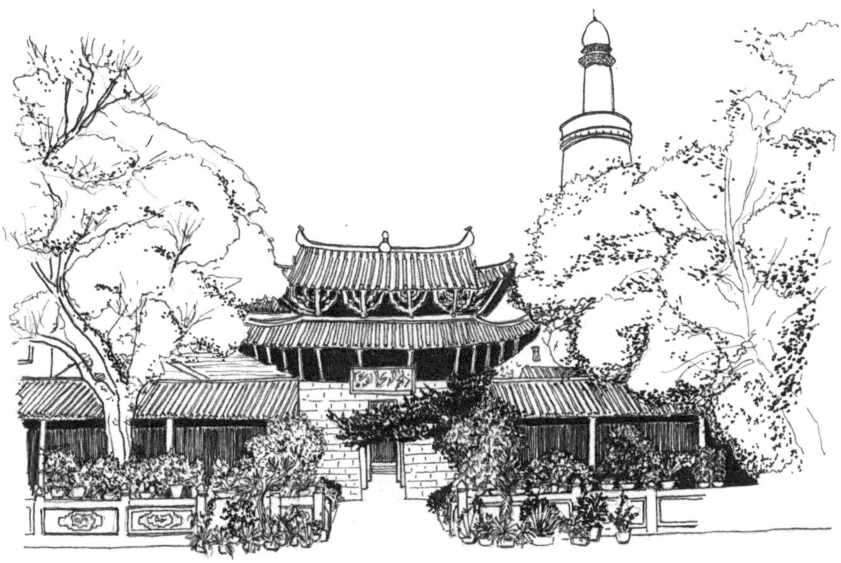

Huaisheng Mosque (also known as the Lighthouse Mosque) in Guangzhou, China

a two-storeyed structure, with a two-tiered hipped roof and double eaves, called the Moon Pavilion. This was the Chinese interpretation of the Islamic minaret, from where the call to prayer is announced and in which vertical visibility is achieved, but here the pavilion served as a multi-functional structure: it was a portal and a moon observatory, as well as a minaret. Through the portal of the Moon Pavilion, one reaches the colonnaded courtyard that ultimately leads to the prayer hall. Such an approach, which preserved the spatial and functional structures of the local culture, demonstrates the governing spirit of design in the premodern architecture of the mosque.

In China, this architecture developed into a fully metabolized Islamic Chinese style during the period of maturity that lasted for 500 years (from the fourteenth to the nineteenth centuries). Luo sums up its dominating spirit as 'in search of mannerism', with spatial, structural and ornamental changes as indicators of the quest for a mature stylistic idiom.[8] This search consolidated what had been achieved previously in terms of orientation, hierarchy of space and multi-purpose utility, culminating in mastery of both technical and aesthetic innovation.

The Great Mosque of Xi'an, in Shaanxi Province, is recognized as the largest and best-preserved early mosque in China. It was built in its current form in 1392, and its architecture represents the typical Chinese walled complex of multiple consecutive courtyards. The prayer hall lies in the fourth and westernmost courtyard, with a capacity of 1,000 worshippers, while the adjacent third courtyard functions as the prayer hall's open space, known as the *sahn*. Both the second and first courtyards were fashioned after traditional Chinese gardens, and alongside them run extensive halls which reflect the mosque's function as a community centre and a madrasa, and include a library, rooms for the imam, and rooms for visitors and for teaching. The *mihrab* is made of carved wood, with bands of Quranic inscriptions in Chinese characters, crowned above the niche with an embellishment of a mandala-like square filled with large Chinese lotuses.[9]

During this phase of maturity, the development of the Chinese mosque architectural idiom included, for instance, the deployment of traditionally Chinese *dougong* (brackets under the eaves) in conjunction

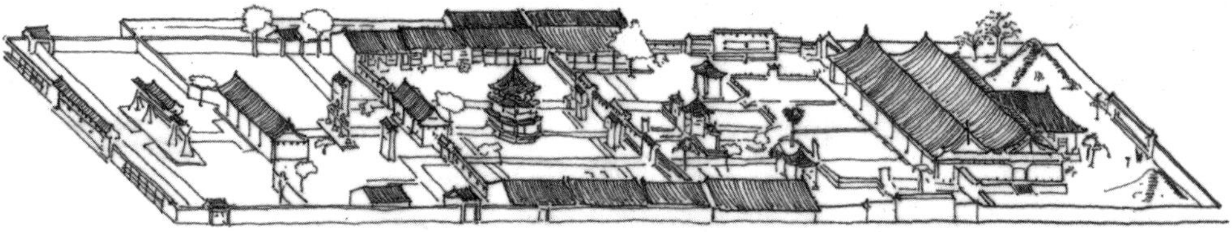

Diagram showing the progression of courtyards in a typical Chinese mosque, here with the prayer hall to the east

with *muqarnas* (traditionally Islamic honeycomb vaulting), so that these decorative elements were emphasized in terms of both height and form. In my view, this aesthetic refinement is an exemplar of how the world view of Islam promulgated the same understanding of structural elegance, in relation to lightness and a combination of slenderness and rigour, as well as efficiency and soundness, all across the Muslim world. At the same time, the concept of flexibility was understood, with an exchange of knowledge, construction techniques, and sometimes individual design elements enjoying a steady flow across cultures, where they were emulated, filtered and morphed into what fitted harmoniously as an expressive whole.

For instance, Luo points out 'a real innovation in both functional layout and building technology',[10] which led Chinese Muslims to build a sequence of halls, one in front of the other, and to join them lengthwise in order to increase capacity and unify space. A complete novelty in terms of construction and spatial order, this experimentation additionally offered sub-solutions such as providing improved roof drainage. Meanwhile, elaborations continued to be made on the multi-purpose minaret/portal/moon observatory, as well as on aesthetically emphasizing the *mihrab* recess – now through light, instead of wood-covered domes. As Luo notes: 'The use of a tower-like timber structure with pointed Chinese roof and clerestory to admit light to the *mihrab* recess was prevalent.'[11]

As previously observed (see p. 110), the mosques in northwestern China did not follow the process of slow metabolism that took place in the southeastern regions. However, it should be noted that in the location from which they were imported the process of configuration did follow a similar pattern, resulting in the brick architecture of the Central Asian style. The Amin Mosque in the Turfan oasis in northwestern China, built in 1778, is representative of those Chinese mosques that embody the cultural spillovers of Central Asian expression into ethnically mixed neighbouring Chinese territories. The minaret of the Amin Mosque features concentric bands of brickwork decoration and a pronounced batter (narrowing of the cylindrical form as it rises), linking it to the most famous Central Asian minaret – that of the Great Mosque of Bukhara, dating from the twelfth century.

The northwestern Chinese mosque is an imported ready-made idiom that conveyed no response to its new locality, because of the migratory character of the local nomadic peoples and the additional lack of stability created by the faultlines of conflicting empires, whereas the southeastern region, characterized by stability and exchanges through trade and town structures, nurtured conditions that were ripe for mosque development (as was also the case in the Levant, for example). Nonetheless, for both types of Chinese mosque, modernity – beginning in the twentieth century – has had a similar effect to that on mosques elsewhere in the Muslim world: identity has been lost and, in order to compensate, a reliance on not necessarily suitable ready-made imported 'images' has become the mainstream.

The story of the Chinese mosque is the story of all pre-modern mosques around the world. Whether in Africa, South Asia or the Levant, the prelapsarian mosque's architecture has consistently followed the same patterns of materialization: it emerged either from the familiar form of the traditional domestic residence or from the abstract layout of a former house of worship, but never from the palace or from any seat of political power. During the emergence phase, it either took its time to digest the surrounding environment and form connections with local systems and common idioms, as we have seen in the example of southeastern Chinese mosques, or it extended externally to connect with a basic neighbouring form that had passed the emergence phase but could still potentially undergo integrative stages of development, as in the case of northwestern Chinese mosques. Between integration and maturity, innovation is governed by how much the architecture of the mosque can

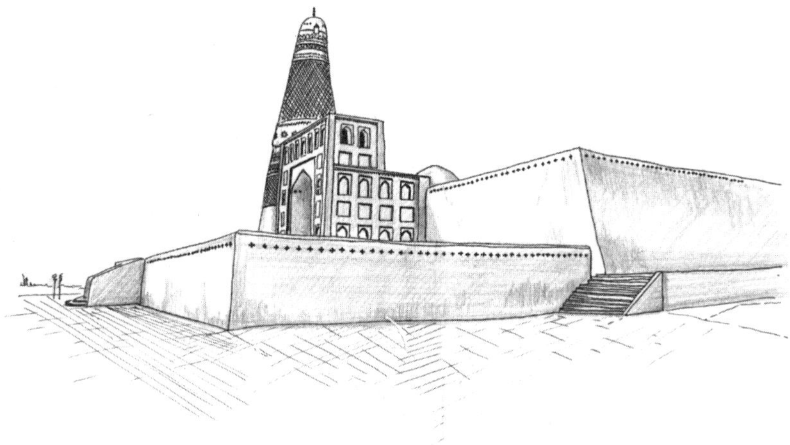

The Amin Mosque in Turfan, Xinjiang Province, China

achieve a renaissance of what exists in all areas of life and for all people, without any sense of exclusivity.

For instance, the highly unusual white minaret of Huaisheng Mosque – a freestanding cylindrical structure that is 36 metres (118 ft) tall – belongs to the early period of the mosque's realization. However, judging by its physical detachment from the building, and its alienated form in relation to the local architecture, art historians have opined that it could have been added at some point during the integration period, alongside one of the rebuildings of the mosque, or it could have been built according to the needs of the growing community. Whatever the case may be with regard to its origins, one aspect of the landmark minaret has become highly pronounced. Due to differentials in its rocky foundations, the minaret exhibits a degree of inclination that has today reached 1.06 metres (nearly 3½ ft) from the vertical. The fact that the minaret has continued to stand, unaffected, for all these centuries is attributed to the ingeniously constructed base, consisting of 3.6-metre-long (nearly 12 ft) stripes of stone, and the body being built with a mixture of soil, glutinous rice, brown sugar and lime.[12] So, even if in this case integration did not take the form of an architectural affiliation with the local environment, the espousal of local techniques, and their usage to help construct a new model of expression, constitute a similar effect.

The emergence of Islam from the domestic sphere, rather than from the realm of power, reveals its place in public life. Through the architecture of the mosque, a clear message is delivered: the mosque is intended for ordinary human life, far removed from the dogmatic power that resides in palaces and is bolstered by military force.

Moreover, domestic architecture was always compatible with the essential layout of the emerging mosque, because it comprises a hierarchy of *revealing* that embodies both a sense of protection and privacy as well as a balancing sense of welcome and hospitality. As a visitor to a home, you earn spatial trust by progressing from the exclusionary outside to the embracing inside; whereas in a palace you remain outside even when you are actually inside, because you can never really negotiate a space that fundamentally does not grant trust, no matter how far you advance. At the mosque, as we have seen in past chapters, an easy transition from the bustling world of mundanity should take you to a place of refuge; a sanctuary where you are able to calm your soul as you cross the physical thresholds of the building.

This process of revealing is often overlooked in modern architecture. Preliminary spaces and subtle elements of guidance are replaced with crude directivity or, in the case of a place like Education City (EC) Mosque in Doha, no directivity at all. Nonetheless, it would be unfair to blame modernity for all the shortcomings in mosque architecture; throughout the different historic dynasties of Islam, there have also been periods of struggle and even failure. In order to shine some light on these periods, it is key to point out that the mosque, throughout its history, has undergone two major metamorphoses; one involving the mausoleum, and one involving the madrasa.

Mosques and mausoleums

I wrote about Khaled ibn al-Walid Mosque in my first book, *The Battle for Home* (2016), because it was a prime site for demonstrations against Bashar al-Assad's regime, as well as a location of fierce fighting between the regime's forces and those of the opposition between 2011 and 2014. The mosque was directly targeted by the regime's forces, leaving much of it, including the central dome and its two minarets, punctured with visible holes. However, what I didn't write about was the story of the rebuilding of the mosque, which began with the regime's attempt at restoration in the aftermath of the civil war in Syria, continued after the fall of the regime on 8 December 2024, and is still ongoing today. The mosque has become an emblem for the city of Homs, not only for being a symbol of the revolution against Assad, but also because it holds the burial place of a Muslim leader and a companion of the Prophet Muhammad: Khaled ibn al-Walid. Indeed, another name for Homs is 'Ibn al-Walid's City'.

In fact, the mosque is situated at the back of a larger graveyard, on what was until recently the northern frontier of the city. In line with the usual purpose of mausoleums, the construction of the first version of the mosque was ordered in 1266 by the Mamluk sultan Al-Zahir Baybars to protect the burial place of Khaled ibn al-Walid within this haphazard cemetery and to perpetuate the memory of the fellow great warrior.

Mausoleum architecture, which developed prominently in the lands of present-day Iran, was spread by two dynasties that had converted to Islam, the Turks and the Mongols. Their active engagement in military endeavours and their cultural reverence for warrior paladins drove their inclination to commemorate those who died for the faith by building mausoleums. The Turks, who had risen to power from their original rank as slave–soldiers in the Abbasid and later Samanid armies in Iran, built an enormous number of mausoleums in their territories.[13] The Mongols, who had once brought all kinds of death and destruction to the Muslim lands they conquered, embraced Islam when one of their leaders, Ghazan Khan, converted in 1295, reportedly building a mosque in every town. However, they were quick to revert to self-aggrandizement when it came to their mausoleums, with the largest in the Islamic world being built in Sultaniyya by Khan's brother and successor Uljaytu.[14]

By contrast, in the lands of the Arabs, where decades of self-discipline under the Prophet Muhammad and his companions were followed by the spiritual civility that was by now deeply rooted in Bilad al-Sham, the tribal sensibility of *asabiyya* and the accompanying warrior mentality were mitigated, without their flame being entirely extinguished, by a constant return to the central judgment of thought for Muslims: the message of Islam. For tribal communities such as those of the Turks and the Mongols, on the other hand, vast distances separating them from key urban centres in the heartlands of Islam – where there was a concentration of *ulamaa* (men of religious knowledge), whose products of thought underwent a constant process of refinement – made it much more difficult for them to master control over the power of *asabiyya*.

In Homs, the first version of the Mosque of Khaled (as it is colloquially called) was made of the local basalt stone and bore the features of traditional Mamluk mausoleum–mosques, in which congregational prayer is not the primary function of the building. The Mamluks' unique ruling system – stemming from their origins as freed-slave mercenaries from the steppes of Central Asia and the Caucasus, who, having gained power, relied for success and succession upon intense rivalry between high-ranking Mamluk elites – meant that those who were bred to rule lived in a constant race towards domination. Initially recruited by the Kurdish Ayyubids, the Mamluks inherited power from them in Egypt, and built some of their most significant religious complexes there. Due to the life of danger they led, their building motivations stemmed from mixed intentions. As scholar Bernard O'Kane has noted: 'For an *amir*, or even a sultan, life was often precarious – a coalition of unfavorable amirs could lead to falling out of favour and banishment, or even execution and confiscation of one's worldly goods.'[15]

As we have seen, mausoleum construction was not part of the architectural vocabulary of early Islam. Tombs had been present in mosques, as at the Prophet's Mosque in Medina and the Umayyad in Damascus, but this is fundamentally different from having the mosque specifically built for the tomb, as is usually the case with mausoleum–mosques. It is with the Mamluks that the building of mausoleums came into full force. The religious hazard of erecting a mausoleum, which ran the risk of leading to 'unseemly pilgrimages and inappropriate intercessionary prayers',[16] was alleviated through the practice of attaching a small mosque to it. Negotiating between the swords of rivals and the frowns of the *ulamaa*, the amirs and the sultans had to build just the right

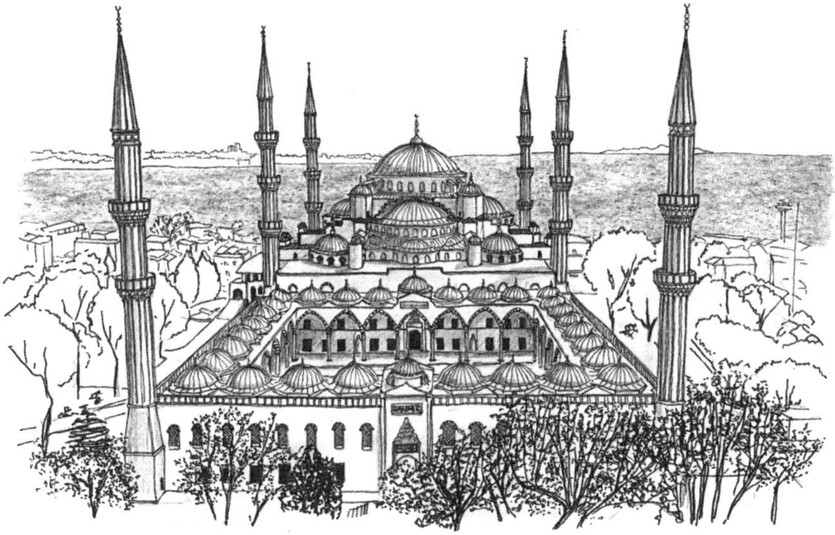

The Sultan Ahmed Mosque (also known as the Blue Mosque) in Istanbul, Turkey

kind of complex, where they could display their blend of personal one-upmanship and religious piety.

In Homs, the Mamluk version of the Mosque of Khaled was demolished in 1903, making way for the prestigious Ottoman rebuilding that was completed in 1913 and still stands today. Its style was inspired by the Sultan Ahmed Mosque in Istanbul, known as the Blue Mosque for its interior adorned by predominantly blue Iznik tiles and painted floral arabesque motifs. As a tourist to Turkey, I visited the Blue Mosque in 2003. At the time, I didn't have my architect's goggles on, but I still remember the sense of wonder and astonishment that engulfed me as I crossed the threshold from the bright light of day and bustling street life to the majesty of the interior beneath the cascading domes and amid the deep blue hues that were illuminated by the typically Ottoman central chandelier, with its circular orbits of light. I also recall fellow tourists flooding the place, and all of us – almost profanely – turning it into a huge museum gallery. As at the Mosque of Khaled, the tomb of Sultan Ahmed lies inside the mosque and is enshrined within a cubical structure that is crowned with a small dome, occupying a corner near the

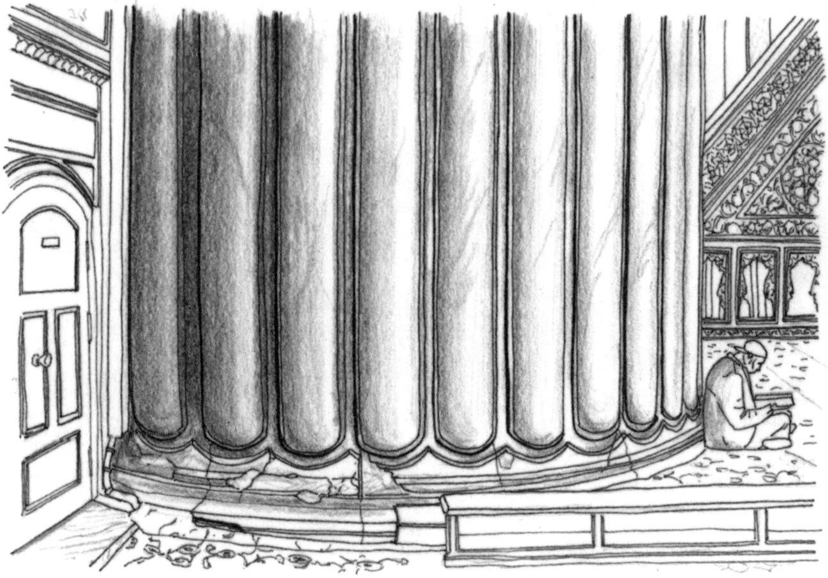

The Sultan Ahmed Mosque: an interior view, featuring a man reciting the Quran

entrance. Completed in 1616, the Sultan Ahmed Mosque is considered the *magnum opus* of Ottoman architecture, but at the same time it is the swan song of the classical Ottoman mosque architecture that was shaped at the hands of the legendary Mimar Sinan.

Sinan's major contribution was his brilliant transformation of the structural concept exemplified by the Byzantine Hagia Sophia in Istanbul, with its central dome and supporting semi-domes. Through masterful innovations, Sinan refined buttressing systems and introduced greater illumination and spatial unity. By turning static Byzantine spaces divided by bulky supports into dynamic, open and harmonious spaces, he established a new, Ottoman idiom of architectural achievement.

The architect of the Sultan Ahmed Mosque, Sedefkar Mehmed Agha, was a disciple of Sinan. 'Sedefkar' is his title, and it literally means (in Turkish) 'one who works with mother-of-pearl'. Mehmed Agha did indeed train in decorative arts, inlaying wood with shellwork (a craft imported from Syria), and this undoubtedly left an impression on his designs. The Sultan Ahmed Mosque has been described as conveying the architect's attention to detail and his 'willingness to break up its elements into smaller parts'.[17] The result is nonetheless a holistically synthesized building of immense size and splendour, with a sculptural quality and a strong decorative impulse.[18] In the same artisanal spirit, Mehmed Agha sought to create a softer profile of Sinan's cascading composition of domes and semi-domes, so he deliberately juxtaposed curved domes with vertical elements that would convey the sense of rigorous power for which Sinan's mosques were famous,[19] but he introduced more curved and multi-tiered supporting elements into the composition of his own domes, producing a sense of upward inclination that draws the eye both inside and outside.

Unlike the 31 by 31 metres (100 × 100 ft) square prayer hall at the Mosque of Khaled – which emphasizes its character as a mausoleum – the prayer hall of the Sultan Ahmed Mosque is a shy rectangle of 64 by 72 metres (210 × 236 ft). Another difference between the two mosques lies in the layout: the Sultan Ahmed Mosque features a prayer hall that is fronted by a colonnaded courtyard, whereas the Mosque of Khaled is freestanding at the back of the cemetery (it has no courtyard or colonnades, and its freestanding form and location surrounded by burial sites indicate its character as a mausoleum–mosque).

The active patronage of Sultan Ahmed (r. 1603–17) is explained by some commentators in the light of implied political motivations. His monumental mosque was the first to be built after a period of pause on grand buildings that had lasted for the reigns of three previous sultans. It is believed that his decision came after the signing of the Peace of Zsitvatorok treaty with the Habsburg monarchy, which has been perceived as an undermining of sultanate prestige. In compensating with a solidified Ottoman image at the monumental Sultan Ahmed Mosque, the decision to include six minarets perhaps went too far, as these were allegedly viewed locally at the time as an affront to the status of the Great Mosque of Mecca (Masjid al-Haram). Regardless of whether he was motivated by the hope of redemption or by piety, the Sultan initiated a comprehensive renovation campaign of the holy mosques of Mecca and Medina, adding an extra minaret to Al-Haram and shipping a new *minbar* made of white marble to be placed at the Prophet's Mosque.

The pair of minarets at the Mosque of Khaled are a rare departure from the idiomatic slender Ottoman minaret, with its fluted surfaces and conical cap. The two minarets are entirely built in limestone, brought from the nearby town of Hama and contrasting elegantly with the body of the mosque, which uses black basalt and the Syrian *ablaq* technique (alternating lines of black and white stone). These polygonal Mamluk minarets look as if they are bidding farewell to the building's older self. Local historians in Homs[20] have noted that the architect who was assigned to the project by the Ottoman sultan Abd al-Hamid was a French-educated Ottoman named Alaa al-Din Ulsoy. The historic accounts also mention the participation of different Christian families in the construction, including the major contribution of the Christian Homsi mason Aref Khzam, who, according to these accounts, was sent to Cairo to view the Mosque of Muhammad Ali and then build the Mosque of Khaled in the same fashion. I find such accounts believable, because the cubic interior space of the Homs mosque, wrapped in the elongated proportions of pointed arches that carry the cascade of the domes and frame the niches of the windows, makes it look more like a chapel than a mosque.

Muhammad Ali, the Albanian governor of Egypt who defected from the Ottomans and is considered the founder of modern Egypt, is also known for the Massacre of the Citadel, in which he orchestrated the killing of hundreds of Mamluk leaders, thus eliminating their influence in Egypt. On the site of the citadel, he built his grand mosque between 1830 and 1857. The initial plans for the building were drafted by the French architect Pascal Coste, and proposed a 'neo-Mamluk style'. The shift to the Ottoman style, which was finally declared for the mosque, was made by Coste's replacement, whose name remains unverified. Nonetheless, the mosque's architecture has ultimately been recognized as 'European–Ottoman', because it is only in its outer shell that it bears any relation to the classic form of Ottoman mosques.

With its cubic space, detached location and French influence, the Mosque of Khaled owes more to the Mosque of Muhammad Ali than it does to the Sultan Ahmed Mosque. Having said that, the skills of Syrian masons meant that the Mosque of Khaled was able to sustain severe

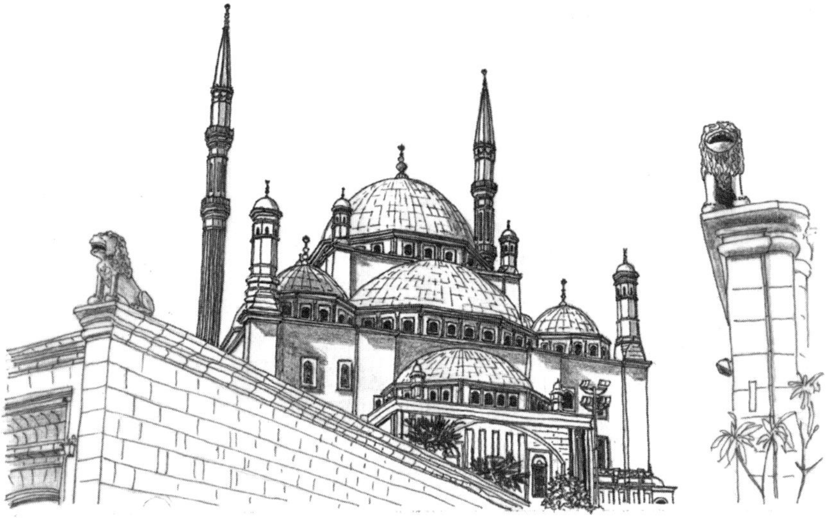

The Mosque of Muhammad Ali in Cairo, Egypt

damage during wartime and, against all odds, remain perfectly sound, whereas the Mosque of Muhammad Ali required restoration work as early as the 1930s (this brings to mind the similar fate of Al-Hassan II Mosque in Casablanca; see p. 82). The questions to be asked here are: do these mausoleum–mosques conform to the phases of integration through which other mosques in both Muslim and non-Muslim lands once went? Was the genesis of their layout of a domestic or worshipful nature, or was it rooted in the contexts of palaces and power? Were their creators guided by pursuit of an egalitarian space, or were they fascinated by impressive spaces?

Similar to the domed cube of the Mamluk mausoleum, the ancient Anatolian mosque offers a centralized space that seems to be inspired more by a nod towards commemoration than by a bow to egalitarian orientation. Despite its brilliance in its own right, there is no doubt that the classical Ottoman architecture pioneered by Mimar Sinan was driven by the quantitative ambition of producing a space to rival the Byzantine Hagia Sophia. Furthermore, despite the evolution from the singular monolithic domed cube to the cascaded space forwarded by a courtyard surrounded by colonnades in the classical mosque, or nestling in a complex of annexes as in the royal mosque-complexes, the Ottoman mosque does not seem to have departed far from that original centrality of the mausoleum.

From the example of the evolution of the Chinese mosque at the beginning of this chapter, we have seen how forging connections with past arrangements of places of worship was common ground for the architecture of the mosque. However, even when the layout or specific elements and functions were retained, spaces were still radically transformed through new visions of the universe (see also p. 72). To use the words of Gülzar Haider: 'Faith is the architect.'[21] Is this to say that classical Ottoman mosques – and their modern replicas – are not spaces of faith? Absolutely not. However, these mosques also tell us something else; namely, that their creators and builders gradually shifted their focus from building places for people to building places of power.

People who look at the form of mosques today are often struck by the magnificence of their soaring central spaces, just as I felt at the Sultan Ahmed Mosque. Indeed, due to the active patronage of Islamic arts, the mosque has historically been *the* place where these various arts have found their finest outlet. As a visual composite, the centralized mega-space with multiple minarets and a gallery of eye-dazzling surfaces constitutes the main stereotypical image for the general public – interestingly, for Muslims and non-Muslims alike. Expert categorization, which divides the mosque's architecture into different 'images', as shared previously (see p. 58), has done little to shift that persistent general perception.

The cube (or polygon) topped with a dome (or multiple domes) has become the instant superficial abstraction of the innovative engineering of the classical Ottoman mosque. Furthermore, with the advent of poured cement and ready-made moulds devaluing the structural feat of the Ottoman achievement, this abstraction becomes even more meaningless. However, it draws attention to the form's possible historical origins in the Sassanid kiosk, where *kōšk* means 'palace', or 'portico' in Persian and *köşk* means 'pavilion' in Turkish.[22] Both refer to a centralized cubical or polygonal space with open walls that are supported by pillars. Although different accounts offer different origins – some refer to the Mongolian yurt; others, less reliably, to Zoroastrian origins – the kiosk seems to offer a direct typology.

Whatever the origin of the domed cubic space from which both the mausoleum and consequently the Ottoman mosque derive their spatial arrangement, the resulting sense of commemoration and focus on monumentality that these mosques reflect seems to connect them with the palace's denial of the gradual embracing act of revealing (in contrast to that of the domestic house). With its confined centralization of space within a cube underneath a dome (versus the elongated orientation of rows of the seminal mosques),[23] this exported anti-mosque quality of 'space of power' in the mausoleum proves challenging to reconcile with the egalitarianism of space as an essence of the mosque.

Back in Homs, in 2016, the regime began what could be one of the clumsiest restoration and rebuilding processes of recent times. The operation was secretive: nobody was permitted to talk about the rebuilding, nor to approach the site (except for monitored prayer, for which cameras were installed everywhere). Funded by Chechnya, the 'rehabilitation' of the mosque (as the regime called it) was conducted by an engineer from Damascus, while the construction works were carried out by the notorious Military Construction Company. There was absolutely zero adherence to the most basic standards of heritage restoration. Everything was handled with carelessness: cement splashes smeared the stone façades; cheap ceramic tiles replaced the marble and stone flooring, with tasteless blue carpet laid on top; and a low-hanging orbital chandelier was installed, whose hideous fluorescent glare turned the space into a hospital. The mausoleum of Khaled ibn al-Walid inside the mosque, which once had a white marble base and finely soldered brass screens, was replaced with what looked like a maquette made of cardboard, crudely painted with black and white stripes in a cheap imitation of *ablaq*. Finally, the box was provided with glass windows and a door, making it look like a doll's house.

Over the decades that preceded this act of vandalism, urban sprawl had already replaced the old village that once surrounded the mosque, turning it – at least in terms of status – into the main congregational mosque of the city. However, this status proved difficult to reconcile with the constrained form of the mausoleum–mosque, which rendered it unable to expand in order to meet the required capacity. Between the 1970s and 1990s, parts of the cemetery were destroyed and turned into terraced areas of lawn and public square, transected by a wide pedestrian axis that connected the parallel street with the western façade of the mosque. This arrangement, as if inspired by the Taj Mahal, emphasized the image of the isolated edifice, but also gave a confusing idea of the location of the main entrance to the mosque. In order to mark the entrance, which actually lay on the perpendicular northern façade, the municipality of the time added a colonnaded courtyard in front of the northern façade, similar to those at classical Ottoman mosques. In so doing, they made two mistakes: the first was that they promptly filled the centre of the courtyard with a large water basin and multiple potted plants, thereby eliminating the prospect of using the courtyard for prayer when the mosque's prayer hall was full. The second was that, in building three colonnades to frame the courtyard (the exception was to the west, where an entrance from the public square was created), the northern façade of the mosque was now fronted by an attached colonnade that broke with the custom of using an uncolonnaded entrance façade to allow rows of congregants to flow seamlessly outside.

These spatial customs are derived from the seed mosque of the Prophet in Medina, and came to fruition at the Umayyad. They comprise what Akel Kahera described as 'spatial Sunnah'.[24] The style of the mosques that followed this spatial Sunnah is defined as the 'hypostyle'. It is composed of two basic parts: on the *qibla* side is the prayer hall (known as the *haram* of the mosque), whose roof is typically supported by rows of columns linked together by a series of arches. The prayer hall is offset by a courtyard that is surrounded by colonnades (porticos), except for the wall parallel to the *qibla* where the main door to the mosque lies. This colonnaded courtyard is called the *sahn* of the mosque, and it serves two main functions: as a preliminary space through which worshippers move from the mundanity of life to the holiness of the act of worship, and as an extra muros space into which the rows of congregants can spill over. In addition, rooms and spaces (galleries) are usually built behind the porticos, and these accommodate the social and educational functions that normally take place around the life of the mosque, as occurred at the Prophet's Mosque and then at later mosques. Notably, employing an architecture of space that relies on the unit or module of bays defined by columns produces a peerless flexibility, as further bays can be added according to the capacity requirements of the prayer hall without affecting the general architecture of the mosque. The Great Mosque of Córdoba is an example of such ingenuity (see also p. 149).

Adjustments and evolutions naturally occurred with regard to the hypostyle mosque. One involved broadening the nave that extends to the *qibla* wall, as well as the transverse nave that runs parallel to the wall, resulting in a T-shaped widening in the plan: art historians thus refer to this as a 'T-Mosque'. Similarly, when the side aisles are extended outwards through the courtyard's galleries and together form a wide U-shaped ambulatory around the prayer hall and courtyard, the mosque is called a 'U-Mosque'. Moreover, a common practice in the hypostyle mosque is to accentuate the *mihrab* area, whether through height (with the use of a small dome, for example) or light (through openings in a structure such as a small dome). Although the southeastern Chinese

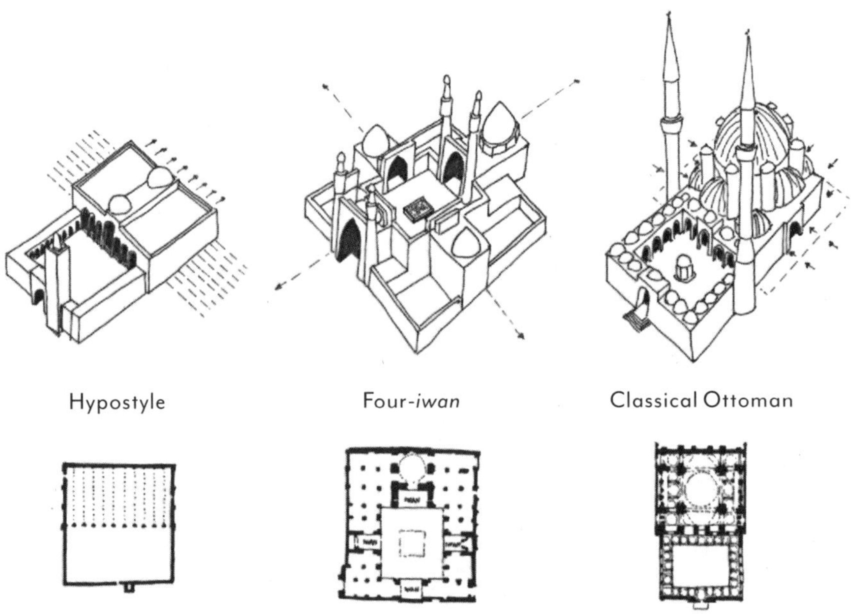

Models of the hypostyle, four-*iwan* and classical Ottoman mosque: exterior and interior

mosque certainly falls into the category that is termed the 'walled complex', I don't think it is a stretch to view it – like the Umayyad – as an adaptation of the hypostyle. This is because it was able to achieve spatial organization in the mediating and integrative terms, thus maintaining the qualities of a unique type of space where acts of revealing, embrace and expansion were possible.

Meanwhile, the mosque that originated in Central Asia produced two models: one is the already explored domed cubic space, while the other has come to be known as the 'four-*iwan*' mosque. If the hypostyle establishes one pole of mosque architecture, then the four-*iwan* mosque constitutes its opposite. The roots of this dichotomy lie in several factors, the most prominent of which is the political and religious division that is the Sunni–Shi'ite conflict.

Dynasties and division

The first time I saw the final outcome of the Syrian regime's so-called rehabilitation of the Mosque of Khaled was in January 2025, when the office of the newly appointed mayor of Homs asked me to give an expert opinion on the site they had formulated according to their plans. It was the first time I had ever been asked by anyone in Syria to share my expertise. In fact, due to my having Apollodorus of Damascus's inclination to defy authority, I had always been thankful that the regime ignored me as much as I avoided them. With the new administration that had toppled the old regime and assumed power in December 2024, I didn't know what to expect. However, I was sure of two things: that if I spoke my mind I wouldn't end up in jail, and that my service would be to my country and not to tyranny.

I stood with my husband in front of the mosque's western façade, looking out over the destroyed square. There wasn't a tree in sight; everything had been burned to the ground, just as we had first seen it when the war ended in 2016. As before, rubble of all the buildings around the mosque stared at us through the black holes of what had once been a wall or a window. Everything looked dead, except for the random market stalls that people had rushed to set up around the part of the square that used to be the cemetery. People were taking photographs with the fighters, with the mosque as their backdrop. An atmosphere of both celebration and relaxation hovered jarringly over a graveyard of a city. But nothing was more jarring than the building that was now attached to the mosque, doubling its length on the western façade. The construction would ordinarily have been understood as the wall of the courtyard (*sahn*), except that here it was as high as the mosque itself. Its entrance was marked by a giant protruding frame, which took us into a gateway that ended with a pointed arch, through which we found ourselves in the *sahn*. Colonnaded on all four sides, the two-storeyed attachment was built entirely of cement that had been left bare; it felt as if the spikes of iron that were erupting through its skin were also piercing ours. Three young men arrived shortly afterwards. Looking sharp, with notebooks in hand, they politely introduced themselves as the municipality team. They asked for our opinion, taking out their pens and placing them on their notebooks. But where to begin?

For years we in Syria had heard of an Iranian orientation within the Ministry of Awqaf (plural of *waqf*) that was allegedly seeking to make social and political changes within Sunni Syria. To some, such

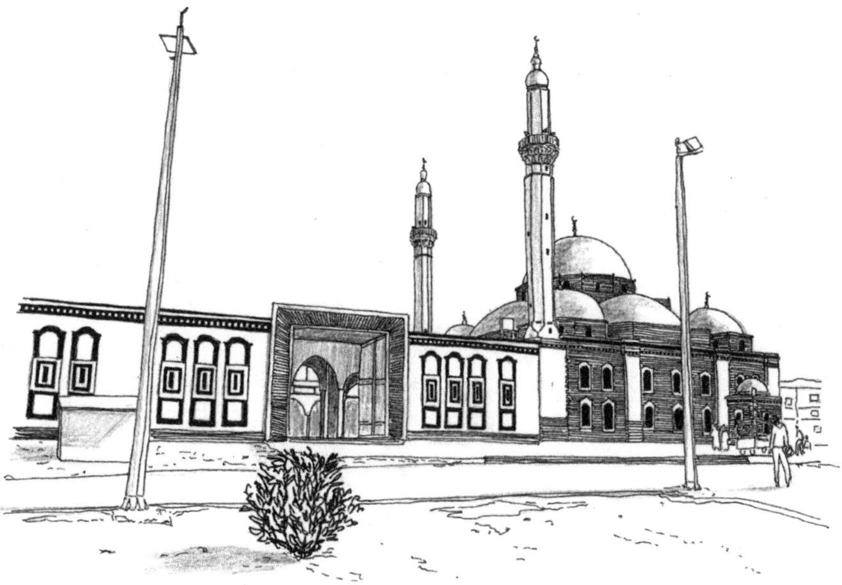

Khaled ibn al-Walid Mosque in Homs, Syria: the new addition can be seen extending from the base of the minarets to the left-hand side

allegations sounded as if they were part of a ridiculous conspiracy theory; however, as an architect, I seek my evidence in the consistently honest and precise realm of buildings. During the years of war and in the aftermath of the conflict, I started to notice how the mosques that the regime selected for repair and restoration were undergoing noticeable alterations: their semi-circular arches (whether of openings or of structures) were systematically being transformed into pointed arches of specific proportions. Their domes were also being elongated, with an upwards stretch in profile. In addition, disconnected protruding gateways were being added to entrances, just like the cement feature that had been imposed on the Mosque of Khaled.

The split between the Sunni (literally, the 'followers of the teachings of the Prophet') and the Shi'a (literally, the 'split group') originally arose over the caliphate; specifically, the merits according to which the succession to the Prophet Muhammad should be decided. Shi'ite communities understood legitimate leadership to lie with Ali, the Prophet's cousin and son-in-law, and his descendants. This view emphasizes hereditary spiritual authority (*imamate*) rather than the elective consensus model favoured by early Sunni tradition (as established by the Prophet's teachings). What started as a political division later evolved into a theological split: the Shi'ites developed a narrative in which they considered the successors to Ali to be divinely guided, for which they were named the 'rightful imams'. The consequences of this split were not only political and religious, but also artistic.

The dismantling of Muslim unity, which had lasted only through the era of the Umayyads followed by the Abbasids, continued with the establishment of two main Shi'a movements: the Fatimids in the west of the Muslim lands, and the Buyids in the east. The Fatimids formed a heterodox religious movement, recognizing seven imams, the last of whom was called Isma'il, hence this branch is still today referred to as 'Isma'ili'. Having initially converted the Berbers of Tunisia, they soon made Egypt their stronghold, establishing the city of Kahera ('the victorious'; which, in English, became Cairo) as their new capital. There they built many royal palaces, as well as Al-Azhar Mosque, where their missionaries were trained. According to architectural historian Doğan

Kuban, the Fatimids can be regarded as 'the founders of a specifically Egyptian architectural style'.[25] Through the architecture of their palaces and a new type of mosque, the Fatimids exhibited the dual character of their rule – celebratory inside, and military outside:

> Cairene domes were built in brick, often on squinches. They had elongated and pointed profiles and were raised on relatively high drums, some of them profusely decorated with a row of arches embellished on their surface with geometric and floral motifs. The domes were decorated on the inside and outside with stucco work. From the late Fatimid period on, fluted exteriors were typical.[26]

Additionally, a gateway protruding from the main façade, at each end of which was a minaret, was used in mosques such as Al-Hakim in Cairo.[27]

Almost all of these features were passed on to the Mamluks, who took power in Egypt from the Ayyubids, who had overthrown the Fatimids in 1171. Interestingly, the Mamluks of Egypt enthusiastically adopted the mausoleum–mosque. drawing from the legacy of the Fatimids:

> The Fatimids introduced the smaller masjid type, such as al-Guyushi Mosque, in which the mausoleum of the founder was integrated into the mosque proper. Contradictory to the tradition of the Prophet this practice gave rise to the most important building type of the Mamluk period (1250–1517), the madrasa-tombs of the sultans, which also served as mosques.[28]

The major difference between the architecture of the mosque that followed the 'spatial Sunnah' of the Prophet's Mosque in Medina and the mosque that developed under the Fatimids comes from the different understandings of religious authority in Sunni and Shi'a traditions. Sunni thought emphasizes communal interpretive traditions rooted in the Prophet's Sunnah, while Shi'a thought emphasizes the spiritual and interpretive authority of the imams. Fatimid patronage introduced architectural forms associated with royal ceremonial spaces and palatial aesthetics, which shaped the development of Cairene mosque architecture in distinctive ways. These differed from the more domestic, courtyard-based models associated with the seminal mosque.

One could argue that the public Muslim sentiment for the Prophet, based on deep love and high veneration, can be seen as an attachment of a sort – i.e. a following of the person rather than the thought or the principle. However, the confusion is resolved as soon as it is realized that this love for the Prophet is directed to his person and not to his status; namely, it is a love detached from the connotations of domination, one that was redeemed from any associations with *asabiyya* or idolization at every juncture during the Prophet's life, and that is sustained through the Quran and Hadith. There is no more perfect testament to this fact than the concise words spoken by the Prophet's most trusted companion and friend, Abu Bakr, when the death of the Prophet was announced and the agitated crowds had to be addressed: 'Those of you who worshipped Muhammad know that Muhammad has died. And those of you who worshipped God know that God is alive and He never dies.'

Under the Seljuks and the Mongols, most Muslim territories became Sunni again. The Seljuks, in particular, oversaw a resurgence of Sunni faith, and to that end they relied on a unique building type: the madrasa. This collegiate complex incorporating lecture and residential facilities for the students, along with some basic liturgical features, developed out of the study rooms and galleries cultivated behind the colonnades of the hypostyle mosques. Nizam al-Mulk, the influential eleventh-century Seljuk vizier, founded a network of religious schools across Muslim lands, in order to counter the dissemination of Shi'ite doctrinal perspectives and train government bureaucrats. He began his enlightenment movement from his native Khurasan and, interestingly, the structural architecture of his madrasa can be seen to derive from the local vernacular:

> The typical Khurasanian house was cruciform in plan, with four arched openings, known as *iwans*, off a central courtyard. Quite fortuitously, this layout coincided with the ideal framework within which to teach the four legal schools of orthodox Islam that enjoyed canonical status: the Hanafi, Shafi'i, Maliki and Hanbali rites. The space between each *iwan* and the corner of the courtyard could be extended to accommodate the students

> in cells arranged in one or two storeys. It is the residential factor that relates the collegiate to the monastic mosque, but whatever its origins Khurasan thus witnessed the birth of a structure combining pragmatism and beauty to a degree seldom seen.[29]

Soon the madrasa structure offered an alternative layout to the hypostyle's 'spatial Sunnah'. More precisely, it was the rebuilding of the formerly hypostyle Friday Mosque in the Seljuk capital of Isfahan, during the twelfth century, that brought the four-*iwan* mosque to prominence.[30]

The transformation was not, in fact, entirely intentional at the beginning. The preliminary act merely involved the creation of a dome chamber on the *qibla* side – a tradition that, as previously mentioned, was quite commonplace in the architecture of earlier hypostyle mosques. However, the scale of this space – occupying a whole sixteen bays – made it the largest masonry dome chamber in the Islamic world at that time. It is said that Malik Shah, the Seljuk ruler for whom Nizam al-Mulk patronized the mosque, had visited the Umayyad in Damascus in 1086,[31] before the rebuilding at the Friday Mosque of Isfahan. The idea of freeing the space in front of the *mihrab* with a large dome

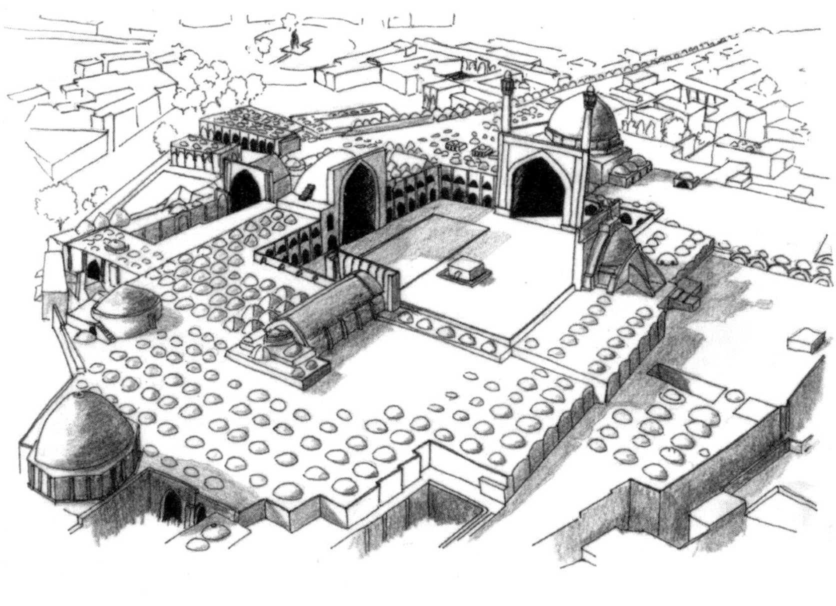

The Friday Mosque in Isfahan, Iran

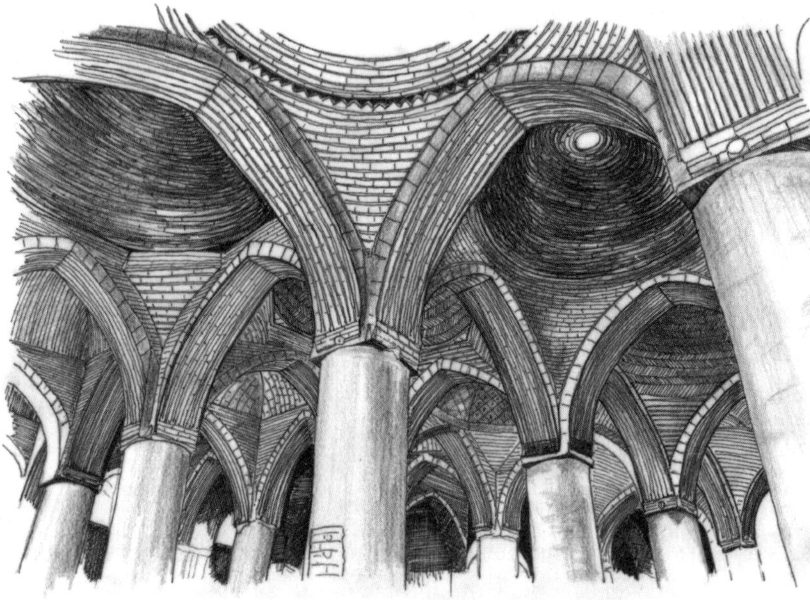

The Friday Mosque: an interior view of the hypostyle hall

may have indeed been inspired by the spacious arrangement seen at the Umayyad.

To enable the enormity of the scale, many engineering breakthroughs were made at the Friday Mosque of Isfahan. The ribbed dome was carried on eight massive piers, and a new type of squinch was introduced, consisting of a barrel vault placed above two quarter-domes, forming an early introduction to the use of *muqarnas*. The rebuilding that followed, which is believed to have taken place after a fire in the twelfth century, was marked by the insertion of the four vaulted halls open on one side to the courtyard, just as in a typical Seljuk madrasa. Breaking up the egalitarian space of the hypostyle with the four *iwans* is a major incongruity when it comes to the essence of the mosque: this cruciform layout not only undermines the unity of the rows of congregants, but it also impedes visual connectivity with the imam in front of the *qibla* wall.

The madrasa building type, which was supplemented most of the time with a mosque facility, was never intended to be a replacement of the mosque. As a collegiate building, it was disseminated across the

Muslim lands to spread enlightenment. Egypt was the place where it 'flourished perhaps more than anywhere else',[32] probably because it was needed there the most after the long reign of the Fatimids. Having started out with two *iwans*, the Egyptian madrasa soon adopted the four-*iwan* plan under the Mamluks, the pinnacle of which was the Sultan Hasan madrasa complex in Cairo. However, due to the Egyptian model being built around a smaller central courtyard, it became possible to cover this and illuminate it with a lantern, which provided early inspiration for the practice in the classical Ottoman mosque.

In what may seem like a bizarre coincidence, the four-*iwan* plan of the Sunni madrasa appeared in Shi'a mosque architecture, after the accession in the sixteenth century of the Safavids – founders of Twelver Shi'ism, which involved belief in a line of twelve infallible imams. Originally a tribe of warrior Sufis from northwest Iran, the Safavids were driven by a fervent loyalty to their leader, Shah Isma'il, who was only fourteen years old when he ascended the throne in 1501. The Safavid state promoted Twelver Shi'ism as the official religious identity, a policy that significantly reshaped Iran's religious landscape.

In 1598, near the Friday Mosque of Isfahan, Shah Abbas, the fifth Safavid shah, initiated a monumental urban transformation that revolved around aggrandizement and centralization. The Shah Mosque (Masjid-i Shah), built between 1611 and 1629, became the jewel in the crown of this scheme, aimed at radically altering the old Seljuk city of Isfahan. The newly formed city, constructed as a deliberate counterpoint to the old Friday Mosque and adjoining bazaar, was an exemplification of state control. The old order, based on decentralization and free trade, was abolished and replaced by the Shah's vision, anchored in two main zones of Safavid polity. The first was Chahar Bagh Avenue, where the Shah's ambitions for economic internationalization took root. All the prominent institutions of the city, including residences for the foreign dignitaries whom the Shah courted both diplomatically and commercially, were located along the grand, garden-lined boulevard. The second main zone was Naqsh-i Jahan Square (literally, 'Image of the World Square'). Lined with two-storey shops on all sides, the colossal rectangular square (400 by 145 metres; 1,300 by 475 ft) had four main portals

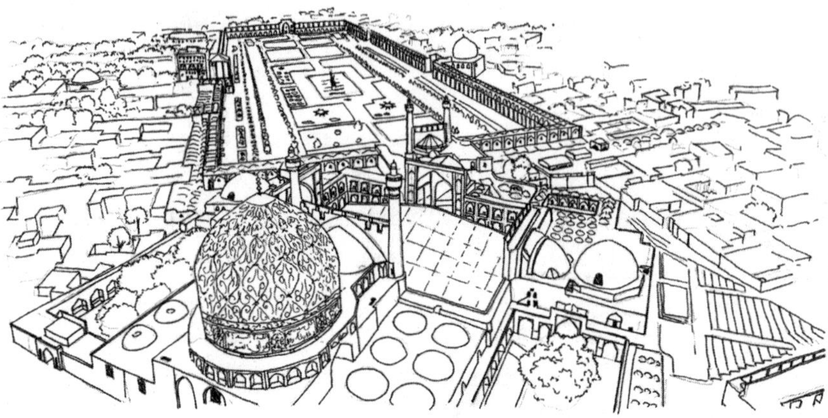

The Shah Mosque (also officially known as the Imam Mosque or Imam Khomeini Mosque), adjacent to Naqsh-i Jahan Square, Isfahan, Iran

that were distributed cardinally. Each of these monumental portals led to a major urban site with a distinct function: the western portal led to the royal palace; the eastern to the small mausoleum–mosque of Sheikh Lutfullah; the northern to an extension of the old bazaar, painted with murals celebrating the Shah's victories over the Uzbeks; and the southern to the Shah Mosque. In this way, both the international and local spheres of the city were brought under the watchful eye and direct grip of the state. As curator and scholar Marika Sardar puts it: 'The four bases of the Safavid state – religion, trade, military, and the royal family itself – were thus united in one monumental visual statement.'[33]

The cruciform design of the four *iwans* around the square, as in the classic four-*iwan* mosque from which Iranian mosque architecture never deviated after the Seljuks, evidently has deeper roots than the spatial arrangement of the madrasa: 'The *iwan*, a rectangular hall closed on three sides, had been used by the Parthians, but attained its ultimate expression in the Sasanian palace at Ctesiphon. Its brick arch is still the largest in the world, and later Islamic patrons strove to outdo it.'[34] The original use of the *iwan* by the Parthians (third-century BCE peoples of Khurasan), which found its evolution in the madrasa, and then 'ultimate expression in the Sasanian palace of Ctesiphon', not only explains the Safavids' enthusiastic adoption of this royal idiom, but also differentiates further between the two routes of development, one of which took the domestic house to the madrasa, while the other concluded in association with the power and centrality of the palace, confirming its lack of conformity with the mosque.

The royal square of Isfahan was oriented on a north–south axis, but the *qibla* direction was south-west. The result was that the two mosques attached to the square (the Shah Mosque and Sheikh Lutfullah) had to turn a forty-five-degree angle from the entrance portal to the interior of the building. From the outside, a false appearance of asymmetry is combined with an instant and complete revealing of the dominating masses, including the huge dome. This is accompanied by the military sense of surveillance that pervades over the space.

The buildings around the square showcase a wide variety of brickwork. It is clear that the use of brick cannot be overlooked as a major shaping (and unifying) factor of the pre-modern architecture of the mosque in the regions that stretched from Mesopotamia (Iraq) to Transoxiana, Iran, and parts of India. In relation to this building material, elongated-profile domes, pointed arches, pillars (instead of columns), and cylindrical or polygonal minarets are common features. Ceramic tiling also became widespread, used to sheath these structures' revetments and protect against erosion, as well as demonstrating high aesthetic quality and extraordinary craftsmanship. These materials were used by the Seljuks and the Timurids (among others), and later by the Safavids, who incorporated numerous Timurid features in their architecture, such as paired minarets, false upper courtyard galleries and side dome chambers. However, the brick construction of the Shah Mosque 'reveal[s] a preference for a more static concept of space',[35] in addition to 'strongly accented, central symmetry',[36] and that belongs in essence to an alternative world view.

The four-*iwan* mosque was also adopted by the Mughals in India, where Sufism was as popular as it was in Mamluk Egypt and Timurid Iran. While Mughal rulers were not themselves Sufis, in the sense of being members of a Sufi order, they had a complex and significant relationship with Sufi traditions and leaders. Sufism developed both as a personal, interior mode of devotion and as a set of organized traditions that, from around the tenth century onwards, coalesced into diverse orders which developed elements of esotericism and mysticism. These orders were typically structured around respected teachers and intimate followers, without implying a formal religious hierarchy comparable to the Shi'a doctrine of Imamate. While the theological foundations of Sufism and Shi'ism are distinct, the value both place on spiritually guided authority may help explain certain resonances in their architectural or institutional expressions.

In the four-*iwan* mosque, Sufis found an architectural plan that mirrored their ideas around symbolic centralized cosmic power radiating to the four cardinal directions, with the dynastic ruler as the central cosmocrator (ruler of the world). In addition, Sufism – which had begun as a personalized way of expressing devotion to God in Islam, then later became marked by the pursuit of various means to perform constant prayer and *dhikr* (the remembrance or recital of the name of God) – found the four-*iwan* mosque functionally compatible with the circles of *dhikr*, which could take place in such mosques' semi-isolated nooks of privacy.

These mosques can therefore be viewed within that understanding of faith and worship being channelled into a public attachment to an individual rather than the principle. In lieu of the unifying worship of rows of congregants, what thrives in the dissociative vision of space at the four-*iwan* mosque is confined circles and distinct hierarchies. Some might regard this as the antithesis of what a mosque should be.

Back in Homs, looking at the Mosque of Khaled, with its hybrid misalliance of Mamluk, Ottoman and Egyptian features, together with some European influences and local interpretations, now combined with a poorly constructed cement box and a distorted attempt at recreating an *iwan*-like expansion of military features, I am dismayed at the plethora of failed experiments and struggle to explain 'what's wrong' to the municipal team. It is not architectural 'purity' that I'm after, but this is no longer a mosque that I see before me.

I find myself preoccupied with what fascinated me when we first arrived at the site: the natural inclination towards inhabitation by people who formed a temporary urban fabric and an economic attachment to the mosque at the first window of opportunity. From the organizational viewpoint of the municipality, this is chaos. I suggest building a proper bazaar, following the traditional symbiosis between the mosque and the market. However, the team's current worry is how dismantling the offending and unsound new mosque addition will be viewed by the public and the media in a country already full of destruction. We stand between the beautifully built mosque and the stolid mass of cracked cement, contemplating in confusion how to rectify the countless blunders of this monstrosity, while trying to avoid unwanted further demolition. What is most perplexing for me, though, is how to expand the mausoleum–mosque – now turned congregational and ceremonial – now that the necessary expertise and language to complete the original statement seem to have been lost.

Chapter 5

The Language of the Arts

'The minarets of Damascus weep as they embrace me; and minarets do, like trees, have souls.'

NIZAR QABBANI[1]

Arabic and the mosque

The first thing I probably heard as a newborn was the *Azan* (the call to prayer). It is the custom of Muslim families to whisper the words of the *Azan* into the ear of the newborn almost immediately after he or she is pulled out of the womb.

The call to prayer was initiated with the first mosque, when the Prophet Muhammad ordered one of his companions, Bilal, who had a powerful and beautiful voice, to climb up onto a neighbouring roof and summon worshippers to prayer, by calling out:

> God is the Greatest, God is the Greatest. I testify that there is no god but God, I testify that there is no god but God. I testify that Muhammad is the Prophet of God, I testify that Muhammad is the Prophet of God. Come to prayer, come to prayer. Come to salvation (success, in self-realization), come to salvation (success, in self-realization). God is the Greatest, God is the Greatest. There is no god but God.

By emphasizing the quality of the muezzin's voice, the Prophet laid the foundations for what has evolved into one of the most cultivated arts in Islam; that is, the art of *Tajwid*. This means 'enhancement' (from the Arabic root *joudah*, or 'high quality'), and it refers to the recitation of the Quran according to the rules of proper pronunciation and vocal harmony. James Dickie considered *Tajwid* 'the phonic equivalent of calligraphy, the Islamic art par excellence'.[2] The mosque thus resides at the heart of a trilogy: language, music and architecture. Dickie noted:

> St Augustine wrote that architecture and music were the highest arts because they were 'the sisters of numbers', an admission which shows he was a Pythagorean at heart. The aesthetic significance of the mosque resides not in the architecture alone but in the fact that it was a place where that art was always to be found in the company of its sister.[3]

To begin with the first part of the trilogy, no real understanding of Islamic architecture – of which the mosque is the crowning form – can be attained without a true appreciation of the Arabic language. This is not only because it is the sacred language of the Quran, as the word of God, constituting the psychic foundation of all Muslim peoples, but also because it is an ancient language with extraordinary characteristics that have enabled it to remain fresh, alive and constantly renewed. As the language of religion, used to utter the word of God, whether in the Quran, in prayer or in the *Azan*, Arabic quickly became the lingua franca of the Muslim peoples, and just as quickly it became the language of science and translation.

As a language of religion, knowledge, science and art, Arabic can be (and, in fact, was and is) a definer of thought and a mode of expression for all Muslims (and non-Muslims) in the heartlands of Islam, regardless of the multitude of their ethnicities. However, 'Arabic' cannot be used as a true definition of a race, for these same groups of peoples. The conflation of Arabism with Islam is a modern phenomenon, which can be attributed to the dismantling of Muslim identity and the resulting vacuum, which nationalist movements have unsuccessfully attempted to fill.

Arabic, with all its already established capabilities, was transfigured by Islam to the unprecedented flourishing that made it the language of civilization in all its fields. Arabic before the Quran is not the Arabic after the Quran. Not only did the holy book focus attention on the use of language and introduce a completely new richness of vocabulary and expression, but it also softened and polished the language, adding clarity and lucidity to its character. At school, when we were children, our teachers – whether Muslims or Christians – used the Quran as a main reference: an inexhaustible spring of plenitude.

Even for the staunchest enemies of Islam – those who opposed the Prophet's message in Mecca, and who were *the* masters of Arabic – the language of the Quran was unassailable. Arabic was the trade of non-Muslim Arabs in Mecca, just as much as their caravan commerce was. They had a special souq for poetry, and it was with well-crafted words – as well as swords – that wars were fought and deals were made.

In the early days of Islam, the Quraysh (the ruling tribe of Mecca) sent one of their highest dignitaries, in terms of both rank and mastery of Arabic, to the Prophet in order to convince him to leave his calling, which they viewed as a threat to their status. This man was none other than the father of Khaled ibn al-Walid ('ibn' means 'son of'), for whom the mosque in Homs was built many centuries later. He went to the Prophet and asked him to recite some verses of the Quran, since this was the cause of the people of Mecca abandoning their old deities. As a language expert and 'critic', Al-Walid ibn al-Mughiera thought he would easily be able to refute the heresies of 'Muhammad's gibberish'. Instead, he went back to the waiting crowd of Quraysh dignitaries and pronounced his verdict on 'Muhammad's Quran': 'By God, I have heard a form of speech that is neither that of man nor of jinn (fairies); it has an attractive sweetness, which enhances its beauty. Its top is fruitful, while its bottom is ripe and unfurling. It rises above everything and cannot be surpassed, and no human being can make this.' The dignitaries replied, in despair: 'Al-Walid has turned, and all of the Quraysh will follow him.'[4] Unwilling to give in, Al-Walid agreed with the dignitaries that this language should be considered a sort of magical craft, for which they would continue to persecute Muhammad.

The point of this story is that, while Arabic was already a superlative art form in pre-Islamic times (so-called 'poetic koine'), facilitated by its unparalleled formal structure, it was through the Quran that the language reached new heights of brilliance and versatility that allowed it to become the generative force of art and synthesis throughout the Muslim history that followed. In his *Art of Islam*, Titus Burckhardt offers an enlightening analysis of the transformative impact of Arabic on the art of Islam. He explains how all languages process vocabulary through two poles: 'auditive intuition', which identifies the meaning of words in relation to a phonetic formula, and 'imaginative intuition', which identifies meanings according to a hierarchy of type-images.[5] While Latin is an example of the latter type being predominant, Arabic relies on auditive intuition, as well as the primacy of action in the language.[6] As Burckhardt puts it: 'In Arabic, the "tree" of verbal forms, of derivations from certain "roots", is quite inexhaustible; it can always bring forth new leaves, new expressions to represent hitherto dormant variations of the basic idea – or action.'[7]

This combination of a logical structure and a derivational mechanism relating to the action verb explains the dynamic character and power of synthesis within the processes of Islamic art. Moreover, the auditive sensibility begets the rhythmic forms of this art. In order to counterbalance this, Arabic has a static foundation, which reveals itself linguistically in what is called the 'nominal sentence'. This consists of two words – the 'name of beginning' (subject) and the 'news' (its predicate) – which are placed side by side with no indication of time. An example might be 'the sky is blue', where 'the sky' is the name of beginning and 'blue' is its news, but in Arabic the verb is omitted. According to Burckhardt, this 'short and concise formula of diamantine clarity' gives Islamic art its 'crystalline' quality.[8]

Arabic became my favourite subject when I was in the tenth grade. Our Arabic course was a comprehensive coverage of the progress of poetry, from pre-Islamic times to modern experimentation. Naturally, we had to understand the lines, and what lay behind and beyond them. However, the fun part for me was 'weighing the poem'. As in music, there are poetic meters, and syllables are weighted according to a metrical system. This is called prosody; in Arabic, it is known as al-arud, or the science of poetry. Studying the meter of a poem determines whether its weight is 'sound' or 'broken'. Syllables are scanned, based on whether letters are vowelled (short, marked with a diacritic) or unvowelled (long, with no diacritic). Essentially, the analysis is phonetic. Even to a schoolgirl like me, pre-Islamic poetry sounded more coarse and convoluted, whereas verses of the Islamic period had a noticeable elegance and a wider range of expression, as well as a certain softness. The depth of meaning also changed, from self-centredness to openness towards the world. It was through the Quran that the Arabic language experienced that cleansing:

> Arab art – poetry and music as well as the plastic arts – loves to repeat certain forms and to introduce sudden and unforeseen variants against this repetitive background. But, whereas art is played out in accordance with easily fathomable rules, the waves of sacred speech may sometimes fall in regular patterns but they arise out of a whole formless ocean. In the same way, the state of inner harmony engendered by the words and sonorous enchantment of the Quran is situated on quite another plane than, for example, perfect poetry. The Quran does not satisfy, it gives and at the same time takes away, it expands the soul by lending it wings then lays it low and leaves it naked; for the believer, it is both comforting and purifying, like a rainstorm. Purely human art does not possess this virtue. That is to say, there is no such thing as a Quranic style which can simply be transposed into art; but there does exist a state of soul which is sustained by the recitation of the Quran and which favors certain formal manifestations while precluding others.[9]

The meters of Arabic poetry, which are called brios (in Arabic *bahr*, pl. *buhur*), are endlessly dwarfed against this 'formless ocean'. The Arabs were frequently challenged in the Quran to compose even a fraction of its verses, not only in terms of construction but also in number: 'Say [Muhammad], if the sea were ink for [writing] the Words of my Lord, surely, it would run dry before the Words of my Lord were finished, even if we brought [another sea] just like it as a supplement.'[10]

In translation, the words of the Quran express only the meaning. In Arabic, not only are the true resonance, rhythm, sonorous tone and synthesis of phrasing revealed, but also the sanctity of the Quran's mastery in conveying ever-unfolding meanings within a remarkably concise and compact form.

The spiritual state that is induced by introduction to the Quran, along with the rational and rhythmic qualities of the Arabic language, constitute a diapason (grand burst of harmony) for the Muslim artist. Indeed, Muslim appreciation of music is influenced by the same mathematical yet dynamic approach. All music uses scales to group ascending and descending notes, but what is peculiar to Eastern music (as opposed to, say, Western classical music) is that it has sub-intervals within a single musical scale. There are quarter, half and three-quarter intervals in Eastern scales (known as *maqam*), which were cultivated under Islam and acquired special importance by being deployed in the *Azan*.

Each *maqam* evokes a distinct emotional state, depending on its rhythm: this could be plaintive, romantic, exciting, and so on. In Turkey, a specific *maqam* is chosen for each prayer time. In Damascus, the *maqam* for the call to prayer varies according to the days of the week. Personally, I find the Turkish system more appealing, as it sits in sympathy with the likely emotional state of the worshipper at each specific time of day. For instance, for the dawn prayer, a slow, tender and slightly wistful *maqam* is chosen in order to gently encourage the worshipper to leave their bed to pray. In contrast, for the noon prayer, a more rousing *maqam* calls for the worshipper to abandon material business and engage in spiritual work. From this perspective, the *maqamat* (plural of *maqam*) were cultivated under Islam through the recitation of the Quran, the call to prayer, and the practice of religious chanting. With regard to the mosque, the mathematical dynamism that is inherent in the language and music of Islam also shapes its architecture. It is this equipoise between the discourse of the mind and that of the heart that is reflected in the interplay of all these arts.

The Great Mosque of Córdoba, built by Abd al-Rahman I in 785, is one of the most famous mosques in the world because of what has been described as a 'forest of columns' positioned throughout its interior space. However, this hypostyle mosque can be considered the pinnacle of mosque architecture because it achieves the ultimate refinement in mosque space: hierarchy is absent, direction is unified, plenitude unfolds

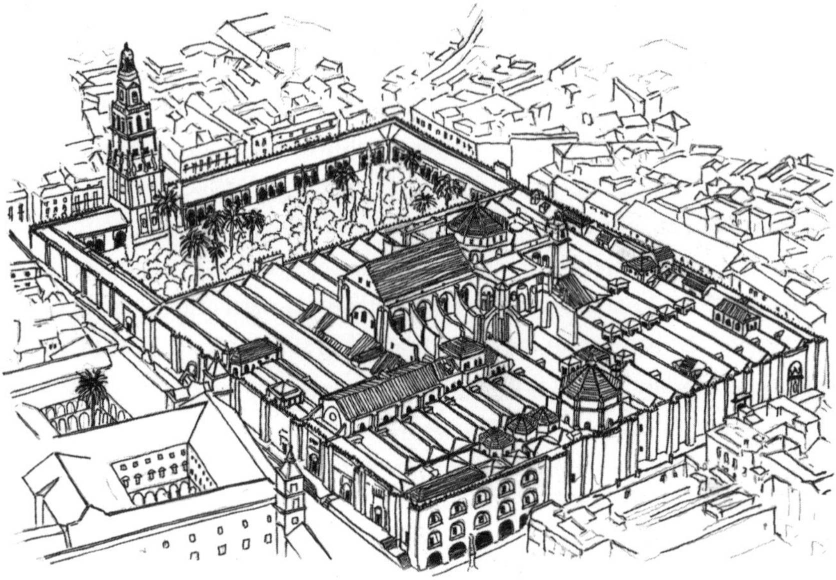

The Great Mosque of Córdoba, Spain: an overview featuring the added structures of the Catholic cathedral that was imposed in 1236, including the bell tower that encases the remains of the former minaret

and dynamism is anchored, all while capturing that inner, flowing state of the soul.

The Great Mosque of Córdoba represents a form of maturity in mosque architecture, just as the Umayyad in Damascus does. The nexuses with Damascus begin with the fact that Abd al-Rahman I was the only Umayyad prince to escape Abbasid persecution, fleeing first to North Africa (where his mother was from) and then settling in Iberia, along with the Syrian cavalry who accompanied him. The nucleus of the mosque was already there, as a Muslim community of Berbers and Arabs was present before Abd al-Rahman's arrival in Iberia. The prince was appointed a leader of the community at the then-primitive mosque of Córdoba. However, having already gone through the emergence and integration phases, the mosque was able to reach the point of maturity quickly.

As in the case of mosque development in northwestern China, the model at Córdoba – built by Abd al-Rahman to replace the temporary structure – was inspired by the Syrian masons whose millennia-old skills had been transfigured by Islam, just as the Arabic language had been for the Arab poets. Those who visit the old cities of Al-Andalus in present-day Spain speak of 'a walk in the heart of Damascus'. But contrary to Western assumptions, which mistakenly read the Great Mosque of Córdoba as a materialized dream of the banished Umayyad prince, its resemblance to the Damascene was achieved beyond Abd al-Rahman's lifetime, through the spirit of an art that looked at the universe as a place of sacred beauty and at the human being as a humble servant seeking to achieve the task of *imar*. This art does not sanctify beauty, nor is its purpose to attain beauty. Its spirit is open and embracive, dynamic and unchangeable.

In the courtyards of the Muslim houses of Damascus, naranj trees are planted. The origins of this citric orange (Citrus × aurantium) are reportedly Chinese, but it is in Damascus that this tree was cultivated in every Muslim house, and it is from Córdoba that it was introduced (and duly became known as the Seville orange), along with other types of orange, to the west of Europe. Indeed, the courtyard of the Great Mosque of Córdoba is now referred to as the Patio de los Naranjos (Courtyard of the Naranj). This is where Abd al-Rahman and his Syrian companions planted the trees they had brought from home, having noticed the close resemblance in terms of landscape, soil, air, water and weather.

Springing from this realization, the architectural response took off on the banks of the River Guadalquivir just as it once had over the basin of Barada. Picking up from where others had left off, the builders of the mosque at Córdoba deployed Visigoth and Roman columns, just as old Roman columns were used at Al-Aqsa for the Dome of the Rock and the Qibli Mosque. Here, the architectural challenge was to achieve the required height in proportion to the space, as the existing columns offered only a fraction of what was necessary. A 'double-decker' treatment had already been used to that end at the Umayyad (and also at Al-Aqsa), but at Córdoba the two-tiered arches achieved a new type of space that was totally undefined by its boundaries.

Through their capitals, each column of the lower deck is connected to the equally spaced neighbouring column via a horseshoe arch made of alternating voussoirs of white limestone and red brick. In order to

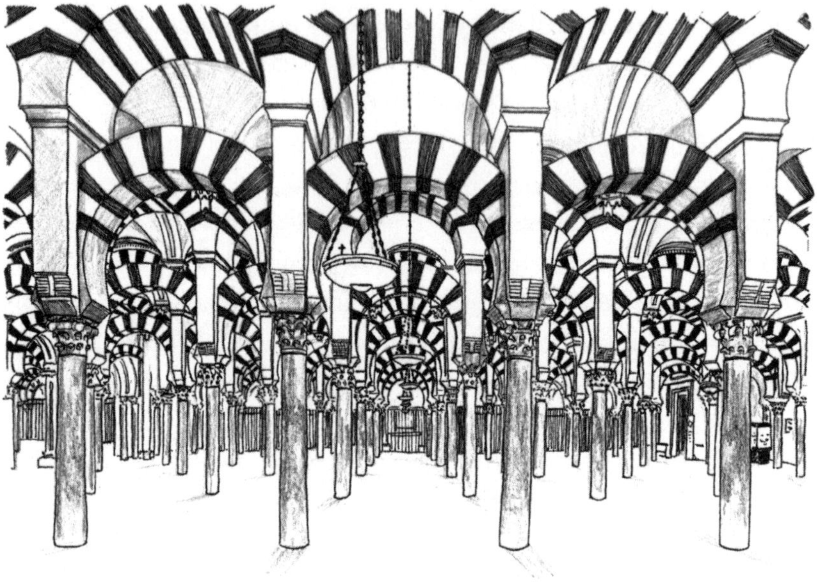

The Great Mosque of Córdoba: an interior view

distribute the weight of the roof so that it does not risk crushing the short columns, but at the same time achieves the required height, the upper deck springs from the columns' capitals in the form of protruding masonry piers that carry an upper set of semi-circular arches. The effect is to make it seem as if the capitals of the columns are 'sprouting' the lower arches to either side, but, in a balancing perpendicular effect, the protruding upper piers carry the weight, as well as the eye, to the second tier. The alternating voussoirs are reminiscent of Syrian *ablaq*, but at the same time they connect with the local use of brick. The resulting interior is an encompassing and yet unfolding space that constitutes the very essence of the Islamic world view, and has proven to challenge the best of Western efforts to rationalize it.

In contrast to the Islamic approach to architecture, the classical Western perspective is inherently anthropomorphic. It is governed by a world view that revolves around the supremacy of the human form as a divine shape. Therefore, buildings are designed so that the architectonics of the building mimic those of the human body. For example, the relationship between the elements of support and the weight that they carry is clearly denoted not only through the proportionate scale, but also through the ornamental indication of sites of exerted forces, such as capitals, keystones and cornices. Space is further rationalized according to a concept of corporeity by distinguishing the vertical from the horizontal within the support system. For example, pillars in their verticality are clearly distinguished from the horizontal beams they support. Many scholars, influenced by this perspective to architecture, tend to evaluate the architecture of the mosque as one that dissolves structural 'barriers', overriding material circumstance – whether in terms of structure or ornament – leading to what has been termed the 'aesthetics of transfiguration'.[11]

The Great Mosque of Córdoba is a prime example of such an architecture, which defies all the classical rules. It belongs to an entirely different world view, in which God is above and beyond all human definitions, where human beings are not at the centre, and where nature is not to be represented per se, rather an experience of it through the divine presence. This is an architecture that believes in no dichotomies: between space and surface, element and material, supporting and non-supporting. There is no presupposed idea that this architecture seeks to represent: no 'forest of palm trees', no theological symbols, no sacred mathematical schemes. Nor is there any preoccupation with power: no triumph over material, gravity or scale that this architecture needs to emphasize by pointing it out. Instead, it is preoccupied with delivering elevation to its environment; building systems, fitting in, and sublimating.

After Abd al-Rahman I, the Great Mosque of Córdoba was enlarged four times over a span of two hundred years. From the original approximately 5,850 square metres (63,000 ft^2), the prayer hall combined with the courtyard reached 23,400 square metres (some 252,000 ft^2) by the time of the last expansion. The flexible dynamism of the mosque's structure and the arcaded zigzagging gables of its roof (identical to those at the Umayyad) allowed the building to grow without inhibition or alteration to its character. It was primarily the effect of the Arabic language on the Muslim mentality that produced this level of repetitive yet rhythmic interlacing, and saturated its creations with a unique dynamism,

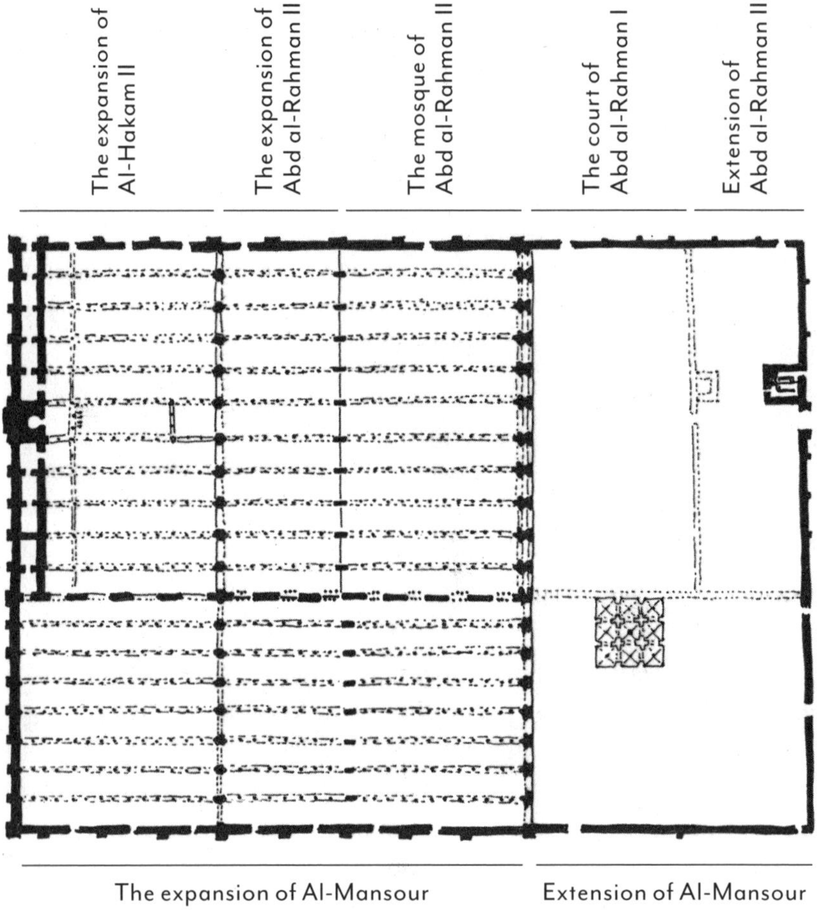

The Great Mosque of Córdoba: a plan showing the various stages of expansion undertaken by the Muslim rulers Abd al-Rahman I, Abd al-Rahman II, Abd al-Rahman III, Al-Hakam II and Al-Mansour

balance and harmony. Titus Burckhardt considered the Great Mosque of Córdoba to be 'composed of arabesque',[12] an art form through which architecture derives dynamism by using the structure of fractions, which lies – like internal joints – at the heart of music and poetry, and enables all these arts to become as energetic as they are, capable of expanding, contracting and springing forth with both ease and harmony. This is manifestly a state of the soul that belongs to the language of the Quran as well as to the world view of Islam.

The arabesque and nature

There may be no more concrete example of the immediate manifestation of the Arabic mentality than the art of arabesque. This is also the art form through which Islam's outlook on nature is best understood. Although it is considered an art of ornament, arabesque also reflects the interlacing of language and of space, as seen at the Great Mosque of Córdoba. Generally speaking, there are two types of arabesque (both being works of interlace): the first is enacted with stylized plant forms that can unfold in any direction, whereas the second takes the form of geometrical interlacing. In both types, 'sprouts' form, divide, then are reintegrated again, just like the double-tiered arches in Córdoba. 'Balanced' and 'free of tension' are descriptors that are repeatedly used to describe the phenomenon of arabesque.

On the one hand, arabesque design defines movement through its forms:

> In the arabesque, perhaps more than in any other design associated with Islam, it is clear how the line defines space, and how sophisticated three- dimensional effects are achieved by differences in width, colour and texture. Shapes left in the background contribute to this effect, as in geometric patterns, adding another dimension to the overall design.[13]

On the other hand, definition is diffused through the omission of centrality and boundaries, and through the deliberate act of unfolding:

> [I]f the formal logic of geometric interlace has the effect of provoking the perpetual dissolution and recomposition of shapes, it also possesses the characteristic of recognizing neither center nor limit, and the ability to spread out virtually forever. Thus, the spectator who enters into the logic of the interlace is enticed into mentally continuing its development beyond the limits of the decorated surface. In other words, the geometric interlace possesses an existence which goes beyond material reality. It is, properly speaking, a conceptual art.[14]

Two major developments elevated the art of arabesque to a level of sophistication and intricacy that made it a distinctly Islamic art; namely the Muslim development of mathematics and the formation of the Islamic view of the natural world through *imar* and all that it entails. As Islam's view of the natural world remains unique to its system of thought, it is the understanding of mathematics that provides shared and common ground for all humanity across cultures and civilizations. Between the general abstract construct of mathematics and a unique empathy towards nature, all human art is formulated.

In 2022, I was invited to speak at a conference for architects and interior designers in Abu Dhabi. The event was organized by a British company, and its audience was mainly individuals from international firms who were operating in the UAE. My talk held a message that challenged the general climate of constantly wanting to build for power. And perhaps for that reason it raised some interest. A visit to the Sheikh Zayed Grand Mosque was on the sightseeing itinerary prepared for attendees. Having matured since my youthful visit to the Sultan Ahmed Mosque in Istanbul, I didn't think that mosques should be treated like museums, but, driven by my plans to write about mosques, I tagged along.

The group of four women architects and designers I was with seemed to be better informed than I was. They knew that arriving at the mosque's site didn't mean arriving at the mosque. It took us almost an hour to actually reach the mosque, from the curb where the taxi dropped us. Time was of the essence, because visiting times are arranged between prayer times: this aspect alone made me think of the double life this mosque was leading. To access the gigantic white building on the horizon, we had to enter a bulbous glass dome, a bit like I. M. Pei's pyramid at the Louvre in Paris. From there, we descended via escalator. The underground world was like a metro station: I couldn't tell if its atmosphere was due to the work history of the consulting firm Halcrow, which took over design management after 2001. As we passed Starbucks and Subway, I noticed my companions starting to wrap the scarves that had been around their necks up over their heads. Finally, we reached the travelator of the 'Path of Tolerance', which is another name for the long corridor

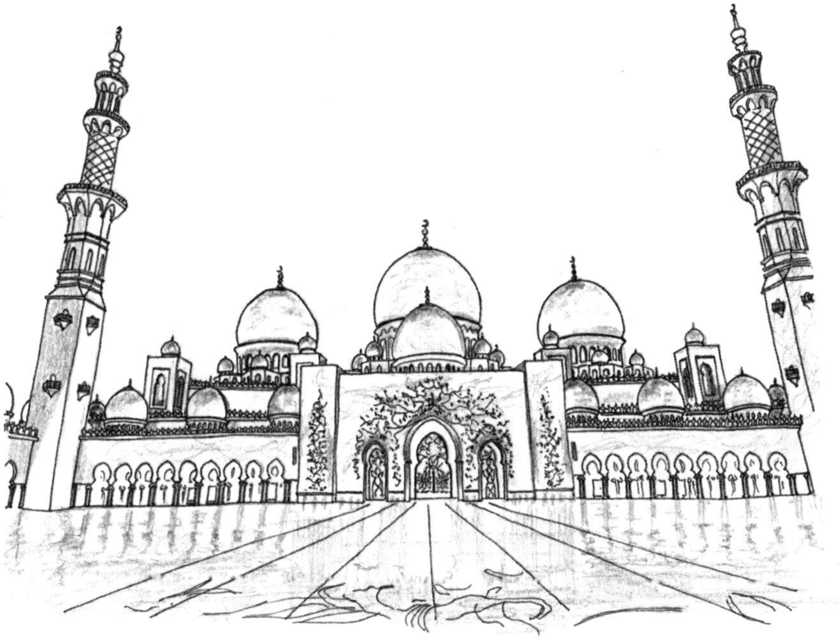

The Sheikh Zayed Grand Mosque in Abu Dhabi, UAE

that leads to the security checkpoint at the end. Beyond that were the elevators that would take us up to ground level, outside the mosque.

By the time we emerged from underground, the sun had set and the building had been illuminated with an elegant lighting scheme. A reflection of the white mass of the mosque rippled with flickers of light in the enormous pool of water that surrounds it on three sides. 'It's amazing what a body of water can do,' said one of the visiting designers. I thought to myself, this place is meant as a palace, not a mosque. As the only Muslim in the group, my growing sense of shame at the tasteless grandeur we were passing was matched only by the growing amazement of my companions. I ventured to share my criticisms of the vast stretches of white marble we were covering, making our way past endless rows of gilded capitals in the form of artificial palm fronds, the disjointed designs of swirling plant ornamentation that compulsively filled every surface without any apparent logic, the way in which everything around us contradicted the essence of mosqueness. My comments were met with silence. Whether my companions thought of them as false claims or inconvenient truths, I wasn't sure.

The architect of the first phase of construction at the mosque was a fellow Syrian, the designer and visual artist Yusef Abdelki. Three more Syrian names appeared at later stages of design and development. Unlike the masons in Córdoba, however, the Syrian contributors to the Sheikh Zayed Grand Mosque evidently drew no inspiration from home, nor did they offer any sublimation of the Syrian model. Instead, a Mughal inspiration for the mosque is evident in the general outline, in which the dominant three domes cover most of the area of the approximately 22,000-square-metre (over 235,000 ft^2) prayer hall. At approximately 17,000 additional square metres (183,000 ft^2), the courtyard is clad in white marble from Greece, as is the building. However, there is a deliberate avoidance of a singular source of 'inspiration'.

According to the brief provided by Halcrow to the Aga Khan Committee, inspiration was taken from 'the majority of the most famous and historic mosque edifices throughout Islamic history ... aspiration to any single Islamic style of architecture was rejected, because it is incompatible with cultural diversity'.[15] The result is a patchwork of a building: Mughal in arrangement, Fatimid in elements, with four hybrid minarets (each section, from base to lantern, influenced by a different style), and with overall details that are more suited to a Disney palace than to a mosque. In total, the reinforced cement complex has eighty-two domes, most of which (if not all) have no structural significance and are merely present for stylistic purposes.

When we finally reached the carpeted prayer hall, we were barricaded by rope fencing that allowed us only to peek onto it from a tiled area. Up above, the colossal domes were supported at the neck by a polygonal tier which transferred the load to massive pillars, each of which was composed of four huge columns. These pillars united around a central void, which was crowned with a heavy cylindrical tier dotted with spotlights to shower the void with light, creating the illusion that the prayer hall was full of elevator units gathered around a central circle.

The world's riches were sourced to garland this mosque with record-breaking honours. Thus, the world's largest handwoven Persian carpet

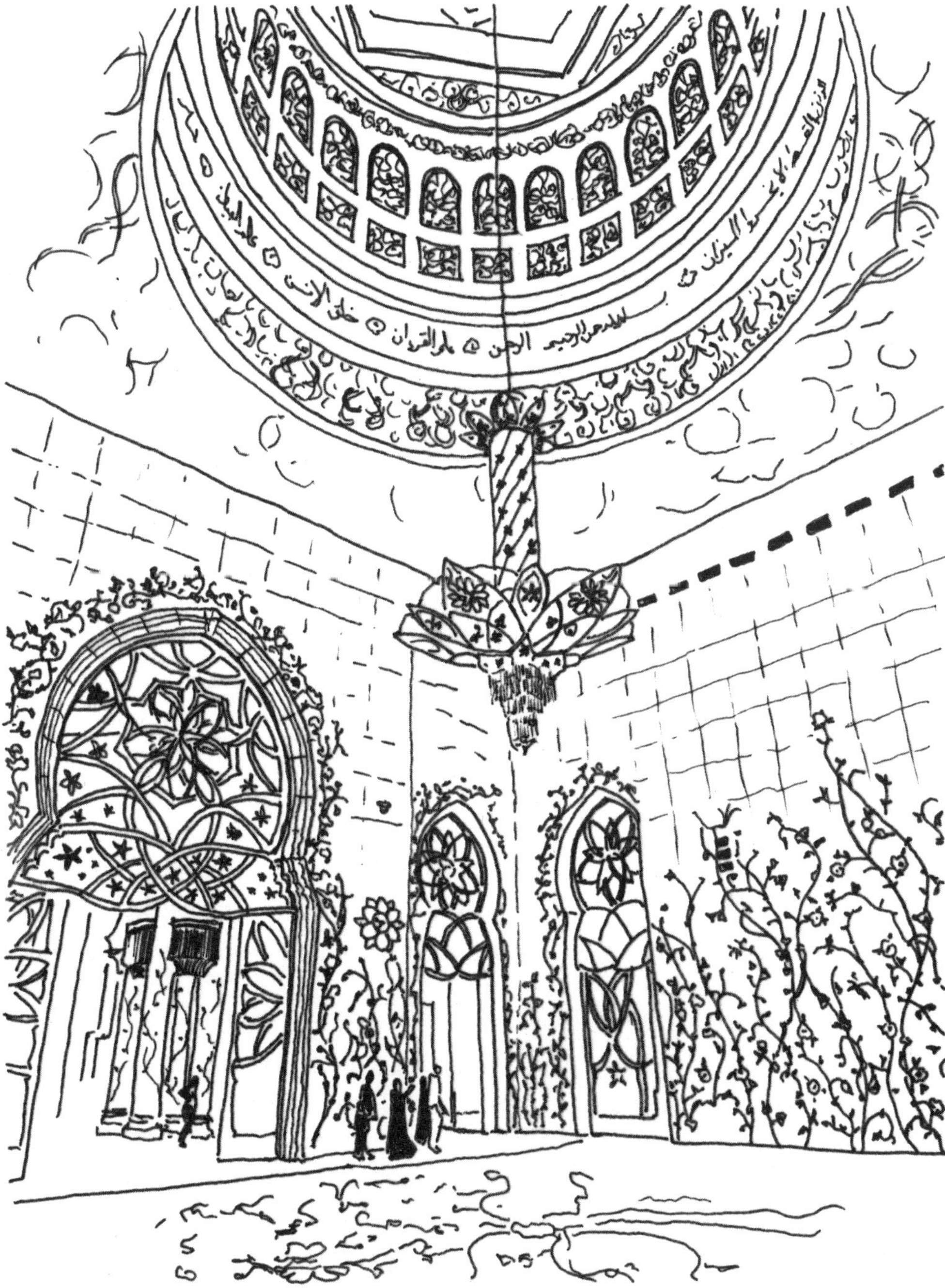

The Sheikh Zayed Grand Mosque: an interior view

keeps company with the world's largest Swarovski crystal chandelier in the prayer hall.[16] Likewise, the world's largest marble mosaic has been created,[17] in collaboration with the British artist who designed much of the mosque's floral marble decoration, including internal walls and floors, exterior archways and the courtyard. This falls in line with the official statement on the mosque's website, which uses the initials 'SZGMC' to refer to the building as a 'Grand Mosque *Centre*' (my emphasis), and explains how the design and construction '"unite the world," using artisans, craftsmen, and materials from many countries, including Italy, Germany, Morocco, India, Turkey, China, the United Kingdom, New Zealand, Greece and, of course, the United Arab Emirates'.[18] The twirling marble rose garden that clambered over the walls and crept along the ground was probably the greatest source of my unease around the design. As I looked at people taking selfies with it, I was taken aback by the jarring scale of the motifs, as much as the impression they gave of an abandoned garden. More importantly, their attempt at realism was divorced from their stony material, which only added to my sense of confrontation with the counterfeit.

During the 'golden age' of Islam, which the creators of the Sheikh Zayed Grand Mosque have evidently tried to reference, the art of arabesque combined the Islamic world of abstraction with the Islamic world of empathy. But before addressing the specific meanings that arabesque embodied, and the extent to which the world of stone gardens and handwoven roses at Zayed is far distant, it is worth noting how the world of art in the West was categorized by the German art historian Wilhelm Worringer in 1906.

In his *Abstraction and Empathy: A Contribution to the Psychology of Style*, Worringer divided art into two main types, which correspond to two opposing human attitudes to the world. The first is the art of abstraction, which comes from regarding the world as a place of unpredictable chaos that threatens human existence, and thus prompts mankind to build its own constructs with an attitude of 'withdrawal from'. As architect and lecturer, Richard Padovan, notes, 'It begins with an overpowering sense of the *terribilità* of the natural world.'[19] The second type is the art of empathy, which comes from viewing the world as a source of benign order and inspiring beauty, thus prompting mankind to 'feel into' organic forms – not by direct imitation, but by acting on an inclination 'toward the truths of organic life'.[20] Without going too far into art theory, which ultimately recognizes overlap in the two categories of Western abstraction and empathy, the conclusion that is of interest with regard to the art and architecture of the mosque is that in which Worringer (citing fellow art historian August Schmarsow) explains all art as 'a disputation of man with nature'.[21]

Contrary to the notions of 'disputation' and *terribilità*, the Muslim approach takes off from a position of embrace. There is no debate, and there is no fear (whether this is expressed in challenge or avoidance). The Muslim outlook on nature is also completely different; it does not seek to withdraw or control, but nor does it seek to idealize or surpass. The task of *imar* imbues its endeavour with a sense of cultivation and respect, with constant reference (and reverence) to the Creator. This is something that Worringer may have appreciated when – citing his (simplistic) portrayal of cultural history through three human types, the 'Primitive', 'Classical' and 'Oriental' – he asserted that 'the Oriental represents a third stage of development, more mature than the Classical: "not *before* all knowledge, but *beyond* it"'.[22] This perspective shifts Muslim 'artistic volition' (to use art historian Alois Riegl's term) away from an engagement with symbolism or a tendency towards representation, and towards a higher concern with what lies *beyond*.

Worringer also posits that the value of art lies in its ability to bestow happiness. For the Muslim artist, the focus lies again in the 'beyond', as ultimate happiness is only achieved through the satisfaction of the Creator, and that again pertains to the task of *imar*. Domination – which, according to Worringer's proposition, must be an implicit tendency in Western attitudes, driven by the fear that he associates with abstraction and the idea of debate that he associates with art in general – does not motivate the art of Islam, which completely trusts the wisdom of the Creator and seeks no alteration or acquisition of His universe. This attitude is what enabled the art of Islam to redefine the relationship between mathematics and the organic form, in the shape of arabesque, which intertwines rhythm and stasis.

Of the two traps that Western scholars repeatedly fall into when it comes to evaluating the art of Islam, the first is to constantly refer to it as a successor to its non-Islamic predecessors, unfairly reducing its contribution to a mere layer added to the solid foundation established by either the Greeks or the Romans. The second is to judge Islamic art according to the Western standards of thought, without viewing it on its own terms and without attempting to understand its world view. Whether it is due to prejudice or to lack of imagination, these Western narratives of the Muslim construct have been a source of endemic misunderstanding.

Early examples of arabesque can be seen at the Umayyad in Damascus, where geometrical interlace is used in trelliswork that protects the windows. Indeed, Renaissance historian Giorgio Vasari identified the trade in a type of decoration that was very similar to the arabesque as *alla damaschina* in 1480.[23] The developments made under Islam in mathematics led to the creation of greater intricacy and a novel sense of dynamism, which was quite uniquely Islamic. As Titus Burckhardt notes: 'Arab interlacement has a geometrical complexity and rhythmic quality quite lacking in its Roman counterpart.'[24] Art historian Dominique Clévenot further points out, with regard to geometry, 'Going beyond the static Greek model, Islam invented the dynamic mathematical concept of trigonometry.'[25] In combining a sense of rhythm and the spirit of geometry, arabesque can be seen to sum up Islam's outlook on nature, in which Islamic abstraction and empathy become one.

Walking through the tangled branches of ornamentation in the Zayed Mosque, where no sense of rhythm or geometry has been adhered to, I found myself thinking about the reductionist overview to which the arts of Islam have been subjected. As I watched my companions looking at the walls as a source of inspiration for their next creations for the region, I felt an overwhelming urge to cover their eyes with my hands and say, 'Please look away; this is not who we really are.' 'We' might sound strange here, since after all I was a visitor like everyone else. However, mosques are central today to the perception of Islam as a universal value for all Muslims, the implications of which are of course the topic of this present book.

Veil and void

This correlation between being a Muslim and being expected to be the arbitrator of the art of the mosque became very palpable to me in Oxford. While I was there for a speaking engagement, I received a kind invitation to visit the Oxford Centre for Islamic Studies (OCIS). Established in 1985, OCIS was initially housed in a wooden hut on St Cross Road, with a mission 'to foster better western understanding of the Islamic world'.[26] In 1990 the organization moved to a temporary home in George Street, before transferring to its new building and current location in Marston Road, next to Magdalen College. The building was finally opened in 2017, after a very bumpy journey: the project had taken thirty-two years to complete.

The problem was the mosque. How could the features of an Islamic building be made to fit within a traditional Christian context? The architect of the project was Abdel Wahed El-Wakil, the renowned Egyptian who had been educated at British secondary schools in Egypt, and was responsible for building twenty mosques in Saudi Arabia, including in Mecca and Medina. OCIS had been offered a 1.6-acre site close to Merton College in 1994, but the plans – which involved El-Wakil's signature use of a brick dome and a Mamluk minaret – led the college to issue a

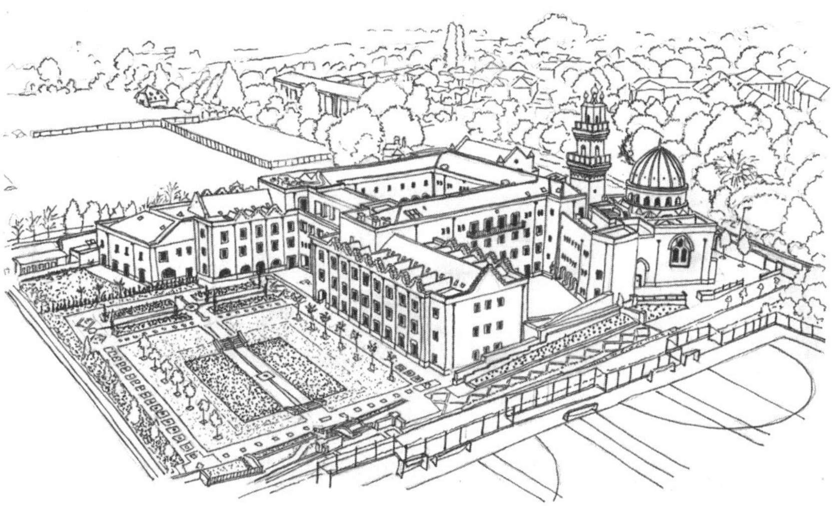

Oxford Centre for Islamic Studies in Oxford, England

high court writ preventing OCIS from using the land, while branding the design a 'mish-mash of eastern and western influences'.[27] Further objections involved concerns about scale and the impact on the skyline.[28] A compromise was reached by granting the project a larger (3.25 acre) and more distant location from the town centre. Making sure that the minaret was shorter than Magdalen's tower, and that Gothic as well as 'Moorish' elements were included, the design was toned down to somewhat acceptable measures.

With King Charles as patron and funding chiefly provided by the Saudi King Fahd, OCIS gave its stated objective as bringing two worlds together. In 1993, King Charles (Prince of Wales at the time) had given a lecture, 'Islam and the West', in his capacity as OCIS patron. In his speech, the issue of misunderstanding between the West and Islam was highlighted. He rightly explained how 'taking ... extremes to be the norm' leads to misunderstanding,[29] and how finding middle ground and unity was possible.[30] Nevertheless, the history of OCIS proved that this was easier said than done.

As I was being driven to the site, I felt as if I was leaving town. At the entrance, first I had to pass through security. Then, coming out of the short entry tunnel, I was immediately confronted by the minaret at the opposite corner, which forces the eye to look up and not around. To my left, the pressing wall of the prayer hall met the short tower of the minaret at an awkward angle. A small dome crowned the prayer hall, in juxtaposition with the minaret, both elements seeming to provide a short statement that they should be quickly taken in and then just as quickly ignored. Stepping away from the cold, shadowy corner of what should have been a welcoming entryway, I turned to my right, where the courtyard space had been defined with an L-shaped building.

The combination of the religious and the collegiate at OCIS was inspired by both the madrasa and Oxford. The architectural treatment of the courtyard immediately conveys the medieval English sense, with Gothic arches and a triangular façade with two small towers. With unassuming details, the façades offer an abstraction of existing Oxford architecture, with the exception of an attached Egyptian Mamluk *mashrabiya* (screened window) and an ornate white marble doorway framed with a high-pointed arch on two columns, presented like valuables on an art collector's wall.

Before I entered the main building through that doorway, I was distracted by the off-centre placement of a water fountain, its location having no rational relationship with its surroundings – as if either the fountain or the doorway was an afterthought. Inside, all the ceilings felt too low, and all the proportions – from individual elements to general spaces – gave the impression of a weighed-down building. I was refreshed from time to time by the sight of inner gardens: one lies inside the main quadrangle, surrounded by cloisters, and the other is a small, square garden. Both have a cruciform walking path, with a small fountain in the centre. Behind the building there is a large open garden, which I was told was inspired by the Islamic gardens of Córdoba – although, unlike those of Córdoba, the trees at OCIS are not fruit-bearing.

The shape and character of the interiors of the building seem to have followed the taste and contributions of the donors. There are Ottoman tiles and Moroccan stucco. The wood and the tiling, the cladding and the carving belong to different worlds, made by disparate artisans. What is supposed to combine these elements and the architecture is the history of high culture and the prowess of superior craftsmanship. As in the approach followed at the Sheikh Zayed Grand Mosque in Abu Dhabi, the amalgam of riches here is political as well as stylistic. The Oxford Centre for Islamic Studies (OCIS) has indeed addressed its mission of 'bringing two worlds together'. It is an interfaith statement.

El-Wakil's personal heroes also come from two worlds, in that they are Hasan Fathy and John Ruskin. In his idiom, blending the vernacular with the classical, the Mamluk with the Fatimid, the Western with the Eastern, is performed by employing traditional craftsmanship and achieving artisanal quality. This has made him a favourite of royalty when it comes to mosque architecture. Purity generally seems to be the overriding concern of El-Wakil's mosque architecture: barren whitewashed buildings, cubic spaces, photogenic exteriors, and a total rejection of modern construction methods. Of course this comes at a high cost: even at OCIS, the initial £20 million budget soared to a staggering £100 million. To me, such puritanical demands seem to contradict the hybridity of styles on which he relies. More importantly, these demands and those mosques exhibit an unwaveringly static viewpoint that contradicts the inherently dynamic Islamic one.

The wrap-up of my tour at OCIS led us to circle back to the mosque near the entrance. Above the interior door, a sign read 'Sheikh Zayed Mosque', referencing the major donor for the building. My host proudly pointed out the brick dome that had been traditionally built by artisans brought by El-Wakil from outside of the United Kingdom. Eyes were on me to comment, and at the risk of appearing stupid I just moronically smiled. I had to conceal my disapproval of this outsourcing, which makes the building not only detached in location but also in creation.

The focus on a participatory collective of artisans and craftsmen is supposed to be a revival of yet another 'image' – that of the age of empires, when free movement in the lands of Muslims and the widespread use of Arabic facilitated collectivity. However, upholding the intermingling of cultures in the Islamic past as a guiding design principle today is, in my view, a piecemeal outlook. By taking the phenomenon out of context, it is overlooked that this was the fruit of the maturity stage, and not the seed of it; in other words, since the phenomenon was the result of complex historical and societal conditions that fostered a culture's overall maturity, it cannot simply be applied to generate that same maturity in the present day.

Moreover, the spirit of indulgence that was humoured in the heyday of certain periods of rule sometimes leads to a contemporary eclecticism that takes the wrong buildings as models, ignoring the fact that these vaunted palaces and mausoleums cannot be conflated with mosques, and that they in any case often represent high peaks that prefigure sharp declines and the sunset of civilizations. Hence, the perils of the eclectic approach go beyond the loss of meaning and can actually lead to the contriving of false meanings. It is important to recognize those short periods in the long history of Islam, when Islam itself was overshadowed. For instance, the fourteenth-century builders of the Palace of the Lions at the Alhambra cannot be conflated with the eighth-century builders of the Great Mosque of Córdoba, even if they shared territory, religion and mastery. The former building exhibits an acquisitive spirit of one-upmanship and indulgence, while the latter is quintessentially *giving*.

Apparent duality in history is only confusing if it is taken out of context. It is by distilling principles, values and meanings that we can appreciate the products of the past with the necessary clarity. Periods of decline that are on the cusp of dissipation, marked by a tendency towards excessiveness, do not represent the values of the engendering essence of Islam that we have been exploring.

As we have seen throughout this book, it is through myths, mysticism and misunderstandings that the field of interpretation of the architecture of the mosque and its arts has become a misleading source of 'knowledge' and 'inspiration' for the mosques of today. It is true that considerable progress has been made since the accounts of the early orientalists, who sneeringly viewed Islamic art and architecture in 'ethnic' (i.e. racist) terms. Their conclusions focused on delivering two main ideas. The first is that the art of Islam exhibits a total disregard for space, and therefore should be regarded as an art of the surface. The second is that the chief characteristics of Islamic art are an excessive veiling and an obsessive need to fill the void: *horror vacui*. In their opinion, these two ideas related to a 'special state of mind', 'spirit', or 'race'.[31]

In essence, early orientalists ascribed the second tendency to a presumed anxiety in the face of the void that they attributed to the Bedouin, for whom, they opined, the emptiness of the desert had to be filled with the compactness of urban life.[32] Here again, the myth of the desert rears its head, with all its biases and contradictions. Firstly, in order to justify this narrative, the orientalists disregard the essentially urban contributions of Islamic architecture. Secondly, they present a false distortion by ignoring the enormous variety of Muslim peoples (urban, rural, nomadic, western, eastern, Arab, Mongol, Turk, Berber, and so on). Thirdly, they assume a *terribilità* outlook on the part of the Bedouin, who in fact are perfectly at home in the plenitude of the desert terrain (one need only read Bedouin poetry – an endless love letter to the desert).

Previous chapters of this book have already challenged such narratives, by shedding a light on the story of civilization, the history of urbanism, and the true mechanism that operates between the urban dweller and the nomad – as part of the history of all humankind – which was brought to remarkable fruition under Islam. Nonetheless, especially when it comes to the arts of Islam, which are primarily nestled at the heart of the mosque, the cobwebs around old interpretations still conceal much of the true meanings of these arts.

Art historian Dalu Jones explains how the image that was disseminated in Europe in the nineteenth century resulted in a confusion between 'the European idea of clutter, excess and richness, and the careful superimposition and layering of textures and designs' that characterized the Islamic art of ornament:

> [Nineteenth-century European art historians] contrasted the apparent rigour of European neo-Classicism, or the symbolic content of Gothic, with what appeared to be a clutter of different but always 'rich' materials and designs, useful only when copied discreetly and used out of context in 'tasteful' interiors. Yet the clutter was Rococo or Victorian rather than Islamic.[33]

Jones recognizes that what had been perceived as 'clutter' was, in fact, a tool used with precision to achieve smooth, imperceptible transitions across space and between interdependent surfaces. In playing with space like this, light, colour and texture, as well as form, were deployed to filter out any sharp contrasts. As Jones notes: 'Islamic art is an art of repose, intellectual rather than emotional, where tensions are resolved. It is a conceptual art where questions and answers are finely balanced.'[34] While Jones makes a comparison between this 'conceptual and intellectual art' and the vocabulary of textiles such as weaving, and thereby rubs on the stereotypical image of the nomad, she fortunately does not go as far as the orientalists did to call this an inherently 'textile mentality'.

What also needs to be noted here is the effect of the Arabic language of the Quran on 'artistic volition'. The inimitable depth of Arabic – in terms of its expressive ability to convey verisimilitude (the appearance of truth or reality) – is evident when dealing with excess, in relation to nature and the universe. Art, in general, deals with excess; it pertains to the realm of our humanity, which rises above primitive instincts and essential needs. Just as the dynamism and power behind the Arabic language are reflected in arabesque as well as in Islamic space, so layers of ornament reflect the Muslim perspective, whereby qualities of condensed meaning, productive deployment of resources, and apprehension of waste are upheld. All of these are not merely values of thought, but also of language.

Finally, there is a general distinction that must be made in viewing what has been observed as the veiling of the void, and that involves the two worlds of materials that constituted Islamic constructions of the premodern era: the world of stone, and that of brick. *Muqarnas*, for instance, which are often unnecessarily read in metaphysical terms, belong to the world of brick. As is often the case, construction requirements inspired aesthetics. While brick offered speed and standardization, it came with the downside of fragility. For that reason, the regions which predominantly built in brick, such as Mesopotamia, Transoxiana and Iran, devised revetments of stucco and ceramic tiles to protect the brick from erosion. Furthermore, cleanliness and hygiene – key requirements in Islamic culture, and conditions for prayer and entry to the mosque – can be maintained throughout by the cladding of the brick with less porous surfaces. It then becomes an exercise of logic to see how builders throughout the various spaces of an edifice might choose to embellish a technical requirement with artistry. The language of brick, which relies on the arch, cupola and vault, historically used *muqarnas* to achieve an eye-pleasing transition, and at the same time to protect the underlying structural elements. It is the same as in language: *transition* is what defines the rhythm. The less visible the transition, the greater the mastery.

The transition between a square base and a hemispherical dome is another technical problem that arose from a structural requirement. Premodern buildings introduced two solutions: squinches (also called angle niches), to which were later added the sub-support and transition of ribs and *muqarnas*, and pendentives (sometimes referred to as 'spherical triangles'). Squinches were adopted by the brick world, while pendentives were used in the stone world. As we have seen, Syrians were the masters of the latter. From the Levant, they took their skills to Andalusian Spain and to Seljuk Anatolia. Many Western scholars overlook this distinction, and give an abbreviated account of Muslim adoption of squinches across

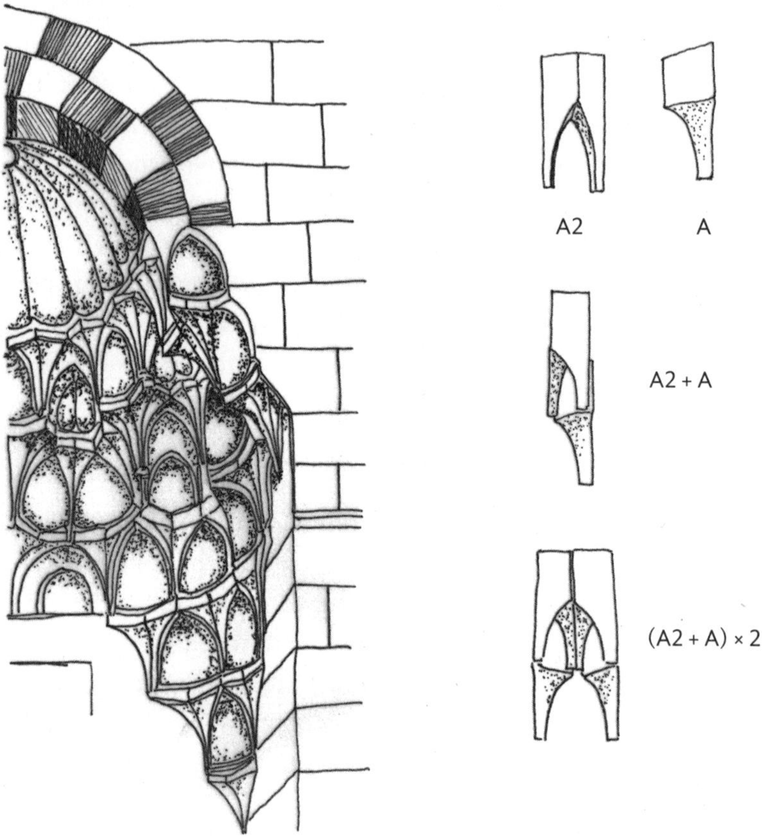

Diagram of *muqarnas* (honeycomb vaulting)

all Islamic regions. Based on this false claim, and thereby ignoring the smooth, curved transition offered by pendentives, they provide a biased interpretation that portrays the Muslim mentality as one that favours 'abstract geometric figures instead of organic spaces'.[35] The result is a reduction of the history of the art and architecture of Islam into a haze of eye-dazzling surfaces, and attempts to philosophize them. By misrepresenting the surface and merely scratching it, these accounts reveal no truths about art, architecture and Islam, and by extension the mosque.

So far, we have tackled two types of mosque: the first are mosques of the past, which belonged to times when mosques were fields of expression and forums for development. Progress, then, was not pre-determined,

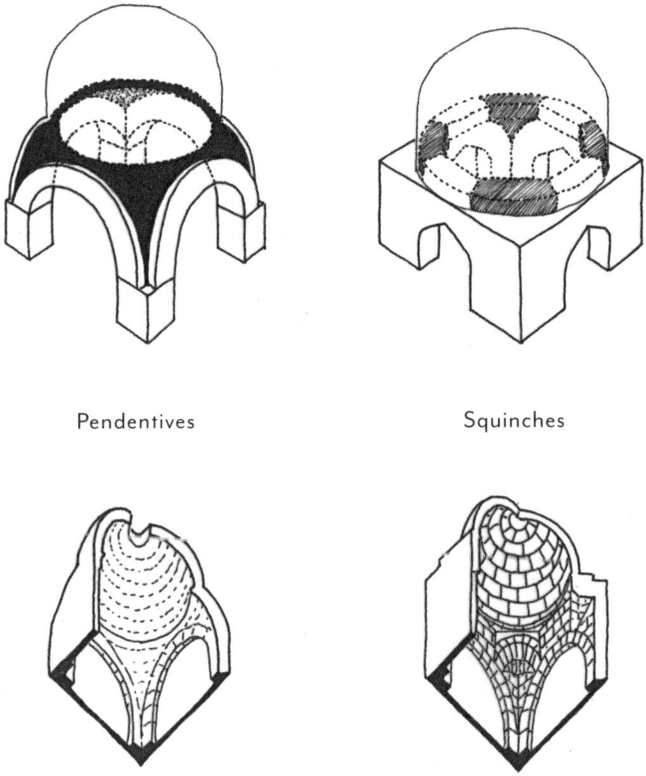

Diagram of pendentives and squinches: exterior and interior

nor was it already concluded; it was a continuous process of layering up. Identity was a natural result of such processes, not an end in itself. Instead, the culmination of these processes revolved around responding to the world and cultivating every element. The second type are mosques of the present day, whether built in the Muslim world or the non-Muslim world. The vast majority of these have been delivered as 'images' of a prescribed ideology, the role of which is primarily political. Whether vernacular, cross-cultural historical or modern,[36] the 'images' that have been generated do not present buildings *for* the world, but rather *of* a world. Efforts to reinterpret the first type were made in order to serve the objectives of the second type.

The basic aspiration of the general public who use a mosque is simply to find a place for prayer, but – as this book attempts to show – this sacred communal act requires a whole kaleidoscope of meanings to be addressed, which need to be reflected in everything around it. Simplifying this requirement to the point of pure utilitarianism means that progress and development will be completely out of reach. In their place, political control will be empowered so that it tightens its grip and smothers the last gasps of freedom of self-expression, and all the other freedoms that go along with it.

Part III

Freedom

Chapter 6

The Mosque and the City

'Islam is an ideology of liberation. It sets the believer free from all the fears and shackles that can be imposed in this world. This freedom however is not complete license to rampage on earth where the strong destroy the weak. It is a freedom that is circumcised by the bounds of law.'

ISMAIL SERAGELDIN[1]

Creating connections

In Taksim Square, at the heart of Istanbul, I find myself between a new Ottoman-style mosque and an old casino turned luxury hotel, contemplating the many divisions that this site embodies. The very name 'Taksim' means 'division' in Arabic, and it explains the original purpose of the location where water was collected from the forested areas and northern parts of the city into Taksim's stone reservoir, then branched off to other destinations.

The square, in its modern arrangement, was designed by the French architect Henri Prost as part of his extensive 'development' efforts for city planning during the premiership of Kemal Atatürk. The monumental space has a forbidding air that suggests a socialist presence, with proud military symbols and a strictly controlled skyline. The view of the waterfront is completely obscured by distant buildings, such as the Atatürk Cultural Centre, each of which constitutes a celebratory object of whichever value is being signified. Symbols of the secular state that replaced Ottoman rule have been forced to compete with the touristic and consumerist ambitions of the modern city. Religion, however, has faced even more difficulty in eking out a place at the square. The first attempts to build a mosque in Taksim Square were made in the 1950s. For decades, the project was met with a series of delays and internal opposition, as the secular elite deemed it 'not in the public interest' and 'unnecessary', arguing that building a mosque at the square would be an act of 'Islamization' of public space.[2]

I walk through the alleyways of boutique hotels and grocery shops selling cucumbers and bananas next to suitcases of all sizes. On each corner lurk a few men, primed to notice the slightest hint of a requirement, for which they will be ready to invite you to solicit their services. As I quicken my pace, I soon emerge into the elongated open space of the square. In front of me is a row of doves lined up on the ledge of a fountain, and for a moment we all look ahead to the raised Gezi Park, from behind which the sun is rising. This location saw a clash between the government and demonstrators in 2013, in what has become known as the Gezi Park Protests. These events were ignited by the government's plans to replace the park with a shopping centre, whose design was to be inspired by the old Ottoman barracks that had once occupied the site but were demolished in Prost's plan.

Fortunately, the shopping centre plans did not go ahead and the park was retained. But when the mosque was finally built in 2017, it looked as if the government had had the final word on the space. To a foreign visitor like me, the mosque seemed to fit in on the triangular corner it occupied. Its design – devised by architects Selim Dalaman and the Turkish–Belgian Şefik Birkiye – has been described as a 'modern interpretation of the traditional form': overt neo-Art Deco features are combined with the Ottoman-style domed structure and its two pencil minarets. The style is a clichéd statement of power, in which historical legitimacy is used in juxtaposition with adopted Western stylization. Classicism, postmodernism, elegance, and a hint of elasticity are the prominent declarations of the mosque complex, which offers a library, café and exhibition hall as an extension to its activities. In a polarized space such as Taksim Square, the mosque does no more or less than any other building or non-building at the site: it simply expresses a representation, while coiled in its corner of space. This is something no

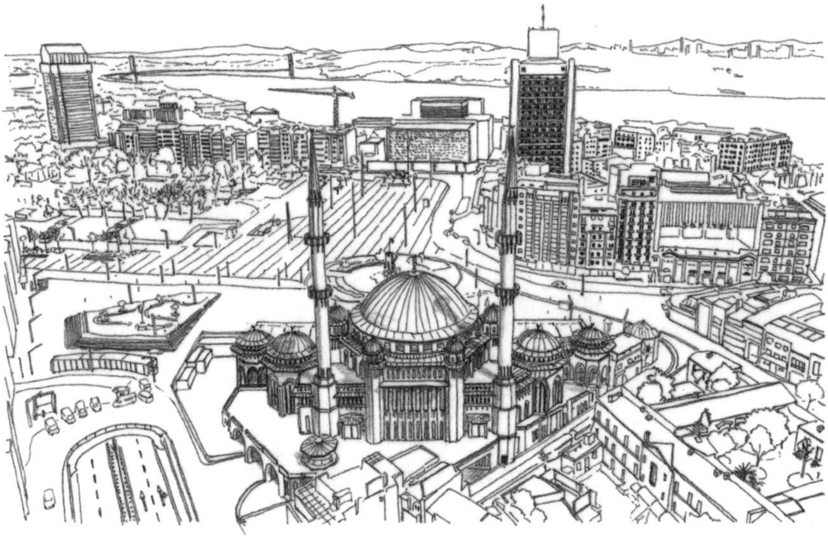

Taksim Mosque, in Taksim Square, Istanbul, Turkey

mosque of the past would have done, for the city of the past was not governed by the politics of segregation, as is the case today.

The Gezi clashes, for instance, were over more than 'just trees'; they represented a last-straw moment in the ongoing conflict between the secular and Islamic camps which has been tearing up Turkey's identity. Since the fall of the Ottomans, Islam has been subjugated and persecuted in the secularized Turkey with the same brutality with which the Soviets have smothered faith and religious practices in their territories. 'Freedom' from the shackles of faith has meant not only embracing postwar Western ideals, but also dismantling all of the political, economic and social systems that were once built by or around that faith. I would like to argue that what constitutes the core of Islam is this very interdependence between freedom and systems, and that by destroying the systemic structures, freedom – instead of being attained – has, in fact, been lost.

In order to explain this, it is worth going back to the point in time when the mosque was the centre of every Muslim town. Even when Islam was new to regions, the mosque was the beating heart of activity for the fledgling Muslim community. In previous chapters, I have mentioned the fellowship between the mosque and the marketplace. It is a spatial correlation that best describes the backbone to the city-building force in Islam; i.e. trade. However, this is not any type of trade: it is a form of trade that is governed by the spirit of worship and Muslim ethics, which has allowed it to nurture its host communities and establish a comprehensive development of all areas of life to all the people around it, regardless of their faith or background. Unlike today's mosques, such mosques were built as an integral part of the urban fabric, with no interest in signifying power. As scholars Nezar AlSayyad and İpek Türeli explain:

> [T]he importance of the mosque within the towns of the Muslim world was muted compared to that of the church within the towns of medieval Europe. The absence in Islam of an institutionalized clergy may explain the difference. The mosque as a physical structure was not an essential part of the hierarchy of governance, and as an institution, it did not possess independent power. Instead, it was intended to serve as a place where power could be transmitted and shared, where the supposed equality between ruler and ruled was manifested. Therefore, the symbolic significance of the early mosque was not represented in its physical qualities; rather, its importance lay in the role it played within the community, a role deeply rooted in the structure of Islamic society.[3]

Certainly, this structure of transmitted and shared power, where no monopoly of any kind could take place, emphasizes the prime objective of mosques as centres of creating connections with their environments and their peoples. This was chiefly accomplished through trade of a similar structure, with no monopoly of power that reflected itself in urban or architectural form.

In her book *Monsoon Mosques: Arrival of Islam and the Development of a Mosque Vernacular*, architect and historic preservationist Patricia Tusa Fels tells the story of the introduction of Islam to the regions of the South Indian Ocean, such as Indonesia, Java, Sumatra and Malabar. Islam arrived there with the ships of Muslim traders, and not only did it build networks of trade that gradually developed those host regions, but it also created an organic prototype of a mosque that was unique to the local culture and responsive to its contexts:

> Large wood-framed roofs and fine wooden craftsmanship distinguish this vernacular, a typology I call the 'monsoon mosque'. This is not a rigid typology but a collection of living, responsive forms; what [architect and design theorist] Christopher Alexander describes as 'good architecture ... well adapted to context, the product of many decisions about form which were tried and tested as those who lived and used buildings sought to adapt them to their purpose'.[4]

The author describes these 'monsoon mosques' as a development of the existing building model, raised above the ground on granite platforms or wooden pillars (depending on the nature of the sub-region), in order to mitigate the risk of earthquakes and to keep insects away from the structures in the wet tropical environment. These mosques had high roofs, so they offered an airy and pleasant atmosphere, using the local materials of wood and porous stone. Connections were made with the environment, as well as with the different communities: 'The relationship between Hindu, Christian and Muslim in Malabar was eased by the longstanding presence of traders along the Malabar Coast. This predisposed the local people to an acceptance of the "other", the alien foreigner.'[5] Connections were thus part of networks of different peoples, different regions and different artistic expressions, with the mosque as the heart of activity:

> In the panorama of the Asian trading networks, the tropical mosque is a unique by-product, a physical reminder of what was once a complex set of international mercantile connections that thrived without telegraph, telephone or Internet. Islam served as a unifying force for large-scale commercial trade and created a chain of caravan and maritime routes that joined far-off ports on the Indian Ocean to the Mediterranean.[6]

In that sense, Islam did not cause a revolution in construction, nor did its arrival import (or impose) any particular tradition; it plugged itself organically into the existing structures and systems, and caused a *free* development from within. Fels compares this model with the Western attitude, exemplified by the Dutch colonization of these regions. The 'trade' of the Dutch was one of complete takeover, exploitative of the natural resources and destructive of local communities: 'The Dutch cleared the cities and countryside of resources, sending tons of gold back to the homeland. They also made sure that rivers and channels drained.'[7]

Notably, when the Dutch looked at the mosque, they couldn't fathom how it was created: 'For many years the Europeans tried to find an outside source for the mosque. Their assumption was that the mosque must have come from somewhere else. Were the colonialists so distracted that they could not see the talents and resources of the local people?'[8]

In my view, the inherent freedom in Islam – which enables the creation of all sorts of connections – is what has allowed the mosque and trade to be 'local'; namely, to belong to local systems and the people who have created them. In that sense, the architecture of the mosque is the epitome of the modern, where modernity is democratic, free, innovative, developing, and above all unifying. These are different connotations from those of Western modernity, which will be discussed in further detail in the following chapter. And it is precisely what the European colonizers couldn't make sense of.

In the South Indian Ocean regions, the Dutch colonialists brought the mosque down to the ground, jeopardizing its structural integrity and putting it back in harm's way. They also brought in metal roofing, with zinc-coated corrugated metal becoming the standard, as well as concrete, which duly replaced the traditional use of wood as the major building material. And then there were the domes, now imported to Sumatra and used to retrofit many of the old mosques: 'Some scholars believe that the Dutch wanted to control Islam by creating their own brand of mosque: one with a mixture of nontraditional [i.e., not widely used in the region] elements, such as domes, arches and minarets. The Dutch colonialists, although often cruel and exploitative, understood the need to support indigenous culture as a means of pacification.'[9]

These means of control and the accompanying policy of pacification continued across the lands of Islam, just as the legacy of the colonizers is being carried through today by the rulers of 'independence'. Fels describes the aftermath of colonial policies: the monsoon mosques are no longer local expressions, their metal and cement roofs necessitate air conditioning, children no longer play in their courtyards, the doors are closed, and the gates are guarded for fear of 'radicalization'. This new reality of the mosque is true across Muslim lands. The pattern has been that, in place of the rule of the colonial powers, the so-called independent governments enforce a rule that does not depart from the interests of those former colonizers. As the tool of pacification, the mosque is limited to providing a shell for controlled religious activities – a point that is restated by Nezar AlSayyad and İpek Türeli: 'In the modern era, as many of their former functions have been assumed by state authorities, mosques have restricted their work to religious activities, leading to the "secularization" of public services and spaces, or, alternatively, to the "sacralization of the mosque."'[10]

Before going into more detail regarding the shape of the modernization process and the ensuing models, I want to focus on the meanings of freedom, and how these have moved from being inherent in the systems under Islam to becoming means of control under the Western counterpart. The most obvious manifestation of freedom is, as previously discussed, freedom from the fear of the unknown and the apprehension of uncertainty. Embodied in the fundamental monolithic message of Islam – that there is no god but the one God to whom everything reverts – uncertainty is embraced rather than feared, because there is trust in the caring hands of the Creator. This message liberates the believer from the threatening shadow of any other authority over his or her being. This is a liberty of spirit whose expressions were examined in previous chapters, but the liberty I am interested in here is one that relates to systems and processes, which reflects itself directly onto the world of building and onto matters of style.

In a study that examined the archives of the municipality of Nablus in Palestine, researcher and architect Abdalrahman Kittana sought to find alternative urban descriptions of the old Islamic city, where previously adjectives such as 'labyrinthine, labyrinth-like, maze-like, unplanned, formless, irregular, spontaneous, organic, chaotic, and similar labels have been employed to describe its complexity'.[11] Just as such labels indicate the Western perception of Muslim urbanization as one which lacks order or systematic development, they also obscure the true generative process of that environment, which Kittana sums up in one word: freedom. This freedom is based on the Islamic land code, which classifies property ownership into three levels of exercise of rights: the right to own, to use, and to control. In turn, there are three different levels of authority in the decision-making process: the public, the private and the collective.[12] Scholar Guy T. Petherbridge backs this point by stating that:

> Islamic settlements are neither fortuitous nor amorphous in their organization, and reveal a consistent underlying order of hierarchical sequences of access and enclosure responding to patterns of social intercourse and allegiance particular to Islamic society.... Islamic urban organization is the physical manifestation of the equilibrium between social homogeneity and heterogeneity, in a social system requiring both segregation of domestic life and participation in the economic and religious life of the community.[13]

The aforementioned 'physical manifestation of the equilibrium between social homogeneity and heterogeneity' is indeed the very definition of Islamic urbanization, and urban freedom is how it is manifested. In his research, Kittana brings to the fore the urban theory articulated by Besim Hakim, which highlights the Islamic principle of 'freedom to act'; namely, that 'any party, be it individual or collective, possesses the right to act and decision-making concerning the development and use of their spaces. However, this freedom is judiciously counterbalanced by the right to react as guided by the principle of prevention of harm and damage.'[14] Interestingly, Kittana's research of the archival records reveals 'multiple instances wherein the right to react is practiced concerning property matters', and where processes of mediation and public negotiation 'frequently play a pivotal role in achieving closure'.[15] The fact that Muslim urban configuration has historically been determined through a dynamic paradigm of decision-making, which relies on all actors in the urban sphere, contrasts with the top-down

Western model of city-building. In the same spirit, mosque-building as an act of freedom cannot be separated from city-building.

Principles such as 'parts of a whole' and 'reciprocity' are introduced by Kittana's research as tenets upon which the dynamics of the creation and development of the Muslim city depend. As indicated by the language that is used (as found in municipal records and court archives), the Muslim urban perspective views the components of city structures through the lenses of both interdependence and dynamism. Buildings are not categorized as 'units'; rather, they are spaces, elements and parts, constituting many facets that can be freely shared, exchanged and negotiated. A section of a wall, an arch, and even the air over an entrance are all examples of urban components with associated stories, as Kittana's research recounts, of the transfer of rights, sale, leasing, construction, or shared usage. Civil conflicts are resolved through hierarchical levels of negotiations, and urban solutions are devised in a free realm of architectural innovation:

> The fluid nature of the decision-making process, shaped by the paradigm of 'decision and counterbalance' and intensified by the possibility of dividing the whole structure into parts, bestows an array of boundless intervention options upon ordinary individuals.... Consequently, the intricate interweaving and apparent irregularity within the urban fabric of the *Kasbah* [old city] emerge organically over time through the cumulative impact of numerous micro-level decisions. These decisions are frequently motivated by mundane everyday requirements rather than deliberate intent to create complexity.... The research concludes that the urban landscape's physical attributes of the city in the Islamic World, encompassing labyrinthine characteristics, irregularities, and intertwinements, are rooted in deeply embedded socio-spatial norms, religious endorsements, and hierarchically controlled rules.[16]

At the heart of this intricate and sophisticated manifestation of urban freedom lies the mosque, as both an urban and cultural centre. The way it is built is part of this network of connections, and involves the same level of economic freedom that freedom of property allows, when it comes to the making of transactions. By contrast, the Western approach to property shows a highly dogmatic attitude, which refuses Islamic intricacy and resorts to rigid zoning and authoritative bureaucratic approaches.

In Istanbul, where secularization has created a rigid paradigm shift towards comprehensive top-down zoning, freedom has become a scarce currency. After delivering the talk I was invited to give, I was approached by a fellow architect. Like me, she wore a headscarf. She found my presence as a speaker most bizarre: how had I been accepted by the Turkish 'elite'? How come the West found my thoughts worthy of recognition? She rightly concluded that the latter was a cause for the first; namely, that because the West had studied my work and validated me, it was possible for my words to be heard in her city. Another woman followed me out, and without any preamble she informed me that I should know that I was not an Arab, and that Syria is not Arabic. It wasn't clear to me why she thought it was so important for me to 'know' this, but it was enough for me to see how disdainful she felt about embracing an identity that was not chauvinistically supported.

Perhaps this misapprehension of my Arab and Muslim identity could explain how piety in Turkey had become attached to materialism[17] and economic achievement. Private schools, gated communities and shopping malls have become associated with the new religious class,[18] as the Gezi protests also indicate. The old association between virtue and austerity and self-reliance is no longer valid. The reason for this could be a reaction against the prejudice that once correlated modernity with secularism. One can see this race towards materialism as a form of self-validation in a game that was initiated by the secular elite who inherited Muslim lands.

Meeting modernity

Independence and freedom were the vaunted principles of the new order that followed the dismantling of the last Islamic ruling system – that of the Ottomans. Across Muslim lands, the era of empires was terminated by the advent of Europe-infatuated ruling classes, who were soon overtaken by colonizers including the British, the French, the Italians and the Dutch. As we have seen in the example of the South Indian Ocean regions (see p. 176), the focus of these colonizers was the extraction of wealth, which involved application of the harshest of means. Ruling native elites, who were installed in order to control the ensuing public independence movements and to maintain the interests of the withdrawing colonial powers, belonged to one of two opposing Western camps: socialist or capitalist. For example, Soviet interests were forwarded in socialist republics such as Syria, Egypt and Algeria, whereas American interests focused on oil-rich countries where monarchy was the rule of choice:

> As new territories were implicated as puzzle pieces within the shifting map of U.S. and Soviet influence during the Cold War, the newly post-colonial states of the Arab and Persian Gulf gained importance both as potential allies, buttressed through the developmental framework of foreign technical assistance, and as sources for the increasingly valuable strategic currency of oil.[19]

Architecture was used to map out an environment where control could be exercised over the various fields of life: the term used was 'modernity'. Two main objectives lay behind the modern building model: a) control of extracted wealth, and b) control of the masses and the narrative. The previously discussed urban freedom, which allowed the participation and active engagement of ordinary citizens, did not fit the agenda of control. Furthermore, the mosque – as a centre of such public freedom – represented the risk of the expression of anti-state sentiments. All aspects related to the mosque were therefore made subject to state control: the content of sermons was dictated by the new regimes, and the mosque personnel were appointed by Ministries of Religious Affairs. Private/public initiatives were now restricted to applications for authorization to build a mosque or to raise funds for its construction, while architectural style could generally only be determined by the ruling authority; in addition, the mosque was always to be kept closed after prayer hours.

As a child of the 1980s, I witnessed the hysterical control that the Assad regime imposed on mosque attendance in the wake of the Hama massacre, in which the regime meted out indiscriminate punishment on members of the opposing Muslim Brotherhood. Young men were followed by informants, with the aim of reporting on whether they were frequent attendants of any mosque. Prayer became the activity of 'terrorists', at which point mosques were only open briefly to the elderly and to undercover agents. China is today applying an extreme version of this approach on its Muslim Uyghurs, with reports of state persecution and detention contrasting shockingly with the past when Islam was freely practised.

'Modernization' was the overarching project under which the new regimes exerted their control over free societies. New development projects were planned in all the Muslim nations. The mosque was retained as a centrepiece of the new towns and neighbourhoods, but it was a government-controlled type of mosque, built as part of the 'modern' image of the country, where style was not so much the issue as the obliteration of urban complexity through new legislation and new models of urban governance that stripped away freedom and replaced it with the so-called modernity.

Design competitions were an essential part of this process. The international competition for a state mosque in Baghdad in 1982 is considered one of the most important architectural events in the region and in the history of the modern mosque, because it generated a great deal of debate around the issue of style. Although the state mosque was never built, the proposals from the participating A-listers remain of relevance to this day.

As part of the Baghdad Pact (a pro-Western military alliance which was established in 1955 and dissolved in 1979), Iraq had already come under British and American influence: indeed, the master plan for Baghdad was produced in 1956 by the British firm of Minoprio, Spencely and Macfarlane, as the Iraqi Development Board had hired the British civil servant Lord Salter as an advisor. During the same time period, the United States Operations Mission (USOM) was operating in Iraq, with a technical aid programme that focused on infrastructure and community 'development'. The architectural scene was comprised of an elite class of foreign-educated professionals, such as Qahtan Awni (trained at the University of California Berkeley), Jaafar Allawi (trained at the University of Liverpool) and Rifat Chadirji (trained at the Hammersmith School of Arts and Crafts in London), among many others.

Chadirji initiated the state mosque competition, and acted as convenor and chairman of the jury. He also appointed the selection committee to evaluate the entries. 'Monumentality, strong identity, and synthesis of past and present' were the main requirements of the brief.[20] The proposals of Robert Venturi, as well as those of the German-trained Jordanian architect Rasem Badran, stood out for the boldness of their aesthetic choices. Even though the project was abandoned, I believe that the importance of this competition lies in that it marks the beginning of a transformation in how mosques were built, and who built them.

In Baghdad, starting in 1958, Walter Gropius and his team The Architects Collaborative had undertaken the design of the University of Baghdad – a commission that was facilitated by the Harvard-trained son of the Iraqi prime minister, Nizar Ali Jawdat, and his then-girlfriend (later wife) Ellen Bovey. The campus included a mosque, which Gropius designed in the shape of a land-bound dome, resting on the ground at three points, and with its centralized space exposed through large glazed façades. The mosque was conceived as a landmark more than anything else: the beginnings of pastiche with a reductionist abstraction outlook can clearly be seen. Together with the monumental eclecticism that was predominant in proposals for the design of the Baghdad state mosque, they make up the two main trends which still dominate the debate around the modern mosque.

Indonesia is the country in which the concept of the state mosque was introduced.[21] With the largest Muslim population worldwide,[22] Indonesia chose to commemorate its independence from Dutch colonization with a design competition, initiated in 1955, to build the Istiqlal Mosque. Istiqlal means 'independence' in Arabic and, as the name indicates, the mosque project was envisioned as a political statement combining the ideals of the secular state and the image of the Islamic nation.

Basing his ideas on principles of the Pancasila (the foundational ideology of Indonesia, formulated in 1945), the nation's leader Sukarno wanted the mosque to embody a statement of both modernity and nationalism. In his biography, Sukarno emphasized the power of symbolism in relation to the new mosque: 'we're people who thrive on symbols', he wrote.[23] The chosen design was therefore packed with symbolism and direct references to concepts that related to the new nation. The architect who won the bid was Friedrich Silaban, the son of a priest. The location selected for the mosque was close to Jakarta Cathedral, on the site of an old Dutch fortress.

At the finished mosque, propaganda went hand in hand with modernism: in place of systems that produced outcomes, images were imposed to indicate labels. Religious harmony and the 'message of tolerance' are highlighted in crude symbolism, as also seen at the Sheikh Zayed Grand Mosque in Abu Dhabi (see p. 152). The two rectangular courtyards that precede the square prayer hall are oriented towards the neighbouring Merdeka Square National Monument, in order to indicate their interconnected national significance. The architectural language and treatment – post-and-lintel concrete structures, with flat roofs and unadorned concrete piers that rise to the height of the building – are reminders of socialist rational architecture. A monumental dome raised over twelve pillars, symbolizing the Prophet's birthday (the 12th of Rabi' al-Awwal, the third month of the Islamic calendar), joins with the single pencil-style minaret as a remnant of an Islamic image that pertains to the victorious Ottomans. Numerical symbolism continues to riddle the design: from the five floors of the five pillars of faith, to the seven doors of the seven heavens, and so on.

Government manifestos, design competitions, foreign advisors and a foreign-trained architectural elite are the components of the modernized era in Muslim lands. The location and the style of new mosques have been determined as part of a political scheme that uses a policy of pacification in parallel with a policy of control. Architects such as Le Corbusier, Michel Écochard and Constantinos Doxiadis were handed regions of Muslim lands to reshape accordingly.

The Greek-born Doxiadis had a significant impact. He is known as the father of ekistics, the urban theory he devised to introduce his ideas

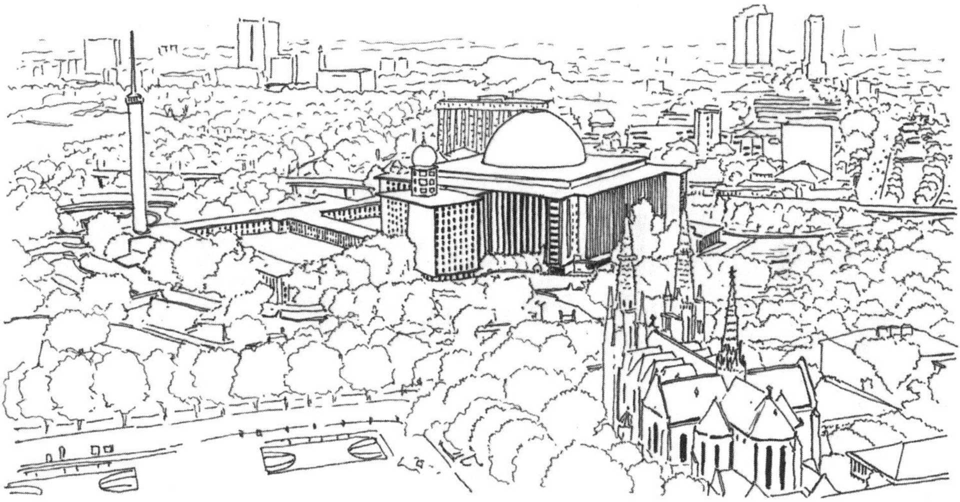

The Istiqlal Mosque (Mosque of Independence) in Jakarta, Indonesia

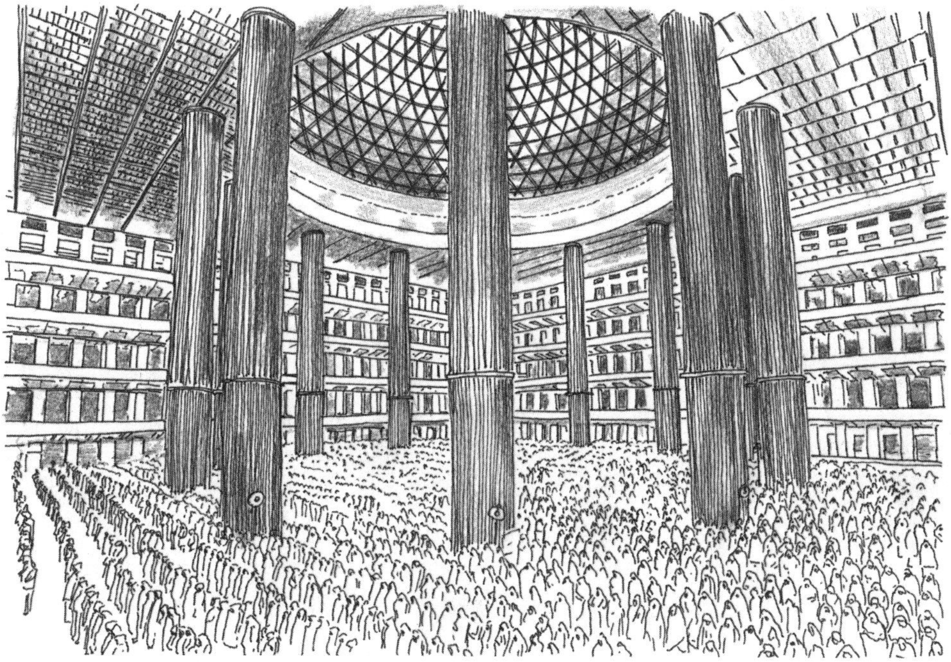

The Istiqlal Mosque: an interior view of the Indonesian congregation (half men, half women) lined up for prayer

about human settlement and global cities. Part of Doxiadis's appeal was his use of computer data to illustrate his concepts for building communities and gauging adaptation to the growth and pace of the postwar city. In the 1960s, Doxiadis Associates (DA) ran The Human Community, a computer-assisted study project that was in the vanguard for architectural offices at the time: 'Doxiadis belonged to a cohort of international architects and intellectuals appraising the implications of new digital technologies for the future of cities.'[24] His planning ventures, which were guided with the type of technological determinism that would dominate the project of modernization in Muslim lands, were funded through his association with an American-run philanthropic organization: 'Constantinos Doxiadis' affinity with Ford Foundation's officials was the driving reason behind the expansion of DA in the developing world.'[25]

Indeed, '[i]n the Middle East, "D" stands for Doxiadis and development'[26] went the phrase. Apart from his work in Iraq and Saudi Arabia, Doxiadis's main contribution was the planning of Islamabad, the city which symbolizes the partition of British India into Muslim Pakistan and Hindu India. Control was the chief concern; instead of Karachi the port city, the Pakistani military regime wanted a more controlled city: 'The site for the new capital was chosen in 1959 by a Commission headed by General Mohammad Yahya Khan, then Chief of Staff of the Army, and advised by Doxiadis and Sir Robert Matthew, the chief co-ordinating architect.'[27] This abandonment of the free-trade-facilitating port city for one that would be under the watchful eye of the state instantly brings to mind a comparison with the history of Islam that was experienced at the monsoon mosques (see p. 177).

The national mosque – named after King Faisal of Saudi Arabia – was completed in Islamabad by 1986. Its location was part of Doxiadis's master plan, imagined against the backdrop of the Margalla Hills and combining both the image of a monumental state mosque and an isolated dramatic landmark. As the name implies, the project was sponsored by Saudi Arabia. The international competition for its design, which was initiated in 1968 and restricted participation to Muslim architects, was won by the Turkish architect Vedat Dalokay. His proposal, which incorporated a tent-like structure pinned to the ground with a

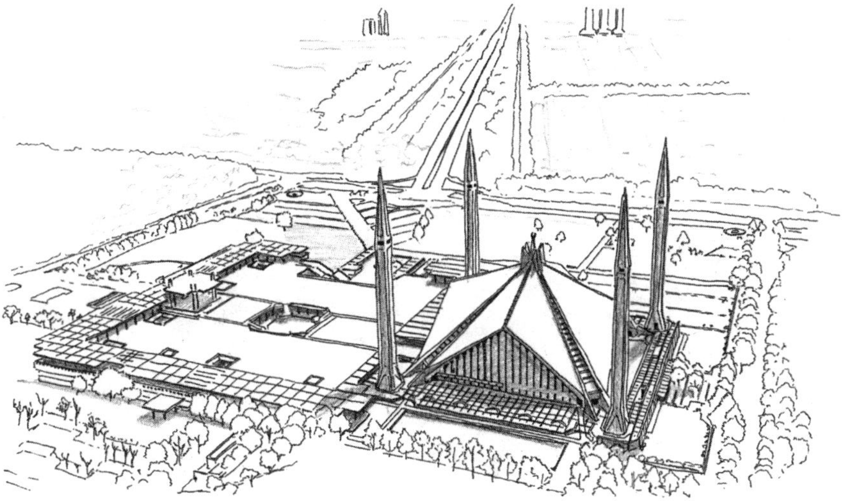

The Faisal Mosque in Islamabad, Pakistan: a view featuring the setting, which consists of a vast expanse of empty landscape away from the city

minaret at each of its four corners, is a reminder of Gropius's grounded dome but taking the abstraction a step further.

The prayer hall is 61 metres square (200 × 200 ft), spanned by triangular-shaped concrete panels that meet at the apex 40 metres (130 ft) above ground level. The glazed intervals between the panels are treated like screens, admitting natural light without exposing the space to the distracting outer world. Inside, a central spherical chandelier adorns the dramatic space, uninterrupted by any columns or pillars, thanks to the innovative engineering of the pyramidical structure. Sculptural qualities are emphasized through the freestanding *minbar* and the 'floating' platform-elevated *mihrab* in the form of an open Quran.

Dalokay's design for the mosque was in fact a recycled entry, having already won the Kocatepe Mosque competition in Ankara in 1957, albeit with a slight alteration from a shell dome to a tent-like structure. After ground was broken for the Kocatepe Mosque in 1967, Dalokay's modernist proposal was shelved and replaced with a historicist design by Hüsrev Tayla and Fatin Uluengin. This prompted an enduring controversy, as to whether the new mosque competed with the secular national emblem of Atatürk's Mausoleum.

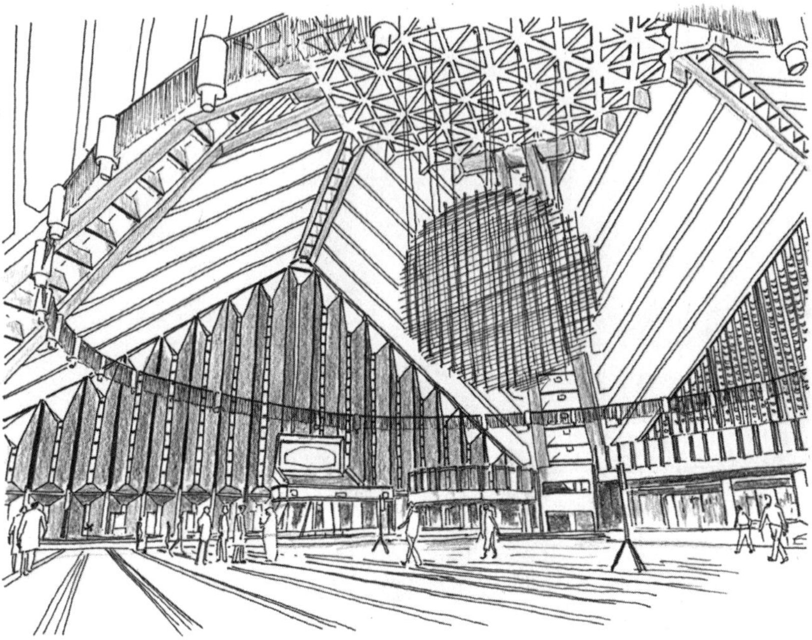

The Faisal Mosque: an interior view of the prayer hall

Turkey has been marching towards regimentation and centralization from as early as the sixteenth century. More precisely, this has been occurring since it became – in deviance from the spirit and systems of Islam – possessed by a lust for power, a power that it sought to convey through its mosques, thereby destroying their transmissive and distributive nature, as discussed above. Scholar Gülru Necipoğlu notes:

> [T]he unprecedented centralization of building construction associated with the establishment of the Hassa Mimarlari (Corps of Royal Architects) meant that the earlier pattern of decentralized patronage was at an end. Architects trained in the capital spread the Ottoman imperial style across the empire, which by then extended from central Europe to western Iran and dominated the whole eastern Mediterranean basin. This style no longer represented the regionalism of a frontier principality absorbing rather than generating influences, but a trans-regional idiom expressing the hegemony of a world empire.[28]

This centralization explains why it was so easy for modern Turkey to develop two such contrasting images in fierce competition for control; that of a secular past, and that of a religious past. Interestingly, the religious image seeks to resolve a hankering after the victorious Ottomans and an adaptation to economically high-achieving modernism. This marriage between the objectives of modernism and Islam is most bizarre, because the severances created by modernism cannot be compatible with the connections achieved by Islam.

In my book *Building for Hope* (2021), I describe the urban effects of modernism in terms of the 'Factory system': this relies on the machine-oriented reality that was created in the aftermath of the Second World War to take human settlement into strict production mode. The cost of this is a severance of all connections between humans and nature, as well as collective and personal endeavour. The values of 'individualism' and 'innovation' became marketing labels for what is, in essence, nothing other than a brutal regimentation of the environment in order to bring it to optimal production and to seize control over it. However, this has meant that everything must be explained in utilitarian terms; even spirituality. By the state's leaving nothing beyond the mathematics of immediate utility, religion has become a means to an end – a very dangerous thought.

It is misleading to think of modernism as merely a style; it is a mode of thought. I cannot think of a better example in this regard than New Gourna in Egypt, designed by Hassan Fathy. The new village was designed around a mosque, the whole concept being envisaged as 'an idealized vision of an arts and crafts ideology involving a rural community

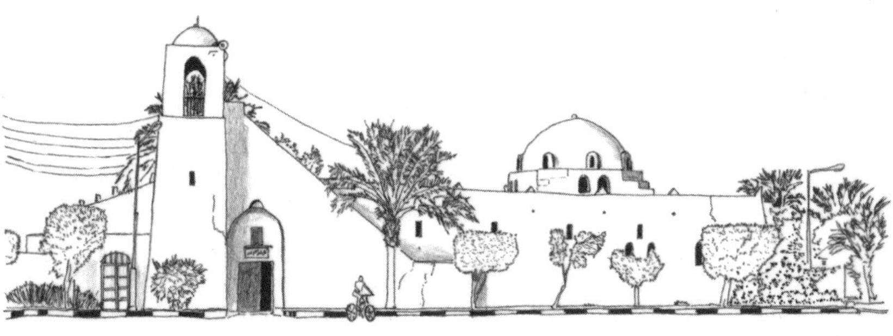

The New Gourna Mosque in Luxor, Egypt

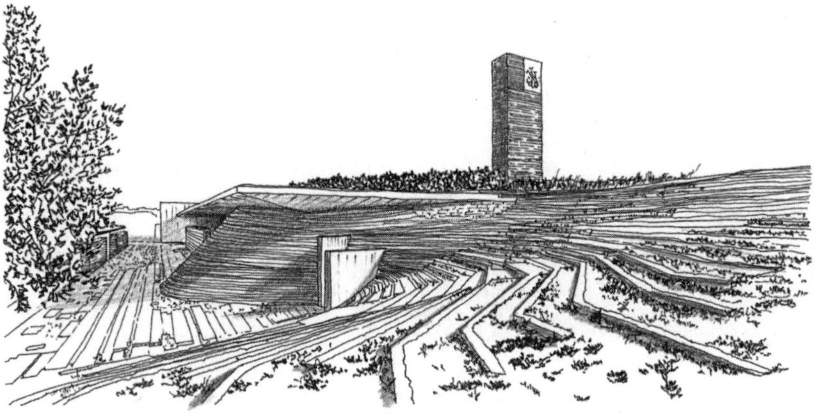

The Sancaklar Mosque in Büyükçekmece, Istanbul, Turkey

in which villagers were encouraged to participate in the process of planning and building'.[29] In fact, the project – which was undertaken by the Egyptian Department of Antiquities – was devised to stop local residents from looting and despoiling the neighbouring Tombs of the Nobles at Luxor. The entire population of the old village was thus displaced to New Gourna, which Fathy designed as a tribal village made of four sections, each led by an imam/tribal chief with the mosque at the centre. The mosque itself was also divided into four *iwans*, each belonging to a section of the village. New Gourna was never fully inhabited: Fathy's romanticized vision of an 'architecture for the poor' became a 'utopia' to inspire the elite but not the simple man. In my view, this type of separative thought belongs to modernity and not to Islam, where freedom is attached to connectivity.

The Sancaklar Mosque on the outskirts of Istanbul, designed by architect Emre Arolat and completed in 2012, is an award-winning mosque. Situated within a neighbourhood of gated communities, the mosque was commissioned at the request of the wealthy Sancaklar family. The architect outlined his vision as aiming to 'address the fundamental issues of designing a mosque by distancing itself from the current architectural discussions based on form and focusing solely on the essence of religious space'.[30] This essence is created through an array

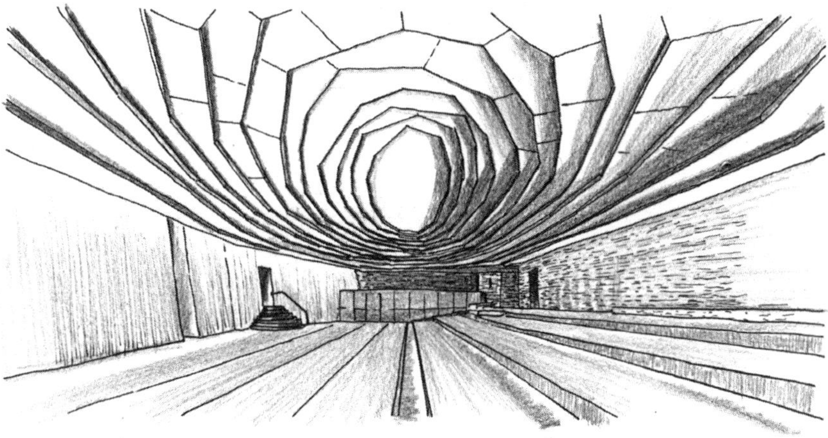

The Sancaklar Mosque interior of the prayer hall

of cast concrete walls and a contoured ceiling framing a 'cave-like' prayer hall. The building, which is clad with a combination of light grey stone and reinforced concrete, overlooks a plaza made up of shallow terraced steps, and it is entered via stepping stones over a pool of shallow water.

The minimalist, concealed mosque resembles the Mosque of the Grand National Assembly in Ankara, which conforms with the policy of pacification in which governments resorted to attaching a trophy mosque to their modernist parliaments. For this Parliament Mosque, the natural slope of the site was used to conceal the building's structure, which takes the form of graduated platforms fronted by an open plaza with a large pool of water.

Similarly, abstraction and reduction were chosen to express the modern character of the Sancaklar Mosque. In terms of urban planning, it is separated from the surrounding gated communities by a busy highway and tall stone walls. A freestanding monolithic tower signifies the abstraction of a minaret and indicates the otherwise concealed presence of the building. The architect explains this minimalist approach as a displacement of historical familiarity. However, to me it makes the building seem more like a cultural pavilion that is loaded with the burden of 'not saying' something, rather than actually saying it. The metaphor of the cave invokes the image of solitude and the act of separation, in contrast

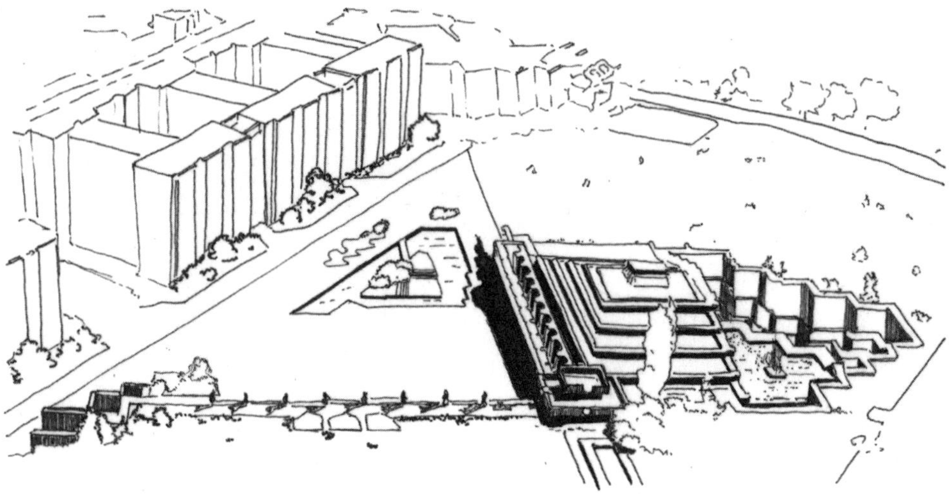

The Parliament Mosque (officially known as the Mosque of the Grand National Assembly) in Ankara, Turkey

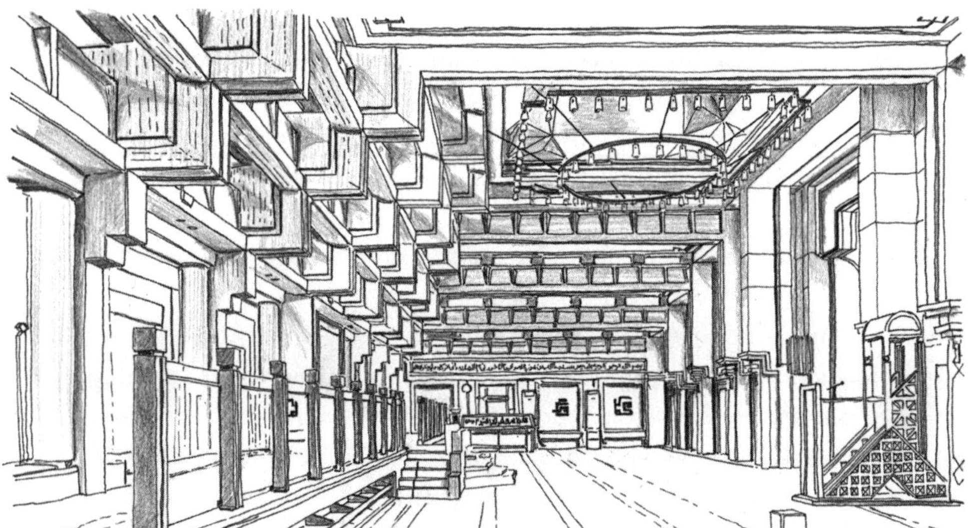

The Parliament Mosque: an interior view of the prayer hall

to the mosque's traditional pursuit of connection. This level of abstraction – whereby the building becomes emotively detached, deliberately not responding to its context but instead making the response about itself – is a symptom of the utilitarian mindset, which restricts expression to ideology instead of ideals.

Chapter 7

The Mosque and Modernity

'Architecture is more than a history of form and style: it is a product of cultural and environmental factors and an expression of the way of life of the people for whom it is built. The architecture of the Islamic world is the architecture of the Muslim people – from rulers and warriors, saints and teachers, merchants and travelers, to the modest family unit.'

GEORGE MICHELL[1]

The mosque of the 21st century

On the clocks of every Syrian, 6:18 am was the time after which the world was no longer the same. 'Syria without Bashar al-Assad' were the incredible words which marked that historic moment. The cage was finally open, and freedom was attained. The prisons were emptied, young men were able to leave their hideouts where they had been escaping military conscription, the displaced were free to come back, and people could finally speak without fear of persecution. The mosque was free again, too: sermons, preachers and congregants were no longer under the radar of surveillance. The media showed people dancing and chanting in the public squares, but what they didn't show was the squares of the universities.

All over Syria, students aligned in tight rows; young men, and behind them young women, turned towards the *qibla* and performed a group prayer. They were expressing their newly acquired freedom to pray, where this had previously been taboo. Indeed, reports were unearthed from the secret police archives giving instructions to delay the graduation of certain students and to penalize certain professors, either for praying or for going to the mosque. Praying in prison led to additional administration of torture, and praying at university could lead to arrest and incarceration; at the very least, it raised an eyebrow.

For one year, between 2021 and 2022, I taught at a private university located between Homs and Damascus. I was driven by the thought that it was through education that we could rebuild, even while the regime was in the midst of destroying. To my surprise, I discovered that my boss was the owner of the university and the son of the first secretary to Hafez al-Assad (father of Bashar, and himself president of Syria from 1971 to 2000). Whenever my boss appeared, a sense of fear and apprehension loomed over the teaching halls. He made a habit of mocking the appearance of employees who didn't dress up to the nines, especially if they were head-scarfed. Speaking in the local dialect of the village from where he and most of the students came was prohibited. Everyone was to speak in 'white dialect', which was the closest to the speech of the capital, preferably throwing in an English expression every now and then to prove 'enlightenment'. Any diversion from these 'standards' would be met with violent scolding and public shaming.

On my first day, I wore jeans, an oversized shirt and trainers. When the *Azan* was called, I enquired as to where I could pray, and whether the campus's mosque was open. I asked my question casually, after a staff meeting, and eyes widened. I was told that prayer was 'not OK' on campus, and that the mosque was permanently closed 'after some events'. Naïvely, I thought I would ask the boss himself where I could pray; after all, we were Muslims, so why should it be a problem to ask the question? 'You can pray wherever you want' came back the answer. Just like that, I was given permission, my casual style was never scrutinized, and in the moment it seemed like 'special treatment'. After a while, it became clear that, as had happened to me in Turkey, my reputation as someone who was 'accepted in the West' gave me a green card in non-religious contexts where prestige and Islam were otherwise not compatible.

For the lesson plan, I had to come up with project ideas to be designed by the students as assignments. One of my projects was 'how to design a mosque': I realized that we were never taught how to design one, although new ones were constantly being built. From my office windows I looked out at the campus's mosque, which – like the rest of the buildings – was designed in a brutalist style: exposed cement and rigid forms were set against the backdrop of bare mountains. In the midst of the arid steppe all around, this university was the project which revitalized the village of its owner; everyone worked for him. The students were asked to design his dreams: a tower so high that it could be seen from Lebanon; the diversion of the Assi River so it would flow into the limestone desert lands of the village; merging all the surrounding villages into one metropolitan area; and creating an artificial ski slope with a snow machine. As the perfect modernist, he loathed all that was organic, local or natural; for him, machinery was the ideal replacement for humanity.

When I proposed the mosque project, he quickly dismissed it, saying that I was 'going to get the university into trouble', alluding to the secret service. I replied sarcastically, 'How about a prison design project then?' Undeterred by the rejection of my request, I later took the students to the campus's mosque. I asked them to reimagine it on their drawing pads, proposing an alternative image. As expected, what I got back were either further abstractions of the current design or a throwback to a classic original. I tried to explain to the class that what they were doing was producing imitations of an existing image, and not an actual response. These were not answers to my question; they were simply echoes of another distant echo. One student responded, 'How would *you* design a mosque?' I took a moment, then said to her, 'I don't know. I don't have an answer to the question either. I simply know what's missing, but I don't know how to fill the void.' Silence fell over the class, as we all pondered the dilemma in a shared moment of confusion.

It is a confusion that conjures two internal debates: one is around architecture, and one is around Islam. The bungled state in which architecture has found itself, after embracing modernism as the aftermath project of the Second World War, raises the question of the style of our times. Some advocate recourse to historicism – as seen in certain trends in mosque design – and believe that retrieving some sort of classicism might rescind the harms done by modernism to the environment and to society. Others seem to try and avoid architecture altogether, by reducing its activity to that of the vernacular. To many, architecture is gauged by the level of rectification it can provide – how 'green' or how 'advanced' it is – and not by its qualification as an *art*, in the sense of invoking higher meanings and creating connections, whereby it forms a real response and an experience.

What it means to be 'modern' is just as confusing when it comes to the question of how to be a Muslim today. Being associated with regression is something most Muslims have to resist. However, this is the product of our times, rather than of Islam itself. As we have seen (p. 176), Islamic modernity brings in innovation, progress and freedom; and this is never imposed from the outside as a top-down tool, but rather emanates from within as a pronounced state of the soul. Islamic modernity does not 'start', as Western modernity started (within a relatively recent time period). Islam, when followed correctly, is timeless, and therefore always 'modern'. Colonial modernity embodies the exact opposite, in both its own lands and the lands of Muslims. The evidence for this claim can be easily traced in buildings, as in systems.

Therefore, the conundrum of how to be a modern Muslim is not actually a question of how to be a Muslim of the current time and place; it is, rather, a question of how to be subjected to an imposed project while carrying the inherent freedom of Islam within. The mosque represents this challenge at its apotheosis. As scholar Azim Nanji states: 'The mosque, perhaps more than any other form of building in contemporary Islam, reflects the inherent tension between two aspects of the modernization process: the growing differentiation in and separation of spheres of activity and life and the seemingly contrary desire to reintegrate these spheres with "Islam".'[2]

DIFC Grand Mosque, completed in 2019, is located on the upper floor of the Dubai International Financial Centre on Gate Avenue. Designed by RMJM, who also worked on the broader Gate Avenue retail, dining and entertainment complex, it is an example of the current trend in mosque building, whereby appearing conspicuously modern is the goal. The mosque is a white cube coupled with a freestanding minaret, both dotted with perforations to create what the architects called an

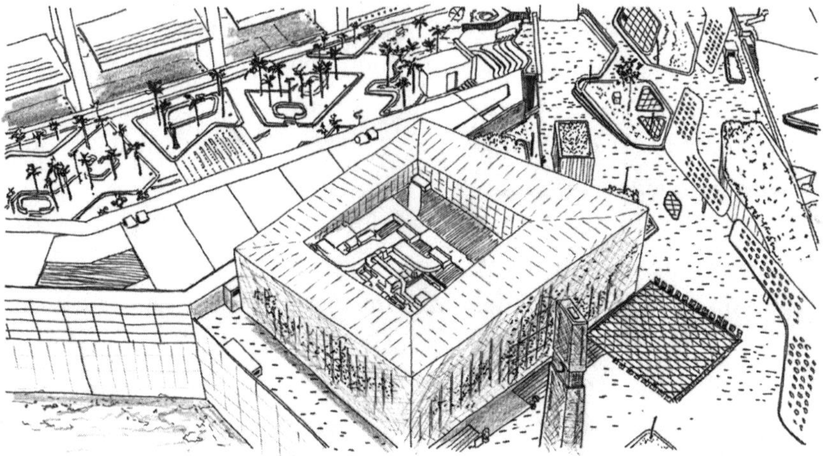

The DIFC Grand Mosque, on the upper floor of the Dubai International Financial Centre (DIFC), Dubai, UAE

'urban lantern at night'.[3] Their objective, as they put it, was to build 'a modern and non-conformist facility'.[4]

On their website, RMJM answered a question about the difference between designing religious buildings and retail or commercial projects by stating that there 'isn't that much of a difference' from a technical point of view. To them, the difference lay in the regulations that they had to consider, and in the 'assigned expectations' with regard to the traditions associated with religious buildings. They noted that they did not have to deal with such expectations in the case of the DIFC Grand Mosque, because they were 'suggesting something new and unique'.[5] In fact, the design was only 'new and unique' and 'non-conformist' in relation to a new trend for mosque architecture; in relation to the modern mainstream, the building is none of the above.

The white perforated box has recently become a favourite theme in the Gulf region, as seen at the Mosque of Mohamed Abdulkhaliq Gargash, also in Dubai. Completed in 2021, this mosque was designed by Dubai-based studio Dabbagh Architects; the UK-educated Saudi architect Sumayya Dabbagh represents a rare appearance of a female practitioner in the field of mosque design. The brief for the project,

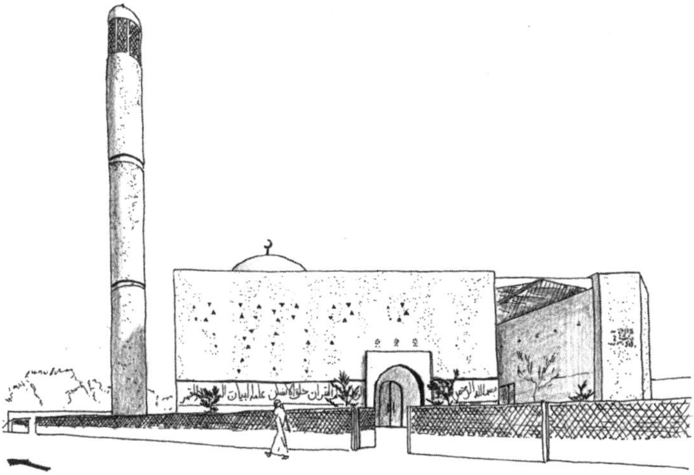

The Mosque of Mohamed Abdulkhaliq Gargash in Dubai, UAE

which was funded by the Gargash family, called for a departure from opulence and status toward a preferred simplicity and minimalism, according to the architect.[6] With regard to the layout, the prayer hall is separated from the ablution facilities and service amenities by an open corridor that contains a water feature and is covered with a perforated canopy. A band of calligraphy, featuring verses from the Quran, wraps around the exterior. 'The intent is to evoke a sense of the sacred … [an] intangible end result is created through these tangible means,' explains the architect.[7]

Remarkably, the twin examples of the DIFC Grand Mosque and the Mosque of Mohamed Abdulkhaliq Gargash have two contradictory backdrops – one lies at the heart of opulence, and the other departs from it – and yet they use almost exactly the same language, form and aesthetics. With their bland white boxes, they are reminiscent of the 'white dialect' enforced in the halls of the university between Homs and Damascus; a deliberate act of conformity, and no freedom of expression. This says more about modernity than it does about its architects: in our mosques, as in our houses, we are left with the white cubes of a dentist's office, decorated with fine lines of gold and beige, where 'light is filtered'

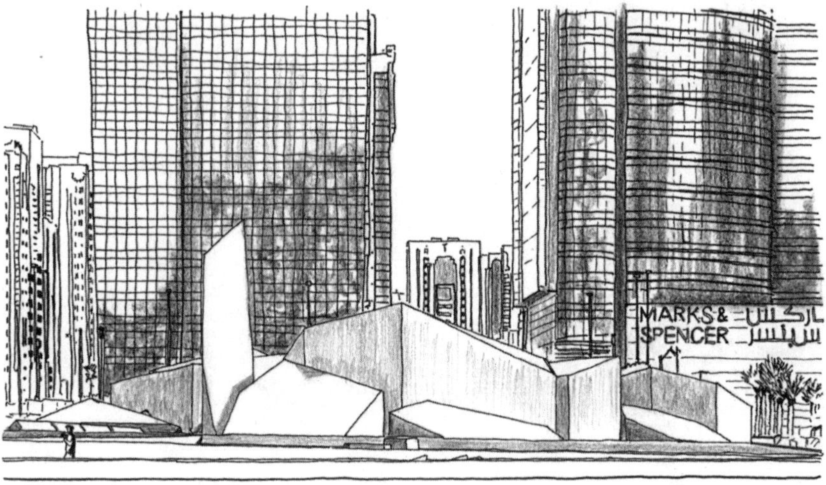

Al Musalla Mosque in Abu Dhabi, UAE

in order to create atmosphere and achieve 'elegance'. But do these tactics add any meaning to our lives? Do they hold any mystery, or induce any wonder? On the contrary, they are abrupt white-dialect responses that are almost robotic in their essence.

Meanwhile, the Danish studio CEBRA built the ultimate abstraction of a mosque in Abu Dhabi, on the Qasr al-Hosn site. Completed in 2019, Al Musalla is part of a wider masterplan commissioned by the Department of Culture and Tourism of Abu Dhabi. The development zone is bordered by grid-planned highways, isolating the square plot of land where the adjacent historic landmark of the Qasr al-Hosn fort sits, surrounded by a forest of glass towers. The architects divided the plot diagonally, creating a dualistic programme that features two contrasting landscapes. In the zone around the fort, they left the landscape of the desert, reinstating the building as a freestanding landmark in the sand. The opposite zone has been paved and programmed in a gradual transition that aims to combine the desert landscape with the structure of the modern city grid.[8] The Musalla Mosque is located within this 'cultural park'. With its series of jagged, interlocking, rock-like volumes, the mosque has been designed to appear as if it is springing from the earth. The rational division of the site continues in the overall layout of the

Musalla: two main 'flows' were created, one for men and a smaller one for women. Connection between the individual volumes of the building was achieved by light-filled glass tubes bridging over water, which, according to CEBRA, 'symbolically purifies the mind when moving from one area to the next'.[9]

The image of rocks rising from a pool of water is apparently the architects' interpretation of 'the mud-crack patterns of Abu Dhabi's coastal desert landscape'. The water is also intended to separate the mosque from its surroundings, in order to 'provide a greater sense of privacy and seclusion'. On the inside, the building is themed to inspire a cave-like experience: rock-like forms hang from the ceiling and outline the walls, which are clad in copper to create what the architects call 'endless reflections of light'. Of their copper-clad cave, CEBRA go on to note: 'It illustrates how man has always looked up into the skies, wondering and reflecting on one's own existence.'[10]

As we can see from the undercover theme of 'complexes' and 'centres', mosque design has become a cultural exercise. Furthermore, abstraction has evolved from the stripping out of historical forms to the

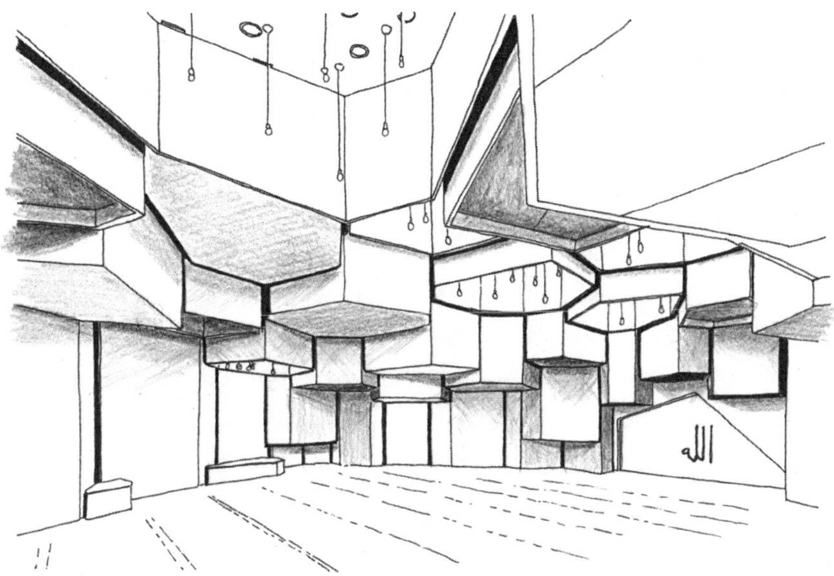

Al Musalla Mosque: an interior view showing the cave-like prayer hall

revival of natural forms, much like an advertising exercise in graphic arts school. When I was teaching, I faced the same challenge with my students, who were taught that architecture can be treated as a graphic exercise, based on the Danish school of graphics which uses diagrams to analyze a site and deconstruct it into a set of components that need to be 'reinvented'. This source of inspiration is the biggest challenge to modern architecture, because it refuses to connect to the world and to the demands of the spirit. Hence its constant attempts to remove shapes from their contexts and to play with their scales and dispositions, calling the entire exercise 'innovation'. However, it is far from innovative to merely disrupt and disconnect. Innovation takes place in the realm of *connection* between the rules of the universe and the rules of the soul.

Humanity's contribution lies in dealing with gravity, the laws of physics and the laws of chemistry in the material world. It transforms the challenge of these laws into service of the multiple functions that are necessary to encompass human activity. The way this service is achieved is the same as the way poetry is composed: the concise and compact can at the same time be rhythmic and harmonious. It is an act of balancing, and an act of dancing. Every culture brings to the fore its distinct qualities depending on its way of connecting with the universe, highlighting what matters the most to its collective spirit and its unique context. Modernity obliterates these connections by subduing the voice of the spirit under the regimented hammer of 'the Factory'. In this world, we are told that all the big questions have been answered, and there is no need for art to deal with any of them. Therefore, when it comes to the mosque, we encounter ideas like the primitive 'cave' chamber, where humanity is still searching for its creator on an isolated island surrounded by water. This doesn't just slash away thousands of years of civilization; it takes the soul and art back to square one.

Social agreement

Foreign architects, systems, trends and education have come to dominate the landscape of contemporary mosque building. Ideology has played its part at both ends: at home, and outside. Thus far, it has become clear that ideology is both the cause and result of the destruction and dismantling of both systems and ideals, as well as the replacement of freedom with control and restriction.

The rift between the past and the present has a parallel in non-Muslim lands. There is therefore a double rift when it comes to the discussion of the mosque in those regions, where one finds a rejection of modernism as well as a rejection of Islam. A false correlation has arisen between the two, with both being perceived as a threat to Western civilization. While modernism – as a cultural movement, signifying grand utopian visions – has been cast aside in favour of postmodernism, the West is still deeply invested in the pursuit of ever-onward growth when it comes to modernity, with its emphasis on capitalism, consumerism, individualism, secularism and technological progress. Those who demonize Islam are mostly those who hold modernity to be the epitome of Western civilization and seek to impose it on Muslim regions. And when the outcome of such a policy is the fragmentation and destruction of those regions, which in effect leads to the migration of their populations to the West, those same Western voices blame deterioration on the migrants, who become accused of being the sole spoilers of two worlds. In contrast to the Eastern regions of the world, where trade and tolerance were the means by which Islam entered established communities, in Europe – as in America and Australia – Muslim communities were formed as a consequence of Western colonial exploitation and destruction of homelands, and the subsequent migration (or subjugation) of native peoples.

Akel Kahera tells the story of the American mosque of the 'slave community': 'Long before the arrival of Muslim immigrants in the 1930s – from the Middle East, the Indian subcontinent, and other parts of the Muslim world – there was a significant Muslim presence in North America.'[11] The over three thousand mosques in America today, which serve the six to eight million adherents from sixty or more ethnic groups,[12] found their way to existence after a long struggle with oppression: 'The American Muslim slave community, although very devout, was hindered by the subjugation and inhuman treatment of slavery and by the restriction placed on religious practice in general among slaves. Furthermore, archaeological evidence that can identify sites where mosques were possibly built in the antebellum period has yet to be discovered.'[13]

To Kahera, who is an African American convert, social agreement is the source of unity in Muslim aesthetics: 'The spatial qualities of Muslim aesthetics have to do with agreement, accord, and conformity. The dialogue among them is architecture, and the unity and ordering of aesthetics perceived in any outcome is necessarily responsive to each quality.'[14] Kahera's idea about social agreement is inspired by the writings of Jaan Holt, the Estonian architect and professor emeritus of Virginia Tech, who, according to Kahera, raises the issue of public gathering from the perspective that suggests that 'the structure of a mosque is very much a part of collective agreement (*ijma*) and that it is indeed human agreement that matters the most'.[15]

The word *ijma* is Arabic for 'consensus', and it is also a term that refers to consensus (among Islamic scholars) as one of the sources for Islamic law (*sharia*): 'Holt's remarks seem to suggest that consensus (*ijma*), not discord, is capable of providing the inspiration for aesthetic comprehensibility. If we explore this reasoning further it is possible that the petition for *ijma* is meant to rescue the client/end user from selfishness, and the architect from the pitfalls of mediocrity, by yielding vigorous and responsible solutions that corroborate the aesthetics of monotheism.'[16]

Rescuing the client from selfishness and the architect from the pitfalls of mediocrity are indeed the main challenges before the project of the mosque, especially in our modern world where the process of creating a building has become far more complex and diffuse in comparison to the relationship of the past between architect and patron, or the simpler and smaller-scale endeavour between builder and owner. Today, the players include a greater number of legislators, contractors and bureaucrats. To achieve social agreement, the mosque project now involves the institution of a committee, whose task is to mediate the interests of all involved, while maintaining the sacredness of the mosque as a house of God. These committees act like civil juries, representing different members and working to reconcile the mundane demands of the project, such as budget, plot and construction requirements, with the spiritual purpose of the mosque as a place of worship and public gathering. It is a modern response to the rifts of our times, but in most instances it proves to mirror the rifts instead of patching them up.

In his essay 'Brother in Islam, Please Draw us a Mosque', Gülzar Haider gives an illuminating account of his experience as a novice filled with the ebullience of modernistic dreams, attempting – with a young Muslim colleague – to design a proposal for the competition for the Grand National Mosque in Islamabad (which became the Faisal Mosque; see p. 186): 'St. Mark's, Ronchamp, Guggenheim, and a heavy dose of abstracted calligraphy; it was sure to win the hearts of any jury, we thought.'[17] Some years later, he went on to design a mosque for the migrant Muslim community in Canada. His vivid and amusing account, replete with details of the strictures imposed by the mosque committee, describes the painful reality of taking a mosque project through to completion, when the committee consists of an assembly of bureaucratic and conflicting camps of arbiters of both faith and style. Haider describes himself as a 'worn-out sailor with many tales to tell', after dealing with eight committees in the span of twenty years.[18] During this time, like any Muslim architect, he was pushed by the various committees 'to perform a minor miracle of designing a mosque with infinite space and zero cost'.[19] All the manipulations drive the architect to declare his frustration: 'Repeatedly, I get seduced by the mosque committees promising me credit in the life "hereafter" and end up in painfully one-sided, almost exploitative contracts in this life "here". A scream remains muffled in my chest, and I am afraid that if it ever escapes it will startle the angels.'[20]

From his excoriating experiences, Haider draws four conclusions that broadly sum up the intellectual and economic disparities he is forced to navigate, with regard to both mosque committees and clients. The first is the mismatch between the clients' 'grand imaginations and harsh realities'[21] – a tragic irony that is best alluded to in Haider's words: 'Little wonder that whenever a Muslim bank or an airline publishes a calendar of mosques, their torn pages start to appear in the mosque committee meetings.'[22] The second is 'the debate on the sources of funds: from total self-reliance' through to approaching 'guilt-ridden princes'.[23] The third identifies the presence of 'the opposing forces of voluntarism and professionalism',[24] where a clash between inexperienced and ignorant volunteers and intellectual professionals is almost inevitable. Finally, there is the recurrent issue of architectural expression, dominated by debate between the *avant-gardists* and the classicists:

> There are generally two positions held by the protagonists of a mosque as an essential symbol of Islamic presence: one that wishes change through technology and modernity, and the other that aims for recognizable imagery. The first forms the majority and upholds change and adaptability as a strong formative force in all spheres of its newly adopted life in the non-Muslim West. And it is precisely this pursuit of novelty, as an end in itself, that has produced mosques with flying saucer domes and rocket minarets.[25]

This pursuit of novelty *as an end in itself* is the scar of the guilt complex – ultimately caused by the pressures of modernity – that Muslims in the West must bear, suffering the same agony that Haider describes. To redeem themselves from the association with retro-Islam, Muslims of the West (whether migrants or native converts) are practically forced to self-stamp themselves with modernity in order to be accepted and fully 'integrated'. This is problematic on many levels, the most obvious issue being the conflict between the *avant-gardists* and the classicists, the socialists and the capitalists, the liberals and the conservatives, around identity and style within Western societies. Although it might appear as if this conflict would be the same within Muslim societies in their homelands, it is in fact very different. Because Islam combines views both of abstraction and empathy – in other words, it stands on middle ground – it combines the ideals of the left and the right in its own unique whole.

I've personally experienced the confusion this causes in the perception of my writings. On more than a few occasions, there have been attempts to categorize my work into one of the opposing intellectual camps: 'she writes about tradition and social cohesion like a dyed-in-the-wool conservative. On the other hand, she writes about colonialism and financialization like an ardent leftist', one article stated.[26] However, the paradox is resolved once my work is viewed in the context of Islam, where both schools of thoughts are brought into balance. Muslims in Western contexts are often drawn into adopting one of the political camps, and this then forces them to live in an internal contradiction, which eclipses an aspect of their faith in the shadow of their political allegiance.

Gülzar Haider describes his own struggle when attempting to reconcile 'mosqueness' within the interior of his design for the Islamic Society of North America in Plainfield, Indiana, with a 'veiled', almost anonymous exterior, in order to avoid the perils of an 'Arabian Nights'-type misunderstanding from the non-Muslim host community. He notes that this discreet exterior later caused his clients to express 'what a Freudian might diagnose as "dome and minaret envy".'[27] These are understandably the words of the 'worn-out sailor', as they highlight the divide within the diasporic Muslim communities, where pressures come from outside as much as from inside.

Just as distance from the heart of Islam once affected the practice of Muslims in the East, so this distance – coupled with pressures exerted on Muslim communities to 'prove their innocence' and to ride the wave of 'modified Islam', often emanating from the UAE and Saudi Arabia – makes it practically impossible to find a balanced and unified vision of how to be a Muslim of one's own time and place. Between the traditionalists' clutching onto outdated and rigid imagery and the abolitionists' anti-mosque stance, the mosque in the West treads a fine line while carrying the weights of two camps: from one end, meeting the expectations of a Muslim community that is striving in search of an identity, while on the other finding a place to fit within an often hostile Western environment. If 'hostile' seems a strong word, I use it because it aptly describes the complex context in which antagonism is the result of a sustained fear of the unknown, amid all the rifts and games of ideology discussed above.

To give an example of a project in the West, the anthropologist Oskar Verkaaik documented the process of building a mosque in the Netherlands. To that end, he attended the mosque committee's meetings and followed the process into the rabbit hole of construction. Right from the outset, social resistance to the idea of building a mosque was notable: 'Regardless of whether it is a modern or conventional building, whether or not it has minarets, or whether architects and commissioners make an attempt to make it fit within its environment, a mosque is by definition seen as something foreign and inappropriate.'[28] Verkaaik noted that this perception is at its peak when the building does not yet exist, whereas protest often declines once the building has actually materialized. He also noticed that this 'anticipation of form is something both Muslims and protesters have in common', in ways that are 'often remarkably similar'.[29]

As in Gülzar Haider's account, Verkaaik's research paints a picture of an internal conflict between two generations and two viewpoints. On the one hand, the younger generation of Muslims aspired to realizing a modern image of Islam that could be a source of pride, as well as a means of integration. On the other hand, the older generation wanted to find a middle ground by using a patchwork of imagery that also included the experimental abstraction of modernity and postmodernism. Interestingly, this latter view was shared by the Dutch architect who was commissioned to design the mosque, as well as by the municipality that oversaw the project and wished to use it to revitalize the area where the mosque was to be located (as is commonplace, its community were inhabitants of an isolated and uninviting far reach of a city suburb).

Indeed, visibility is the number one issue when it comes to the project of the mosque in the West. The Muslim community wants to be *seen* for the combination of identities it embodies, often with an extended hand towards the place it strives to call home. However, this form of 'seeing' is not necessarily something the rest of Western society is interested in: 'Issues about form and design take place in a political sphere in which the presence of Islam is often seen in terms of cultural loss and social disintegration.'[30] There are of course more mundane issues that Verkaaik lists and that are part of the debate around the mosque project across the West, such as concerns about traffic and parking, fears about a drop in the value of real estate, and 'a deep distrust of the local state that is assumed to be sympathetic to Muslims and unresponsive to the desires of that part of the population that considers itself white and autochthonous'.[31] One of the most puzzling paradoxes with regard to the mosque in the West is that, at the same time as it is habitually 'outcast' both in a municipal and logistical sense, it has to defend itself against accusations that it is 'concealed'. For this reason, mosques increasingly feature more glass in their designs, in order to disclose the 'feared secrecy' to passersby and reveal Muslims praying and workshipping – the very activity that many people do not wish to see in their streets! Such irreconcilable demands on the design are met with yet more raised eyebrows if the resulting building appears *too* modern and context-sensitive.

In his book *The British Mosque*, Shahed Saleem follows the journey of the mosque in the United Kingdom from its initial phases of accommodation in converted houses and old properties to the process of integration through purpose-built mosques, where the challenges include sourcing funds, finding a site and commissioning an architect, in addition to addressing the protests of neighbourhood residents, as well as navigating the media and bureaucratic procedures. In all the accounts, the challenges are the same, and the labour of integration has failed to give birth to the anticipated maturity stage. In my view, the shortcomings are not strictly the responsibility of one party; rather, they are the outcome of sinister political ideologies among those who have interests in fanning the flames between different factions and those who prefer to keep a lid on knowing either oneself or the other.

Besides visibility, another of the key sources of contention surrounding the mosque is the issue of women's participation. Although there are different degrees of separation between the sexes in all the monotheistic religions, and the history of Islam is full of female patrons of mosques, as well as the colourful participation of women in all fields of Islamic civilization, the scrutiny of Islam in the West overlooks all these facts and accounts. Muslims often find themselves in the position of defender because of such wilful misunderstandings. There is no need for any defence, but – as regards the particular issue of prayer – it should be noted that, in the seminal example of the Prophet's Mosque, women prayed behind men for public propriety purposes. The separation is not rigid (women's sections can also be found next to men's, as well as above; no complete spatial disintegration is necessary, and many variations have come to exist): its purpose is simply to provide the right circumstances for optimal performance of the act of worshipping, without any unnecessary distractions. In terms of obligation, women have the discretionary right to pray at their homes as well as at the mosque.

The specific criteria for attendance are essentially that all congregants (men and women alike) are required to be in a state of ceremonial purity and to wear proper attire that is in line with Islamic codes of decency and that attracts no attention between the sexes. The freedom granted to women to choose where they wish to pray aligns with the Islamic concept of *satr* (which means the keeping of privacy). During their monthly periods (which are considered a state of non-purity), women are not permitted to perform the ritual of prayer. As one might imagine, a woman who wishes to maintain her privacy may not want others to keep track of her absence from the mosque due to physiological reasons. Of course, this is one simple instance of a whole web of reasons why a woman might not attend a mosque. While modern-day arrangements for childcare and domestic commitments reflect changing family roles that enable women to attend the mosque more frequently, the free choice for women to practise their worship according to their own management of time can be seen as an example of the legislative flexibility of Islam.

Many Muslim scholars have written books that tackle the subject of women's lifestyles and options, and explain them in context. For the interests of this book, and our focus here on both the West and Muslim homelands, it is important to note that the role of the mosque in the lives of Muslim women in the West has become far more vital than for their counterparts in Muslim countries, mainly because what has been outlined here has led to the alienation that women in the West often experience outside of the mosque.

The machine and the craft

On my numerous visits to the West, I have been immensely fortunate to have met countless people who have showered me with their affection and kindness. Every time I have come home, I have carried with me a heart full of gratitude and memories of total strangers with whom a true human connection has happened, even in the space of the few minutes of a brief conversation. In these encounters, I have found a true spiritual longing to meet in that free space of the spirit where no shackles of ideological systems or modes of control exist. I was visiting from a place where no political freedom could be exercised – a place of torture prisons and ruthless monitoring. The places I was visiting knew no such world, but they were prisoners of a different kind of cage – a cage of economic control and a restrictive world view. This is a world view in which humanity is trapped inside the illusion of holding power over the universe, and in which those who are in control will do everything they can to maintain this illusion, including enforcing limits on seeing and knowing.

Machines are the primary tool for maintaining this illusion. In the field of architecture, Le Corbusier's 'machine for living in' (his description of the contemporary home) became a foundational idea for modernism. In our time, however, machines have proven to be intrusive, polluting, and largely destructive. And so more machines have been invented, in order to rectify these shortcomings – 'smart', 'green' and 'sustainable' machines.

The Cambridge Central Mosque, completed in 2019, has been dubbed the first 'eco-mosque' in Europe. This label could be read as being part of the building's marketing campaign to the non-Muslim local community in the United Kingdom. An 'eco-mosque' might be considered less of a 'cultural loss', and more of a high-performing machine. Dr Tim Winter (also known as Sheikh Abdal Hakim Murad) is the founder and the man behind the vision of this 'place for all'.[32] It was designed by Marks Barfield Architects, after they won the design competition held in 2009. Previous projects by the studio include the London Eye and the i360 observation tower in Brighton, which, depending on how you look at it, makes them either an odd or an inspired choice for a mosque design. Sadly, David Marks died in 2017, and the building in its completed state was seen only by his wife and partner Julia Barfield.

As in a typical stage of emergence of any proper mosque, the first mosque in Cambridge was established in the domestic sphere. In the 1970s, it was accommodated in a residential house on Chesterton Road. In 1981, the Abu Bakr Mosque, also known as the Cambridge Mosque, opened in a converted hall on Mawson Road. The importance of the arrival of the purpose-built mosque on Mill Road is discussed by the

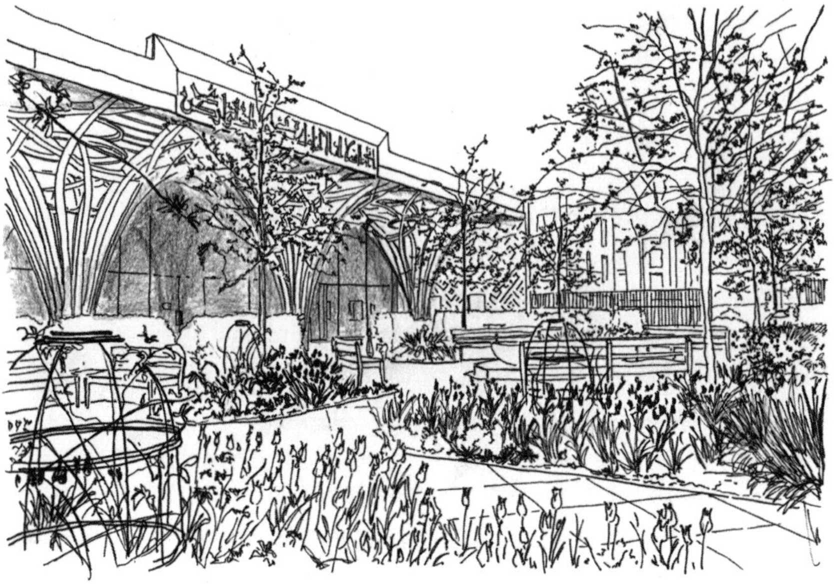

The Cambridge Central Mosque, UK: a view from the front garden

writer Shahida Rahman, who is one of the trustees and the daughter of a Bangladeshi immigrant who used to host prayers at his house:

> Mill Road has always been a 'community of communities' and when the early Muslims arrived, this was a foreign and unfamiliar land. For us, it is our home that we love. I am British, Muslim, and Bangladeshi. However, I do not look to perceive them as individual identities, isolated from one another, but as a combination; a mixture of all. Our Mosque reflects an amalgamation of identities and our journey into this 'community of communities', which is truly inspiring and humbling.[33]

These few lines tell the story of Muslim immigrants in the West. There is no glorification of immigrant communities, but at the same time one cannot overlook the challenges that arise with their arrival at the new locations that host them. While such topics are outside the scope of this book, we can note here the eggshells Muslims have to walk on, in order to bring their presence as *Muslims* to the fore; namely, by the building of a mosque. Importantly, we must consider what having a mosque means to them, and their contribution to the wider community where they feel at home.

The starting point for the architects of the Cambridge Central Mosque was a central truth about mosques – that they were historically characterized by their time and place. The architects were inspired by the diversity they read about in Shahed Saleem's *The British Mosque*, and they were also guided by the vision of Tim Winter. Thus, a 'modern and British mosque' was imagined.[34] The only problem was: how to interpret the Muslim ingredient in this four-worded formula?

The architects chose to combine both Islamic and English religious architectural traditions, by using the favoured 'garden of trees' metaphor and branching columns that 'reach out like the interlacing ribs of English Gothic fan vaults, as in the chapel of King's College at Cambridge University'.[35] The branches, which are made of timber to emphasize the sustainability aspect, are strikingly similar to those used in the design of the Mosque and Islamic Cultural Centre of Rome. The latter was also the result of a design competition, held in 1972. Funded by Saudi Arabia, construction took place between 1984 and 1995. The building had to comply with conditions set by the Vatican.[36] Offering a religious, recreational and cultural programme, it combines the features of a platform-raised colonnaded Roman temple and a space containing thirty-two branched columns topped by a central dome.

The Cambridge Central Mosque also uses its fair share of symbolism: the geometric patterns that were developed in collaboration with Professor Keith Critchlow 'symbolise the infinite'.[37] Despite its merit, Critchlow's work is heavily affected by Sufi writings and draws on mystical interpretations of geometrical design. The theme of a mosque as a 'calm oasis'[38] is similarly immersed in a romanticized (almost orientalist in essence) view of the place of worship, but this was the theme chosen for the mosque in Cambridge. A bulbous timber dome, manufactured in Switzerland, crowns the prayer hall but serves no structural purpose.

Looking at the stretched rectangular plot of land, it seemed to me that the biggest design challenge should have been creating the most elongated space possible for prayer and reconciling that with the short

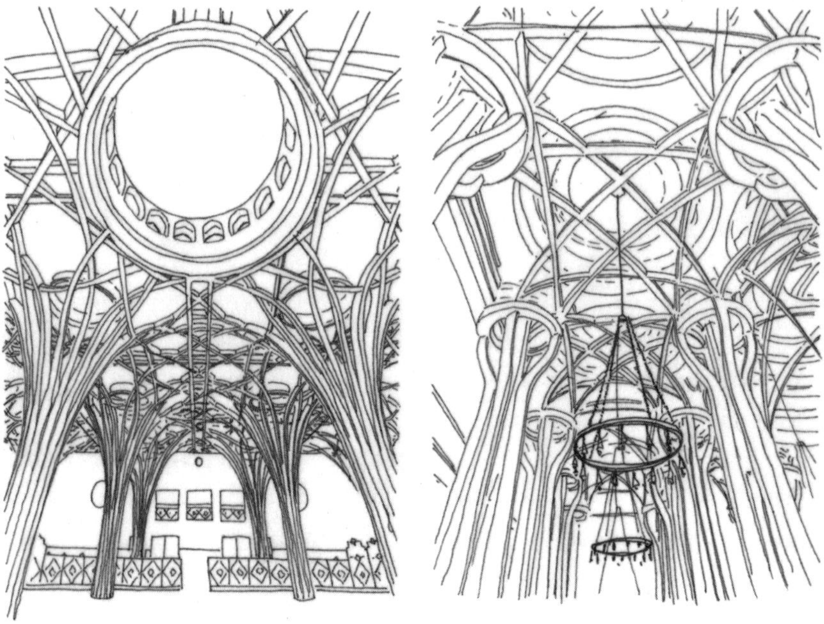

Comparative views of the interiors of the Cambridge Central Mosque, UK, and the Mosque and Islamic Cultural Centre (also known as the Grand Mosque of Rome), Italy

width of the plot and the necessary angled orientation towards the *qibla*. However, the finished design reproduces the common mistake made by non-Muslim architects of selecting a square space for the prayer hall. At the Cambridge Central Mosque, an additional mistake was made by following a spacious canopied space – through which people enter the mosque, as well as the adjacent café – with a cramped narrow neck of an entrance into the prayer hall. The narrow neck appears again between the building and the front garden designed by Emma Clark, creating another congestion point. The sight of footwear scattered in spaces (rather than on shoe racks at the entrance or in personal shoe bags) also halts the flow of movement through the building, and seems to indicate an underestimation of the sheer volume of worshippers. Additionally, the sixteen branched columns inside the prayer hall are not all positioned in relation to the space, leaving small gaps next to the walls, which goes against the natural flow of a mosque.

While it must be acknowledged and commended that this project seems to have been imagined as a new way of approaching mosque design – by bringing in different actors, by attempting to make connections with the existing context, and by highlighting beauty through the means of the current time and place – there still seems to be something missing that prevents the mosque, in my opinion, from achieving its full potential; namely, freedom from ideology, even if the mosque's creators meant well and wished only for acceptance.

By contrast, the Australian Islamic Centre in Newport, Melbourne, opened in 2017 and designed by Glenn Murcutt, is an example of a quite different approach. The mosque was declared 'the first truly contemporary Australian mosque',[39] achieving 'a new perception of Islam in Australia'.[40] Murcutt was commissioned in 2005, by the predominantly Lebanese–Australian community, who wanted a contemporary mosque that would be a representation of their belonging to Australia today. (The first Australian mosque was built by members of the Afghan community in Marree, South Australia, in 1861.) Murcutt's first instinct was to work in equal collaboration with a Muslim architect. The Turkish–Australian Hakan Elevli was suggested, and after a meeting he joined the project. Murcutt's gesture indicated a truly humble admission of one's limits of knowledge, and an ego-free spirit of collaboration.

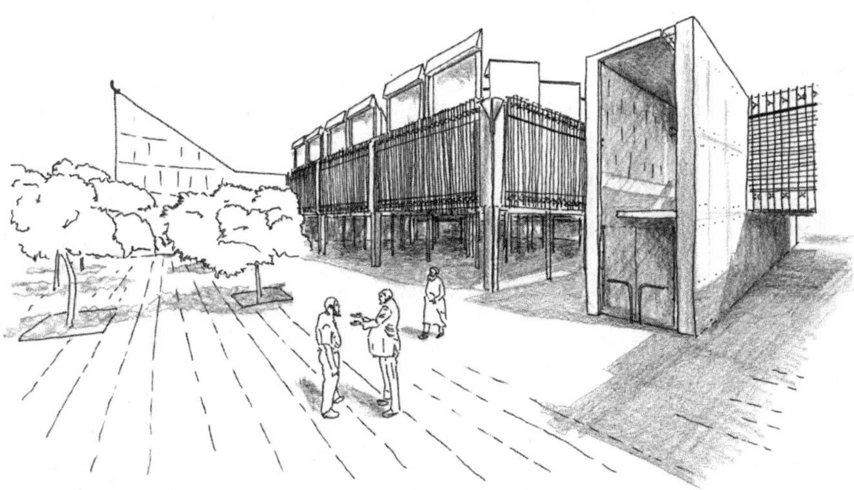

The Australian Islamic Centre in Newport, Melbourne

The story of the building of the mosque is told in a documentary film titled *Glenn Murcutt: Designing a New Mosque – with Pen and Paper*. Importantly, the story of what it is to be a craftsman architect plays in parallel in the background. Murcutt is a modern architect, only if modernity means contemporary. His method of working is not that of a machine; it is that of a craftsman. Using a pencil to hand-draw his designs at his desk at home, where he runs a one-man architectural practice, he ensures that he is sufficiently immersed and that his emotions are involved in his work, which up until the mosque project mostly consisted of designs for small-scale houses. He describes his practice as a 'quiet architecture', having 'calmness, freedom and serenity'.

Before coming up with his vision for the mosque, Murcutt went through historical examples and worked on distilling an essence. His meetings with the mosque committee and with the community resulted in him explaining to the traditionalists among them that, in many instances, the history of the mosque did not involve domes. In proposing to negate the stereotypical image, he instead offered a different experience. In collaboration with Elevli, Murcutt developed a mosque design that featured a spacious rectangular prayer hall, in which the aisles were composed out of his interpretation of order: twenty-four steel columns were arranged to create three bays from east to west and three from north to south.

Inside the resulting module, Murcutt wanted to reimagine the experience of light that is found within the Great Mosque of Córdoba. He created a network of lanterns to bring light from above, like the lanterns that illuminate the space at Córdoba – free of any simplistic symbolism or graphic abstractions. Wrapped in gold-painted metal sheaths, Murcutt's fifty-five roof lanterns are three metres (nearly 10 ft) high, and made of colour-glazed facets to filter the natural light and naturally illuminate the main prayer hall. With different colours used for each cardinal direction, the lanterns draw triangles of coloured daylight into the building, in an ever-changing pattern determined by the sun's movement.

Stained glass is Syria's gift to the ancient world. It is a craft that is associated with Damascus, and the Phoenicians on the coast. Only after

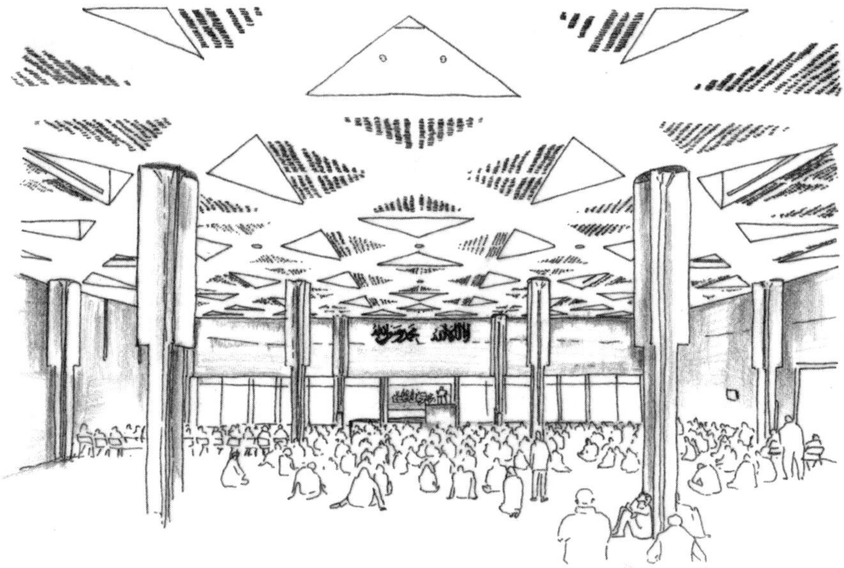

The Australian Islamic Centre: an interior view of the prayer hall, during the Friday sermon

the Mongols' raid on Damascus were the chemical secrets of this refined art revealed and disseminated. It may be that Murcutt saw images of the coloured windows in the Umayyad or at Córdoba, and took inspiration from them.

Inspiration has also come from Murcutt's sensitivity towards his surroundings. Taught by the Australian aboriginals to 'build very lightly', he looks at the Australian landscape and sees how the trees are strong at the base, then 'feather' as they meet the sky. In the film, he says that he had always thought there was something wrong with the way buildings were constructed in Australia: 'very heavy'. His experience in house design proved to be the perfect introduction to mosque design, since the connection with the domestic realm has always been an essential one.

His journey in building the mosque was transformative, not only in a professional sense but also on a human level. He lost his architect son in 2011: Nick Murcutt, whom he saw as an 'extension of himself', died after a short battle with cancer. The Muslim community stood beside Murcutt during this difficult time, praying for Nick when he was sick, and embracing Murcutt in his sadness. 'Why wouldn't you give your all to these people?' he noted.

Delays and overspend on the budget were resolved in community meetings, where Murcutt would remind members of his vision. They independently made donations on multiple occasions, raising money to the point of financial exhaustion. Women even donated their personal jewelry, after their husbands had contributed as much as they could. At the same time, Murcutt was carefully sampling the various shades of coloured glass, hand-picking the 'right degree'. His devotion to his work comes not from a wish to control, but from a place of humility – 'giving his all', as did the community. With the lanterns alone costing over one million Australian dollars, Murcutt explains how all negotiations were conducted 'purely on trust'. It was a labour of love from beginning to end, with Murcutt highly involved at every stage. During the building phase, the construction – with its high walls of poured cement – initially looked like a factory. But it was entirely transformed as space was born: strong at the base and feathering as it meets the sky.

The difference between machine-oriented thinking and a craft-imbued mentality is that the latter is an endeavour that involves responding to the universe, reflecting and engaging. In some sense, it is like prayer, where the door of the spirit is open, and where humans acknowledge their powerlessness and constantly strive to make improvements.

How to design a mosque today is less of an enigma to me than it was when my student asked me in class that day. However, finding a successful mosque, which is a reflection of who we are as Muslims today, has become an extremely difficult task. Our unity has been shattered by decades of colonial policies and oppressive regimes. Mosques are reflections of who we are as Muslims, how we connect to the world, and what we value the most. They are the prime fields of our arts and our expressions of self. They are places of enlightenment and development, not mere shells of activity. They are where we meet – not simply the other, but ourselves. However, our self-image has been placed in a hall of mirrors, and our self-realization now depends on redefining ourselves in a world where freedom is imprisoned either in a gilded cage or in a torture basement.

In my own country, freedom has miraculously escaped the torture basement of the Assad regime. However, like a lost child in the alleyways of the souq, this freedom is being stopped and interrogated, pulled in every direction, while the march from behind is headed determinedly into that dreaded gilded cage. US special envoy Tom Barrack has stated that 'prosperity is the only answer',[41] in place of the illusion of peace, for what he describes as 'tribes and villages'.[42] After a century of the post-colonial vassal states experiencing policies of scarcity, used as a means of control over the masses, it seems the 'endgame' of today might be based on this new conviction that full bellies are less prone to action. Meanwhile, the 'New Umayyads' has become the colloquial brand of the new Sunni rule, and the general mood is charged with an intoxicating sense of popularism.

But while we must be wary of shark fins in those choppy waters between the West and the East, the ocean flows on. As the Prophet Muhammad said, 'What is the example of this worldly life in comparison to the Hereafter other than one of you dipping his finger in the sea?'[43] Swords and crowns rust, and the only things the dollar bill can't buy are the only things that truly matter. Today, the mosques are open again, flocked by students; young boys and girls are going to the madrasas after school; books are no longer banned; and sermons are no longer pre-written. Hope lives in the nest of freedom.

Since we all, as humans, face existential questions of how to be and how to become in a world that seems to get more cruel and more divided with every passing day, it is crucial that we remain free in mind, in spirit and in place. It is a freedom that must be granted to everyone, everywhere: it is not for one nation over the other, or one community over the next, and, most crucially, it must not be blocked by the gates of ideology. The mosque of today is a reflection of how well we will succeed in achieving this paramount goal.

Notes

1. *Masjid* means mosque; literally, 'place of prostration'.
2. Holy Quran, Surah Al-A'raf (ch. 7), verses 30–31.

INTRODUCTION

1. While *sharia* rules are considered divine, following God's instructions in the Quran and the Sunnah, there is a human undertaking – *fiqh*, or jurisprudence – in understanding, interpreting and applying these principles.
2. Terms such as 'Muslim nations' are used throughout the book to refer to Muslim-majority territories, while recognizing that these feature widely differing relationships between Islam and the state. Terms such as 'non-Muslim countries' are used to refer to Muslim-minority territories, where Islam is not the principal or state religion. However, the connotations of the wider, worldwide 'Muslim nation' (*umma*) go beyond modern political definitions of statehood and the statistics of minorities/majorities. In the traditional lands of Islam, the legacy of Muslim nationhood is indicated by the remnants of the systems built by Islamic civilization and social structures, which endured even after the dismantling of the related political, legislative and economic structures in the aftermath of the Second World War. In these countries, Islam relates to place, and not just people. It is not merely the faith of these communities, as it is in countries such as the UK; it is, rather, the core of a built civilization whose traces still permeate all its communities, majorities and minorities alike.
3. Michel Houellebecq, in conversation with philosopher and editor of *Front Populaire* magazine Michel Onfray, published in *Front Populaire*, November 2022. Notably, since then, pig heads have been left on the doorsteps of nine mosques in France, and a worshipper was stabbed to death by a Frenchman inside the mosque in La Grand-Combe.

CHAPTER 1: WHAT IS 'MOSQUENESS'?

1. Hasan-Uddin Khan, 'An Overview of Contemporary Mosques', in *The Mosque: History, Architectural Development & Regional Diversity*, ed. Martin Frishman and Hasan-Uddin Khan, Thames & Hudson, London, 1994, p. 267.
2. Layla al-Sabbagh, 'The Al-Farisiya School in Damascus, Part 1', *The Magazine of the Arabic Language Community in Damascus*, vol. 1, no. 83, p. 56 (published in Arabic, all translations by the present author).
3. The researchers were likely archaeologist Carl Watzinger and architectural historian Karl Wulzinger, who worked on mapping Damascus in 1917.
4. Al-Sabbagh, 'The Al-Farisiya School', p. 57.
5. Ibid., p. 60.
6. Ibid.
7. Ibid., p. 57.
8. Damascus is widely regarded as the oldest continuously inhabited city in the world.
9. Holy Quran, Surah Al-Imran (ch. 3), verse 96.
10. Holy Quran, Surah Al-Baqarah (ch. 1), verse 285.
11. Imam Malik, *Al-Muwatta*, Book 47, Hadith 8.
12. Narrated by Al-Tirmidhi, and Ibn Majah, and authenticated by Al-Albani.
13. As the hadith 'And the earth was made to me a place for prostration and a material for cleansing' confirms, a Muslim can pray anywhere, and dry soil can even be used in place of water for cleansing, where the latter is unavailable. See *Sahih al-Bukhari*, vol. 1, Dar Ibn Katheer, Beirut, 1993, p. 168.
14. Holy Quran, Surah Al-Ankabut (ch. 29), verse 45.

15. Muhammad Metwalli al-Sha'rawi, in a recorded lesson (part of a series on Quranic studies, in Arabic).
16. Gülzar Haider, 'Faith is the Architect, Reflections on the Mosque', *Architecture & Comportement / Architecture & Behaviour*, vol. 11, no. 3–4 [1995], p. 246.
17. Holy Quran, Surah Al-Fatiha (ch. 1).
18. Titus Burckhardt, *Art of Islam: Language and Meaning*, World of Islam Festival Trust, 1976, p. 85.
19. Akel Ismail Kahera, *Deconstructing the American Mosque: Space, Gender, and Aesthetics*, University of Texas Press, Austin, 2002, p. 37.
20. Ibid., p. 36.
21. The idea of building a *minbar* was, in fact, suggested by a woman from Medina. Before that, the Prophet stood before the congregation and, when tired, leaned on a palm trunk beside him. The woman reportedly proposed 'making an object [for the Prophet] to rest on' and said 'that her carpenter son would make it for him'. This way, not only could the Prophet sometimes rest on the second step of the *minbar*, but the rows in the back, including women, were also able to see him. See Ibn Hajar al-Asqalani, *Fath al-Bari Explanation of Sahih al-Bukhari*, vol. 4, Dar al-Rayyan, Cairo, 1986, p. 374 (published in Arabic, translated by the present author).
22. James Dickie (Yaqub Zaki), 'Allah and Eternity: Mosques, Madrasas and Tombs', in *Architecture of the Islamic World: Its History and Social Meaning*, ed. George Michell, Thames & Hudson, London, 1978, p. 33.
23. Burckhardt, *Art of Islam*, p. 19.
24. Dickie (Zaki), 'Allah and Eternity', p. 36.
25. See Kahera, *Deconstructing the American Mosque*, p. 36.
26. Because the sixth expansion mainly involved adding/renovating structures (minarets, domes, walls etc), it cannot be depicted on the general site plan on p. 38.
27. Jerome Taylor, 'Medina: Saudis Take a Bulldozer to Islam's History', www.independent.co.uk, 26 October 2012 (accessed 20 August 2025).
28. Ibid.
29. Extract from a poem published in Arabic, translated by the present author.
30. www.bonner-design.com/projects/sliding_domes.htm (accessed 20 October 2025).

CHAPTER 2: WHAT IS THE NATURE OF ISLAMIC CIVILIZATION?

1. Kamil Khan Mumtaz, *Architecture in Pakistan*, ed. Judith Shaw, Concept Media, Singapore, 1985, p. 194.
2. 'Countries of the World Ranked by GDP/Capita in PPP (2025)', www.worldatlas.com (accessed 7 August 2025).
3. In 1865, the 'Pearl Carpet of Baroda', made using Gulf pearls, was commissioned by the Maharaja of Baroda, intended as a gift to adorn the Prophet Muhammad's tomb in Medina.
4. www.visitqatar.com (accessed 20 August 2025).
5. Renata Holod and Hasan-Uddin Khan, *The Mosque and the Modern World: Architects, Patrons and Designs since the 1950s*, Thames & Hudson, London, 1997, p. 151.
6. Ibid.
7. Ibid., p. 152.
8. Mark Twain, *The Innocents Abroad*, Harper & Brothers, New York and London, 1869, p. 179.
9. Ibid., pp. 177–8.
10. Shahed Saleem, *The British Mosque: An Architectural and Social History*, Historic England, Swindon, 2018, p. 78.
11. Olivia B. Waxman, 'Was Aladdin Based on a Real Person? Here's Why Scholars Are Starting to Think So', time.com, 23 May 2019 (accessed 7 August 2025).
12. Antoine Abu Zeid, 'Who is Hanna Diyab al-Halabi, the Inventor of Some of the Tales of the "Nights"?', www.independentarabia.com, 28 August 2023

(original article in Arabic, with English translation; accessed 7 August 2025).

13. Holod and Khan, *The Mosque and the Modern World*, pp. 13–14.
14. At the time of writing, the Sykes–Picot borders seem to have finally collapsed – not because the historic natural regions have regained their legitimacy, but because colonial/expansionist projects have reinvigorated themselves. Reporting notes that 'Israel is not interested in adhering to the Middle East's established borders set by the WWI Sykes-Picot agreement', and quotes US special envoy Tom Barrack as saying that Israel has the 'capacity or the desire' to take over Lebanon and Syria. See Sean Mathews, 'Israel sees Sykes-Picot borders as "meaningless", US envoy Tom Barrack says', www.middleeasteye.net, 29 August 2025 (accessed 20 October 2025).
15. 'Levant', ar.wikipedia.org (article in Arabic, accessed 8 August 2025).
16. Diana Darke, *Islamesque: The Forgotten Craftsmen Who Built Europe's Medieval Monuments*, Hurst Publishers, London, 2024.
17. See also Sophia Rose Arjana, *Muslims in the Western Imagination*, Oxford University Press, Oxford, 2015, which explores the ways in which Muslim men have been depicted as monsters throughout history; it highlights how Western authors have chosen what to report and which authors from the Muslim world to commemorate in order to fit the manufactured 'savage' narrative.
18. Adnan Al Bunni, *Apollodorus: The Greatest Architect in Ancient History*, Ministry of Culture Publications, Damascus, 1990 (published in Arabic), p. 29.
19. Ibid., p. 41.
20. Gérard Degeorge, *Damascus*, Rizzoli International Publications, Canada, 2004, p. 23. Regarding language, Degeorge notes: 'Greek, the language of the court, administrators, lawyers, major traders, and more generally of all those who found it advantageous to assimilate the politically dominant culture, never percolated down to the mass of the population, who remained faithful to the old Aramaic idiom.'
21. Talal Akili, *The Great Mosque of Damascus: From Roman Temple to Monument of Islam*, ARCOD – Architectural Research Center of Old Damascus, Damascus, p. 14.
22. Ibid., p. 16.
23. Ibid., p. 43.
24. Ibid., p. 44.
25. Ibid., p. 49.
26. Burckhardt, *Art of Islam*, p. 117.
27. Ibid.
28. Akili, *The Great Mosque of Damascus*, p. 7.
29. There were earthquakes in 749, 848, 1157, 1201, 1202, 1302 and 1759 CE, and fires in 1069, 1166, 1174, 1392, 1401, 1479 and 1893.
30. Akili, *The Great Mosque of Damascus*, p. 192 (citing K. A. C. Creswell, *Early Muslim Architecture*, p. 518).
31. Burckhardt, *Art of Islam*, pp. 23, 25.
32. Ismail Serageldin, 'Regionalism', in *The Mosque*, ed. Frishman and Khan, p. 72.
33. Ibid.
34. Ibid.
35. Burckhardt, *Art of Islam*, p. 63.
36. Kahera, *Deconstructing the American Mosque*, p. 116. 'The term *homo universalis* (Latin) or *uomo universale* (Italian) was popularized during the Renaissance; the Greek term is attributed to the philosopher Protagoras.
37. Holy Quran, Surah Al-Ahzab (ch. 33), verse 72.
38. Talal Akili, furthermore, provides images taken in the nineteenth century of mansions on the bank of the River Barada looking very similar to imagery depicted in the mosaics, and he notes that the scene would not have changed much from the time of the mosaics. See Akili, *The Great Mosque of Damascus*, p. 214.
39. Kahera, *Deconstructing the American Mosque*, p. 65.

40. 'Jumma [*sic*] Mosque: John McAslan + Partners', www.theplan.it, n.d. (accessed 14 August 2025).
41. At the Umayyad in Damascus, for example, an elevated octagonal structure known as the 'Dome of the Treasury' still stands in the courtyard.

CHAPTER 3: WHAT IS THE ROLE OF THE MOSQUE?

1. Burckhardt, *Art of Islam*, p. 40.
2. Dickie (Zaki), 'Allah and Eternity', pp. 36–7.
3. Shi'a Islam holds that the imam is divinely appointed and protected from error, a belief that is not accepted in Sunni doctrine.
4. Simona Bordone, 'Djamaâ el Djazaïr: The Great Mosque of Algiers is the Third Largest in the World', www.domusweb.it, 14 December 2020 (accessed 14 August 2025).
5. 'Grand Mosque, Algiers: How Do You Build a Mosque in the 21st Century?', www.ksp-engel.com, n.d. (accessed 14 August 2025).
6. Bordone, 'Djamaâ el Djazaïr' (accessed 14 August 2025).
7. Ibid.
8. 'Grand Mosque, Algiers' (accessed 14 August 2025).
9. Kishwar Rizvi, *The Transnational Mosque: Architecture and Historical Memory in the Contemporary Middle East*, University of North Carolina Press, Chapel Hill, 2015, p. 9.
10. Ibid., pp. 205–6.
11. Ibid., p. 21.
12. Ibid., p. 23.
13. Holy Quran, Surah Ghafir (ch. 40), verses 36–7.
14. Burckhardt, *Art of Islam*, p. 104. For further reading, see *Building for Hope: Towards an Architecture of Belonging* by the present author (Thames & Hudson, London, 2021).
15. Burckhardt, *Art of Islam*, p. 101.
16. Ibn Khaldoun, *The Introduction*, vol. I, Dar Yaarob, Damascus, 2004, p. 338 (published in Arabic, translated by the present author).
17. Francis D. K. Ching, Mark M. Jarzombek and Vikramaditya Prakash, *A Global History of Architecture*, Wiley, Hoboken, NJ, 2017, pp. 32–3.
18. Burckhardt, *Art of Islam*, p. 105.
19. Ibid., pp. 105–6.
20. Ibid., p. 106.
21. Ibid.
22. Holy Quran, Surah Al-Baqarah (ch. 1), verse 125.
23. Holy Quran, Surah Al-Baqarah (ch. 1), verse 127.
24. *Al-Harām* (with a long 'a') refers to the divine prohibition on fighting within the territory of Al-Haram Mosque, whereas the word *haram* (with a short 'a') means 'sacred precincts'.
25. See Oleg Grabar, *The Dome of the Rock*, Thames & Hudson, London, 1996.
26. 'Did 'Abd al-Malik build Dome of the Rock to divert the Hajj from Makkah?' islamic-awareness.org, 18 February 2001 (accessed 22 October 2025).
27. Raafat Miri and Abdullah Maarouf, *The Atlas of Features of the Holy Aqsa Mosque*, Al-Fursan Publications, Amman, 2011, p. 10 (published in Arabic, translated by the present author).
28. News agencies in the region have reported on Israeli excavations under Al-Aqsa (part of the City of David settler colonial project), aimed at actively inducing the mosque's collapse, in order to build the Third (Solomon) Temple and fulfil biblical prophesies. See, for example, 'Palestinian Government Denounces Settler Threat to Al-Aqsa Mosque', aljazeera.com, 19 April 2025 (accessed 4 November 2025).
29. Burckhardt, *Art of Islam*, p. 12.
30. Rizvi, *The Transnational Mosque*, p. 85.

CHAPTER 4: THE ARCHITECTURE OF THE MOSQUE

1. Cited by Vincent Monteil in *L'Islam noir*, Editions du Seuil, Paris, 1964, p. 41 (published in French, translated by the present author).
2. Bernard O'Kane, *Treasures of Islam: Artistic Glories of the Muslim World*, Duncan Baird Publishers, London, 2007, p. 204.
3. Luo Xiaowei, 'China', in *The Mosque*, ed. Frishman and Khan, p. 209.
4. Ibid.
5. Ibid., p. 210.
6. Ibid.
7. The other three are traditionally regarded as Qingjing Mosque in Quanzhou, Xianhe Mosque in Yangzhou and Fenghuang Mosque in Hangzhou.
8. Luo Xiaowei, 'China', pp. 220–21.
9. Ibid., p. 223.
10. Ibid., p. 221.
11. Ibid.
12. 'Introducing Huaisheng Mosque, Huaisheng Mosque Guide, Huaisheng Mosque Travel Guide'. Article from Guangzhou Municipal Commission of Tourism: www.islamichina.com/guangzhou/guangzhou-attractions/guangzhou-huaisheng-mosque.html (accessed 9 September 2025).
13. O'Kane, *Treasures of Islam*, p. 108.
14. Ibid.
15. Ibid., p. 67.
16. Ibid.
17. Doğan Kuban, *Ottoman Architecture*, Antique Collectors' Club, Woodbridge, Suffolk, 2010, pp. 363–5.
18. Ibid.
19. Ibid., p. 364.
20. See, for example, Faisal Sheikhani, *Homs and its Khaled*, Dar Al-Ershard Publications, Homs, pp. 98 and 241.
21. See Haider, 'Faith is the Architect, Reflections on the Mosque', pp. 243–8.
22. en.wikipedia.org/wiki/Kiosk (accessed 19 September 2025).
23. The elongation of rows was perfected at the Prophet's Mosque, which became the prototype that other mosques built upon (the seed from which the fruit grew). However, despite the spatial logic that the elongated prayer hall displays, versus the squared format, this does not qualify the elongated format as some kind of 'rule of thumb'. There are no rules of form (religiously speaking) that grant more legitimacy to some forms over others. Our comparison between the development of the hypostyle mosque versus the other types, such as the mausoleum-derived (and later the madrasa-derived) mosques, provides us, though, with an indication as to the difference in emphasis that each typology may ultimately convey.
24. Kahera, *Deconstructing the American Mosque*, p. 10 and passim.
25. Doğan Kuban, 'The Central Arab Lands', in *The Mosque*, ed. Frishman and Khan, p. 96.
26. Ibid., p. 97.
27. Ibid.
28. Ibid., p. 96.
29. Dickie (Zaki), 'Allah and Eternity', p. 38.
30. O'Kane, *Treasures of Islam*, p. 115.
31. Ibid.
32. Dickie (Zaki), 'Allah and Eternity', p. 40.
33. Marika Sardar, 'Shah 'Abbas and the Arts of Isfahan.' In *Heilbrunn Timeline of Art History*. New York: The Metropolitan Museum of Art, 2000: www.metmuseum.org/toah/hd/shah/hd_shah.htm (accessed 14 September 2025).
34. O'Kane, *Treasures of Islam*, p. 17.
35. Dominique Clévenot (with photographs by Gérard Degeorge), *Ornament and Decoration in Islamic Architecture*, Thames & Hudson, London, 2000, p. 43.
36. Ibid.

CHAPTER 5: THE LANGUAGE OF THE ARTS

1. From 'The Damascene Poem'.

2. Dickie (Zaki), 'Allah and Eternity', p. 37.
3. Ibid.
4. 'The Testimony of Al-Waleed bin Al-Mughira [*sic*] with the Eloquence of the Holy Quran', islamweb.net, 19 February 2008 (accessed 27 October 2025).
5. Burckhardt, *Art of Islam*, p. 42.
6. Ibid.
7. Ibid., p. 43.
8. Ibid., p. 44.
9. Ibid., p. 46.
10. Holy Quran, Surah Al-Kahf (ch. 18), verse 109.
11. Clévenot, *Ornament and Decoration in Islamic Architecture*, p. 193.
12. Burckhardt, *Art of Islam*, p. 127.
13. Dalu Jones, 'Surface, Pattern and Light', in *Architecture of the Islamic World*, ed. Michell, p. 171.
14. Clévenot, *Ornament and Decoration in Islamic Architecture*, p. 147.
15. Rizvi, *The Transnational Mosque*, p. 178.
16. Ibid., p. 181.
17. Amrutha Loganathan, 'Sheikh Zayed Grand Mosque, Abu Dhabi', www.re-thinkingthefuture.com, n.d. (accessed 16 September 2025).
18. www.szgmc.gov.ae/en/islamic-architecture/overview (accessed 16 September 2025).
19. Richard Padovan, *Proportion: Science, Philosophy, Architecture*, E & FN Spon Press, London, 1999, p. 25.
20. Wilhelm Worringer, *Abstraction and Empathy: A Contribution to the Psychology of Style*, translated from German by Michael Bullock, International Universities Press, London and New York, 1953, p. 17. This text was originally written as a doctoral thesis in 1906, and published in 1908 in Germany as *Abstraktion und Einfühlung*.
21. Ibid., p. 12.
22. Padovan, *Proportion*, with citation from Worringer, p. 22.
23. Jones, 'Surface, Pattern, and Light', p. 172.
24. Burckhardt, *Art of Islam*, p. 61.
25. Clévenot, *Ornament and Decoration in Islamic Architecture*, p. 148.
26. James Meek, 'Islamic Centre Shifts Its Ground', www.theguardian.com, 14 August 1999 (accessed 17 September 2025).
27. Ibid.
28. Ibid.
29. 'A Speech by HRH The Prince of Wales titled "Islam and the West" at the Oxford Centre for Islamic Studies, The Sheldonian Theatre, Oxford', www.royal.uk, 27 October 1993 (accessed 17 September 2025).
30. Matt Oliver, 'Prince Charles Urges Population to "Rediscover Unity" as He Opens Oxford Centre for Islamic Studies', www.oxfordmail.co.uk, 17 May 2017 (accessed 17 September 2025).
31. Mohammad al-Asad, 'Application of Geometry', in *The Mosque*, ed. Frishman and Khan, p. 67.
32. Ibid.
33. Jones, 'Surface, Pattern, and Light', p. 175.
34. Ibid., p. 162.
35. Clévenot, *Ornament and Decoration in Islamic Architecture*, p. 197.
36. Khan, 'An Overview of Contemporary Mosques', p. 238.

CHAPTER 6: THE MOSQUE AND THE CITY

1. Ismail Serageldin, *Space for Freedom: The Search for Architectural Excellence in Muslim Societies*, The Aga Khan Award for Architecture/Butterworth Architecture, London, 1989, p. 217.
2. 'Mosque to Finally be Unveiled in Istanbul's Taksim Square', dailysabah.com, 19 April 2021 (accessed 25 September 2025).
3. Nezar AlSayyad and İpek Türeli, 'The Mosque in the Urban Context', 2021, p. 25: spatialjustice.research.mcgill.ca/assets/writing/2021_Mosque_AlSayyad&Tureli.pdf
4. Patricia Tusa Fels, *Monsoon Mosques: Arrival of Islam and the Development of a Mosque*

Vernacular, Mapin Publishing, Ahmedabad, 2020, p. 13.

5. Ibid., p. 32.
6. Ibid., pp. 13–14.
7. Ibid., p. 123.
8. Ibid., p. 15.
9. Ibid., p. 59.
10. AlSayyad and Türeli, 'The Mosque in the Urban Context', p. 29.
11. Abdalrahman Kittana, 'Exploring the Intricate Architectural Fabric of a Historic Arab Medina: A Study of Nablus Old Town', *Journal of Islamic Architecture*, December 2023, p. 584.
12. Ibid., p. 585.
13. Guy T. Petherbridge, 'Vernacular Architecture: The House and Society', in *Architecture of the Islamic World*, ed. Michell, p. 195.
14. Kittana, 'Exploring the Intricate Architectural Fabric of a Historic Arab Medina', pp. 585–6.
15. Ibid., p. 586.
16. Ibid., p. 593.
17. Christopher de Bellaigue, 'Turkey: "Surreal, Menacing ... Pompous"', *The New York Review*, 19 December 2013: www.nybooks.com/articles/2013/12/19/turkey-surreal-menacing-pompous/ (accessed 25 September 2025).
18. A segment of modern-day Turkish society, often associated with the ruling Justice and Development Party (AKP), has risen in economic power and now openly displays its religious identity in public life, in a break from the secular elite who have traditionally dominated public space and wealth.
19. Michael Kubo, 'Genius versus Expertise. Frank Lloyd Wright and The Architects Collaborative at the University of Baghdad', *Histories of Postwar Architecture*, no. 8, 2021, p. 15.
20. Holod and Khan, *The Mosque and the Modern World*, p. 85.
21. Ibid., p. 64.
22. K. Caileigh Stirling, '5 Facts about Muslims and Christians in Indonesia', Pew Research Center, 28 March 2024.
23. Cited in Holod and Khan, *The Mosque and the Modern World*, p. 65.
24. Wolfgang Saxon, 'Constantinos Doxiadis, City Planner, Is Dead at 62', *The New York Times*, 29 June 1975, p. 34.
25. Lefteris Theodosis, 'Victory over Chaos? Constantinos A. Doxiadis and Ekistics 1945–1975', Universitat Politècnica de Catalunya, Barcelona, 2015, p. 99.
26. Ibid., p. 98.
27. Holod and Khan, *The Mosque and the Modern World*, p. 76.
28. Gülru Necipoğlu, 'Anatolia and the Ottoman Legacy', in *The Mosque*, ed. Frishman and Khan, p. 153.
29. Holod and Khan, *The Mosque and the Modern World*, p. 108.
30. Cited in Jessica Mairs, 'Terraced Landscaping Surrounds Concrete and Stone Structure of Emre Arolat's Sancaklar Mosque', dezeen.com, 6 April 2015 (accessed 25 September 2025).

CHAPTER 7: THE MOSQUE AND MODERNITY

1. George Michell, 'Preface', in *Architecture of the Islamic World*, ed. Michell, p. 7.
2. Azim Nanji, 'Contemporary Expressions of Islam in Buildings: What Have We Learned?', in *Expressions of Islam in Buildings: Exploring Architecture in Islamic Cultures*, Concept Media/Aga Khan Award for Architecture, Jakarta and Yogyakarta, 1990, p. 221.
3. 'Interview with the Architect: Enayat Ghaedi on the DIFC Grand Mosque', rmjm.com, n.d. (accessed 25 September 2025).
4. 'RMJM's Grand Mosque and KSA Pavilion Projects Shortlisted for d3 RIBA Gulf Architecture Festival 2020', rmjm.com, n.d. (accessed 25 September 2025).
5. 'Interview with the Architect', rmjm.com (accessed 25 September 2025).

6. Tom Ravenscroft, 'Dabbagh Architects Creates Calligraphy-covered Contemporary Mosque in Dubai', dezeen.com, 26 August 2021 (accessed 25 September 2025).
7. Ibid.
8. 'Qasr Al Hosn: Al Musallah Prayer Hall / CEBRA' www.archdaily.com, n.d. (accessed 28 September 2025).
9. Ibid.
10. Jon Astbury, 'Prayer Hall Sits Inside a Cluster of Rock-shaped Buildings', dezeen.com, 27 December 2019 (accessed 25 September 2025).
11. Kahera, *Deconstructing the American Mosque*, p. 148.
12. Ibid.
13. Ibid., p. 147.
14. Ibid., p. 135.
15. Ibid., p. 155.
16. Ibid., p. 159.
17. Gulzar [*sic*] Haider, '"Brother in Islam, Please Draw us a Mosque". Muslims in the West: A Personal Account', in *Expressions of Islam in Buildings*, p. 156.
18. Ibid., p. 157.
19. Ibid.
20. Cited in Kahera, *Deconstructing the American Mosque*, p. 151.
21. Haider, '"Brother in Islam"', p. 157.
22. Ibid., p. 158.
23. Ibid., p. 157.
24. Ibid., p. 158.
25. Ibid.
26. Dan Hitchens, 'One Woman's Fight to Rebuild Syria', compactmag.com, 24 January 2025 (accessed 29 September 2025).
27. Haider, '"Brother in Islam"', p. 160.
28. Oskar Verkaaik, 'The Anticipated Mosque: The Political Affect of a Planned Building', *City & Society*, vol. 32, no. 1, The Political Materiality of Cities, April 2020: anthrosource.onlinelibrary.wiley.com/doi/10.1111/ciso.12241 (accessed 29 September 2025).
29. Ibid.
30. Ibid.
31. Ibid.
32. 'The Story of the Cambridge Central Mosque', Latest TV, n.d.: www.youtube.com/watch?v=DYY4h_ae2mI (accessed 29 September 2025).
33. Shahida Rahman, 'A Community of Communities', cambridgecentralmosque.org, 5 December 2019 (accessed 29 September 2025).
34. 'The Story of the Cambridge Central Mosque' (accessed 29 September 2025).
35. 'Cambridge Central Mosque', arquitecturaviva.com, n.d. (accessed 29 September 2025).
36. Holod and Khan, *The Mosque and the Modern World*, p. 255.
37. Cajsa Carlson, 'Marks Barfield Architects Designs Cambridge Central Mosque to Be "Place of Tranquility"', dezeen.com, 20 January 2021 (accessed 25 September 2025).
38. Ibid.
39. Ewan McEoin, 'The Australian Islamic Centre in Newport, Melbourne', www.ngv.vic.gov.au, 8 August 2016 (accessed 29 September 2025).
40. 'Australian Islamic Centre / Glenn Murcutt + Elevli Plus', www.archdaily.com, n.d. (accessed 29 September 2025).
41. 'Tom Barrack on Israel, the Middle East and What's Next', The National News, 22 September 2025: www.youtube.com/watch?v=1qM3iosGloU (accessed 28 October 2025).
42. Barrack is quoted as saying 'There is no Middle East. There [are] tribes and villages'. See '"Tribes and Villages": US envoy Tom Barrack Questions Existence of Middle East', english.alarabiya.net, 26 September 2025 (accessed 28 October 2025).
43. Riyad as-Salihin, *The Book of Miscellany*, Hadith 462.

Glossary

ablaq: alternating (or fluctuating) rows of light and dark stone, prevalent in Syria with the use of limestone and basalt

amana: entrusted responsibility; the obligation to faithfully and ethically carry out a duty

amir: leader, governor (literally, commander)

aqeedah: creed; faith in Islam

asabiyya: social solidarity, forged by kinship and blood ties; a concept defined by fourteenth-century scholar Ibn Khaldoun as the binding force of human society

Azan: the Muslim call to prayer

Five Pillars of Islam: the core beliefs and practices that form the foundation of the Islamic faith: *shahada* (declaration of faith), *salat** (prayer), *zakat* (charity), *sawm* (fasting) and *hajj** (pilgrimage)

Hadith: the sayings of the Prophet Muhammad

hajj: annual pilgrimage to Mecca, which Muslims – if physically and financially able – are expected to undertake at least once in their lifetime

hijra: start of the Islamic calendar, marking the migration of the Prophet Muhammad from Mecca to Medina in 622

imam: religious leader, primarily responsible for leading prayers in a mosque, but also providing guidance and counselling on religious and personal matters

imar: the act of building, maintaining and restoring the earth, and all that is on earth

Jummah: congregational prayer (obligatory for Muslim men) performed on Friday, replacing the regular *Dhuhr* (midday) prayer

khalifa: the role of the human being as steward or vice-regent of God, entrusted with managing and taking care of the earth; plural *khulafa*

khan: type of inn, functioning as a trading post and hostel for traders and travellers

madrasa: religious school, usually attached to a mosque

maqam: Eastern musical scale; a melodic framework that dictates the specific pitches and patterns to be used to evoke a particular mood

masjid: Arabic word for 'mosque'

mihrab: niche carved into the *qibla** wall

minbar: pulpit in a mosque

muqarnas: honeycomb vaulting

qibla: the direction of the Kaaba in Mecca, thus indicating the direction Muslims should face when praying; the prayer hall wall is known as the *qibla* wall

sahn: prayer hall courtyard

salat: Arabic word for 'prayer'

sharia: the legal and moral framework of Islam, derived from the Quran and the Sunnah*, and guiding every aspect of Muslim life, from religious practices to personal ethics, business and family matters (literally, the 'correct path')

souq: traditional marketplace or bazaar

Sunnah: the teachings and practices of the Prophet Muhammad (literally, 'ancestral precedent', 'custom')

surah: one of the 114 chapters of the Quran, each chapter being divided into verses

tawaf: ritual circumambulation of the Kaaba in Mecca, to be performed counterclockwise seven times

tawhid: the consciousness of divine unity

ulamaa: Muslim scholars, learned in Islamic doctrine, law and tradition

umma: the worldwide community of Muslims, united by faith in Islam

waqf: Islamic endowment to be used in perpetuity for a charitable or religious purpose (literally, 'imprisonment', 'prohibition')

Timeline of the Ruling Muslim Dynasties

THE ARABS AND THE 'HEART OF ISLAM' REGIONS

The Rashidun, 632–661. Rashid, the singular form of Rashidun and Rashidin, means 'the good and committed one'. The term is used to refer to the companions of the Prophet Muhammad who ruled after his death in 632. These are Abu Bakr, Umar, Uthman, and Ali and his son Hasan. Their territories stretched from Khurasan (encompassing modern-day northeastern Iran, southern Turkmenistan and northern Afghanistan) to Tunisia. Medina was their capital until 657, when it was moved to Kufa in Iraq under the leadership of Ali. When Ali was assassinated in 661, Hasan gave up his seat as a caliph to Muawiyah, with whom there had been a conflict over the caliphate since the death of Othman in 656. The Rashidun built new systems and institutions, and established new cities and mosques.

The Umayyads, 661–750. Muawiyah had been the governor of Syria for twenty years before he became the first Umayyad caliph in 661. The dynasty takes its name from Muawiyah's great-grandfather, Umayya, and it marks the change in the ruling system from the democratic election of the Rashidun to the hereditable seat of the dynasties. With their capital in Damascus, the Umayyads grew an empire that eventually stretched from central Asia to Spain. They built great new mosques such as the Dome of the Rock and the Umayyad Mosque of Damascus, among others, and renovated and expanded many more.

The Abbasids, 750–1258. Muhammad ibn Ali al-Abbasi, a descendant of the Prophet Muhammad's uncle

Al-Abbas, was responsible for the initial movement that called for rule to be retrieved and kept within the clan. After taking over the province of Khurasan in 747 through revolt, the Abbasids hunted the Umayyad ruling class and killed them all, except for Prince Abd al-Rahman I who managed to escape and flee to Córdoba, where he established his emirate in 756. The Abbasids moved capital four times, starting in Kufa in Iraq and then moving to the newly established city, Madinat al-Salam (now known as Baghdad), in 789. From 836 to 892, they were based in the city of Samarra, during which time the Great Mosque of Samarra was built (848–851); it boasted a minaret with a spiral ramp, a form borrowed from the Babylonian temples. Finally, the Abbasids returned to Baghdad. The Abbasid era is often described as the Golden Age of Islam, due to its people's celebration of knowledge and the great advances in science and art put forward.

The most notable insurgence against the Abbasids was led by Ahmad ibn Tulun, a Turkic slave-soldier raised at the Abbasid court and appointed governor of Egypt in 1868 by a distracted Abbasid caliph. In 872, Ibn Tulun declared independence and, followed by his son, ruled over Egypt and parts of the Levant from 872 to 905. He built the Mosque of Ibn Tulun in the capital of Al-Qata'i, just north of the old capital Fustat; it was greatly influenced by the mosque of Samarra.

The sovereignty of the Abbasids diminished with the establishment of two Shi'ite states: one in the east, the Buyids of Iran , who conquered Baghdad in 945 and ruled over Iraq and Iran; the other in the west, the Fatimids, who ruled over Egypt. Other insurgents included the Seljuks.

The last Abbasid caliph was killed at the hands of the pagan Mongols who invaded Baghdad and wreaked havoc in 1258. The Abbasids remained nominal heads of state under the subsequent Mamluks until 1517.

The Fatimids, 909–1171. Claiming to be descendants of the Prophet Muhammad's daughter Fatima, wife of Ali, this Shi'ite dynasty recognizes a line of seven imams, viewing them as possessing divinely guided authority, the last of whom is Ismail, hence their other name, the Ismailis. In 909 the Fatimid caliphate was founded by Abd Allah al-Mahdi (a self-appointed nickname that means 'the guided one'). Al-Mahdi first attempted to establish his state from Salamiyah in Syria, but his ideas were met with opposition. The support that was not gained in Syria was eventually found in Tunisia among the Berbers, where the Fatimid state was established in 912 with a capital, named Al-Mahdiyya, built on a coastal promontory. Exploiting an unstable political landscape, the Fatimids conquered Egypt in 969 and established Cairo as their new capital, where they built Al-Azhar Mosque (972). Their expansion continued into Syria and the Hejaz (the western part of modern-day Saudi Arabia). However, an offshoot of the caliphate, the Qarmatians (899–1077), who revolted against Al-Mahdi in 899 and ruled over eastern Hejaz and parts of Iraq, snatched Syria between 970 and

973. The Fatimids were ultimately able to take it back. In 930, the Qarmatians raided Mecca, attacking the Kaaba and stealing the Black Stone, a revered rock set into the building's eastern corner, in an act condemned by the Muslim world and all mainstream Shi'ite groups.

THE TURKS AND THE MONGOLS AND EASTERN ISLAM REGIONS

Central Asia was the primary source of slave-soldiers (largely pagan Turks) who converted to Islam, served in the military (from the time of the Abbasids) and rose to positions of power. This is how dynasties such as the Samanids in Transoxiana (corresponding to modern-day eastern Uzbekistan, western Tajikistan, and parts of Kazakhstan and Kyrgyzstan) and Khurasan (819–1005), and the Ghaznavids in eastern Afghanistan stretching to northern India (977–1186), were formed.

On the other hand, the Shi'ite Buyids (932–1062) originating from the mountainous region at the Caspian Sea, and the Sunni Ghurids (1100–1215) descending from the mountainous regions of central Afghanistan, can be considered native to Persia.

The Seljuks, 1040–1194. A Turkish tribe living in the central Asian steppes who converted to Islam at the end of the tenth century and who filled the power vacuum created through the struggles among the Ghaznavids, Samanids and Buyids. They established their capital Isfahan in Iran, where they greatly modified the Jamah Mosque, first established by the Abbasids. They are known for introducing madrasas, a religious education system to counter the influence of the Shi'a religious movement.

The Seljuks who dominated in Anatolia (modern-day Turkey) after defeating the Byzantine army and who established their capital in Konya were referred to as the Seljuks of Rum, distinguishing them from those ruling in Iran.

The Zengids and the Ayyubids, 1127–1250. Founded by Imad al-Din Zengi (1127–46), these groups belong to the Seljuk Atabegs of Mosul. The Atabegs were army commanders who taught the young Seljuk princes military strategy, religion and governance. The Zengids, and the Ayyubids who worked under them and later extended their rule (the sultanate was founded by Saladin, of Kurdish heritage, who adopted the name Ayyub in honour of his father), fought and defeated the Christian Crusaders and the Fatimids. They ruled over Egypt and the Levant. They built many madrasas, hospitals and defensive citadels. They also built an army of Turkish mercenaries from Central Asia and the Caucasus, who became known as the Mamluks.

The Mamluks, 1250–1517. The Mamluks' army took control in Egypt during the transition of power from the last Ayyubid ruler, As-Salih, to his son Turanshah. In addition to Egypt, their territory included the Levant, upper Mesopotamia, Hejaz and Anatolia. The Mamluks were the force that stopped the Mongolian invasion of the Levant in 1260. They built numerous religious complexes and mausoleums, and their legacy is most evident in Cairo, where they built the Mosque of Baybars and the Mosque of Sultan Hasan, among others.

The Mongols and the Mughals, 1256–1857. The Mongol invasion of the Muslim lands in 1258 destroyed many cities and ended dynasties. However, it also resulted in the Mongols converting to Islam. In Iran they established the Ilkhanid dynasty (1256–1336), and they built a mosque in every town; they also built large mausoleums. The Ilkhanids allowed the defeated Seljuks of Rum in Anatolia to exist as vassals. When the Ilkhanids collapsed, smaller dynasties sprang up in their place.

The Turco-Mongolian tribal chief Timur (also known as Tamerlane) eliminated the petty dynasties and established a rule from his base in Samarkand (Uzbekistan) that included most of the territory between Syria and India, sacking cities such as Damascus and Baghdad. In 1398, Timur invaded India, leaving behind a weakened sultanate that broke into petty kingdoms. This Timurid territory was later reclaimed by his descendant, Babur, who established the Mughal dynasty (1526–1857). Central Asia was back in the hands of the Uzbeks, while the Mughals ruled over India and built an extensive array of distinguished buildings there, among them the world-famous Taj Mahal. During the Mughals' rule, India was invaded by the Iranian Nadir Shah in 1738, and the British in 1798.

The Ottomans, 1298–1922. As a branch of the Seljuks of Rum located in northwestern Anatolia, the Ottomans belonged to one of the twenty-four Oghuz tribes and their history begins under the leadership of Ertugrul – a Turcoman who settled away from the Mongols in western Anatolia. His son, Osman I, gives the Ottomans their name. At its peak, the Ottoman empire stretched from central Europe to Iran in the east and Maghreb in the west. Their capital was initially Bursa, then later Edirne, and lastly Istanbul. During their long reign, they built extensively, including structures such as the Green Mosque, the Suleymaniye Mosque, and many others.

The Safavids, 1501–1722. A Turkish-speaking tribe of warrior Sufis from northwest Iran. They made Shi'ism the religion of state, led by their leader Shah Isma'il. They believed in a line of twelve imams. Buffered by the Ottomans in the west, Safavid control stretched from eastern Iraq to western Transoxiana. Their capital was moved from Qazvin to Isfahan, where they built a modernized complex and the Shah Abbas Mosque. The Safavids were ultimately replaced by the Qajars (1779–1925), who favoured European styles and influences.

THE BERBERS AND WESTERN ISLAM REGIONS

North Africa was a region that came in and out of Muslim rule via the Rashidun, the Umayyads, and later the Abbasids, the Fatimids and finally the Ottomans. Not all of the local

Berber tribes accepted Islam; some of them kept allegiances with the Roman and Byzantine empires, while others contained figures, like Tariq ibn Ziyad, who became Muslim leaders. Islam first reached Spain in 711, when Ibn Ziyad crossed Gibraltar (a mispronunciation of the Arabic *Jabal Tareq* (mountain of Tareq) into Iberia.

The Umayyads in Córdoba, 756–1031. The escaping Umayyad prince Abd al-Rahman I established an Umayyad emirate with the nascent Muslim community initially introduced by the Berbers. The Umayyad dynasty of Abd al-Rahman included seventeen amirs and caliphs, who brought the legacy of the Levant to Iberia. Under their reign, Madinat al-Zahra near Córdoba and the Great Mosque of Córdoba were built and an era of intellectual, cultural, artistic and scientific flourishing ensued, similar to the renaissance experienced in the Abbasid Golden Age. The caliphate collapsed into petty kingdoms in the early eleventh century.

Almoravids, 1056–1147. A group of Berber tribes that spread from Mauritania upwards to Andalusia and downwards to western Africa. Their founder was Yousef ibn Tashfin; the name Almoravids comes from *al-murabitun*, which means 'those who stay and defend the strongholds'. Their capital was the newly established Marrakesh in Morocco. They rebuilt the Qarawiyyin Mosque in Fez (1134–43) and introduced the use of *muqarnas*, a structural and decorative vault seen across Islamic architecture.

Almohads, 1121–1269. Replacing the Almoravids, the Almohads (*al-muwahhidun*, meaning 'the believers in one God') were founded by the Berber leader Muhammad ibn Tumart who studied in Córdoba and translated Arabic writings into Berber. They made Fez their capital and built the Kutubiyya Mosque in Marrakesh.

Marinids 1244–1465. Deposing the Almohads, the Berber tribe of the Banu Marin ('the people of Marin') were herders from eastern Morocco who captured Fez and made it their capital in 1250. They built madrasas, hospitals and khans. In their place came the Wattasids (another Berber dynasty), followed by the Sadids and Alawids, until the Ottomans consolidated a lasting rule.

Nasrids, 1232–1492. Established by Muhammad ibn Yousef ibn Nasr from the Banu al-Ahmar clan, the Nasrids managed to maintain a last Muslim stronghold in Iberia, with its capital in Granada. The Nasrids enjoyed intermittent support from the Marinids. They built the renowned Alhambra palace.

Acknowledgments

Writing this book has been much like a shell-collecting mission. As I've walked and searched, I've been fascinated by the small treasures I've uncovered and intimidated by the waves unearthing them. And those shells I have found have gradually pieced themselves together in a puzzle that keeps on growing. I thank my Creator for putting so much beauty in my way, and for sending his seagulls, crabs and mighty waves to help me see it. I thank my husband, Ghassan, the most beautiful soul I've ever encountered and the one I'm so blessed to be partnered with for life. Through the writing of this book, as in life, he has been my rock and my lantern, and I don't know what I would do without the cushioning kindness with which he surrounds me. Thank you for being the first person to read my book, one chapter at a time; for encouraging me when I lost confidence, and for guiding me through the confusion of my own thoughts. I also thank my children, my two wings, Naya and Ayk, who helped me so much in making this book. Naya, my best friend in the world, thank you for reading, encouraging, critiquing and illuminating me always. Ayk, my beloved boy, who took on with full commitment the tasks I abandoned in order to work on this book, and who became a 'household chef' for an entire year – thank you for being such a caring, responsible and reliable individual.

I thank my dearest friends, Hanan Hamoud and Ahmad Jmaeil, for their true friendship, and for keeping me in their thoughts and being there whenever I needed help. Their encouragement throughout the process of writing this book cannot be overstated.

I could not be more grateful to my publisher, Thames & Hudson, and all the members of their excellent staff who help ideas become objects of love and beauty. I especially thank Lucas Dietrich for his continuing visionary work, and for the trust, kindness and liberty he so graciously bestowed on the book project so that it might see the light. I'm equally grateful to Helen Fanthorpe for her unwavering commitment and her brilliant skill in keeping the ball rolling. The input of both Lucas and Helen has been invaluable.

My heartfelt and deepest thanks go to my brilliant editor, Jenny Wilson, who elevated the text not only with her magic editorial wand, but also with her piercing eye and inquisitive mind. This book would read much less easily were it not for Jenny's most capable hands.

Thank you to my dear friend Anis Nacrour, who has gifted me many books in the past and who so generously sent me two more for research all the way from France: *The Transnational Mosque* and *Deconstructing the American Mosque*. Shahed Saleem very thoughtfully sent me a digital copy of his book,

The British Mosque, and Dr Akel Kahera also gave me a copy of his *The Mosque as a Place*. Living as I do in the isolation of sanctioned Syria, where shipping and book access is no small endeavour, adds to the profound value of these friendly gestures. Without access to all these resources, my understanding of the subject of the mosque would be much less.

My thanks also go to Dr Akel Kahera (again), Diana Darke and Stefano Serafini for your kind support as well as your friendship.

Lastly, my gratitude is due to all the people who invited me to take part in their events and hosted me in their beautiful cities, and to all the kind individuals I had the pleasure to meet in the different cities of the world, some of whom have become friends for life. I cherish dearly those encounters, as well as the opportunities they afforded. They have expanded my world view and on many occasions have made my heart full.

Picture Credits

Unless otherwise stated, all illustrations have been adapted from the sources stated below.

p. 7 2014 photo by MOHAMMED SALEM / Reuters; **p. 15** 2024 photo by an unidentified photographer published on https://www.facebook.com/trtworld/posts/palestinians-in-gazas-rafah-perform-their-friday-prayers-amid-the-rubble-of-faro/816107723884804/ (Accessed 3 March 2024); **pp. 21, 52, 129, 153, 155** original photos by the author; **p. 38** (above) photo published in MadainProject https://madainproject.com/masjid_al_nabawi_at_the_time_of_prophet_muhammad (Accessed 3 March 2024); **p. 38** (middle) photo by @Erth Tear via MoathAlofi published on https://ar.wikipedia.org/wiki/%D8%A7%D9%84%D9%85%D8%B3%D8%AC%D8%AF_%D8%A7%D9%84%D9%86%D8%A8%D9%88%D9%8A (Accessed 3 March 2024); **p. 38** (below) photo published on https://ar.wikipedia.org/wiki/%D8%A7%D9%84%D9%85%D8%B3%D8%AC%D8%AF_%D8%A7%D9%84%D9%86%D8%A8%D9%88%D9%8A (Accessed 3 March 2024); **p. 42** photo by an unidentified photographer published on https://www.facebook.com/photo.php?fbid=3152119666617737&id=1033802411342458&set=a.120315529440716 (Accessed 3 March 2024); **p. 50** photo by an unidentified photographer published on https://www.qatar.georgetown.edu/from-mosque-to-home-discovering-the-hidden-wonders-of-islamic-architecture-design-and-artisanship/ (Accessed 3 March 2024); **p. 54** unidentified photographer published on https://id.trip.com/guide/muslim-travel/panduan-wisata-muslim-di-qatar.html (Accessed 3 March 2024); **p. 61** source map published on gisgeography.com/middle-east-map (Accessed 4 March 2024); **p. 65** 2024 photo by İzettin Kasım / Anadolu Images; **p. 70** photo published on https://commons.wikimedia.org/wiki/File:Damascus_Umayyad_Mosque_interior_1502.jpg (Accessed 3 March 2024); **pp. 74, 127** diagram in *The Mosque: History, Architectural Development & Regional Diversity*, ed. Martin Frishman and Hasan-Uddin Khan, Thames & Hudson, London, 1994; **p. 79** photo published on https://commons.wikimedia.org/wiki/File:Jumaa_Mosque.jpg (Accessed 3 March 2024); **p. 81** photo published

on https://www.islamicity.org/11185/hassan-ii-mosque-the-gem-of-casablanca/ (Accessed 3 March 2024); **p. 83** photo published on https://thecookandthewriter.com/2024/04/19/visiting-the-hassan-ii-mosque/ (Accessed 3 March 2024); **pp. 86–87** photo published on https://www.ksp-engel.com/en/projekte/grosse-moschee (Accessed 3 March 2024); **p. 98** photo published on https://www.informationen-bilder.de/israel-palaestina/jerusalem.htm (Accessed 3 March 2024); **p. 99** photo published on https://www.worldhistory.org/image/11632/dome-of-the-rock/ (Accessed 3 March 2024); **p. 104** photo published on https://commons.wikimedia.org/wiki/File:Dome_of_Rock,_Temple_Mount,_Jerusalem.jpg (Accessed 3 March 2024); **p. 106** photo published on https://www.facebook.com/photo.php?fbid=421727043435949&id=100067959708418&set=a.421727010102619 (Accessed 3 March 2024); **p. 111** photo published on https://www.islamicarchitecturalheritage.com/listings/the-great-mosque-of-guangzhou (Accessed 3 March 2024); **p. 113** image of Huajuexiangsi (The Great Mosque in Xi'an) by an unidentified artist dated in 1392, published in https://www.khanacademy.org/humanities/art-asia/imperial-china/ming-dynasty/a/the-great-mosque-of-xian (Accessed 3 March 2024); **p. 115** photo published on https://www.islamichinatravel.com/destination-guide/turpan/turpan-masjid/turpan-emin-minaret-mosque/ (Accessed 3 March 2024); **p. 119** 2023 photo by Ali Atmaca / Anadolu Images; **p. 120** 2016 photo by Chris McGrath/Getty Images; **p. 123** photo by @ Didier Marti / Getty Images; **p. 133** photo by Henri Stierlin /Bildarchiv Steffens / Bridgeman Images; **p. 134** photo by Andrea Pistolesi / Getty Images; **p. 136** photo by David Ewing / Getty Images; **p. 146** photo by Richard Mortel from Riyadh, Saudi Arabia published on https://commons.wikimedia.org/wiki/File:Great_Mosque_of_Cordoba,_interior,_8th_-_10th_centuries_(38)_(29721130342).jpg (Accessed 3 March 2024);
p. 148 photo published on https://es.wikipedia.org/wiki/Mezquita-catedral_de_C%C3%B3rdoba (Accessed 3 March 2024); **p. 150** plan published on https://en.wikipedia.org/wiki/File:Mezquita_planta_antes_1236.jpg (Accessed 3 March 2024); **p. 159** photo published on https://www.oxcis.ac.uk/about-us (Accessed 3 March 2024); **p. 166** drawing published on https://www.sciencedirect.com/science/article/pii/S2095263517300584 (Accessed 3 March 2024); **p. 167** drawing published in Kleiner, Fred S. *Gardner's Art through the Ages: A Global History*. 15th ed., Cengage Learning, 2016; **p. 173** 2021 photo by Muhammed Enes Yıldırım / Anadolu Images; **p. 185** (above) photo published on https://www.rvasia.org/church-asia/jakarta-cathedral-istiqlal-mosque-symbols-religious-tolerance-indonesia (Accessed 3 March 2024); **p. 185** (below) photo published by The Jakarta Post Images/Wendra Ajistyatama; **p. 187** photo by Shutterstock; **p. 188** photo published on https://en.wikipedia.org/wiki/Faisal_Mosque#/media/File:Another_interior_view_-_Faisal_Mosque.jpg (Accessed 3 March 2024); **p. 189** photo published on https://www.ne.jp/asahi/arc/ind/1_primer/hassanfathy/xfat_1eng.htm (Accessed 3 March 2024); **pp. 190–91** photo published on https://emrearolat.com/project/sancaklar-mosque/ (Accessed 3 March 2024); **p. 192** photos published on https://www.cinicimimarlik.com/tr/tbmm-camii/ (Accessed 3 March 2024); **p. 198** photo published on https://depositphotos.com/photo/grant-mosque-exterior-located-difc-district-aerial-promenade-gate-avenue-649212066.html (Accessed 3 March 2024); **p. 199** photo published on http://www.dabbagharchitects.com/portfolio_page/mosque-of-light/ (Accessed 3 March 2024); **pp. 200–01** photos by Mikkel Frost; **p. 212** photo by Jason Ingram; **p. 214** (left) photo by Morley von Sternberg; **p. 214** (right) photo published on https://www.romeactually.com/shapes-lights-patterns-romes-grand-mosque/ (Accessed 3 March 2024); **pp. 215, 217** photos by Anthony Browell

Index

N

O

P

INDEX